KOOKS AND DEGENERATES ON ICE

KOOKS AND DEGENERATES ON ICE

Bobby Orr, the Big Bad Bruins, and the Stanley Cup Championship That Transformed Hockey

Thomas J. Whalen

ROWMAN & LITTLEFIELD
Lanham • Boulder • New York • London

Published by Rowman & Littlefield
An imprint of The Rowman & Littlefield Publishing Group, Inc.
4501 Forbes Boulevard, Suite 200, Lanham, Maryland 20706
www.rowman.com

6 Tinworth Street, London SE11 5AL

British Library Cataloguing in Publication Information Available

Library of Congress Cataloging-in-Publication Data

Names: Whalen, Thomas J., 1964– author.
Title: Kooks and degenerates on ice : Bobby Orr, the big bad Bruins, and the Stanley Cup championship that transformed hockey / Thomas J. Whalen.
Description: Lanham, Maryland : Rowman & Littlefield, 2020. | Includes bibliographical references and index. | Summary: "This book celebrates the 1969–70 Boston Bruins. While the country seethed from racial violence, war, and mass shootings, the "Big Bad Bruins," led by the legendary Bobby Orr, brushed off their perennial losing ways to advance to the playoffs and defeat the St. Louis Blues in the Stanley Cup Finals for their first championship in 29 years"— Provided by publisher.
Identifiers: LCCN 2019048435 (print) | LCCN 2019048436 (ebook) | ISBN 9781538110287 (cloth) | ISBN 9781538110294 (epub)
Subjects: LCSH: Boston Bruins (Hockey team)—History. | Orr, Bobby, 1948– | Stanley Cup (Hockey) (1970)
Classification: LCC GV848.B6 W53 2020 (print) | LCC GV848.B6 (ebook) | DDC 796.962/64—dc23
LC record available at https://lccn.loc.gov/2019048435
LC ebook record available at https://lccn.loc.gov/2019048436

In loving memory of
Herman T. Whalen,
inspirational dad and hockey player extraordinaire

CONTENTS

PREFACE

In the pantheon of all-time Boston sports greats, none is bigger than Theodore Samuel Williams. The last man to hit .400 in a Major League Baseball season, the famously temperamental Red Sox slugger won six batting titles and hit 521 homers in a brilliant 19-year career that spanned from the New Deal era of the 1930s to the dawn of the Space Age in the 1960s. "I wanted to be the greatest hitter who ever lived," he wrote in his autobiography, *My Turn at Bat*, with John Underwood. Williams had long since accomplished that goal when he sat down for a live 1992 television interview with fellow Beantown legends Larry Bird of the Celtics and Bobby Orr of the Bruins.

This once-in-a-lifetime gathering of athletic prowess had been put together by local sports broadcaster Bob Lobel for a popular weekly show he hosted called *Sports Final*. A usually breezy performer in front of the camera, Lobel was all nerves on this particular day. "That's because I was the only one who could screw it up," Lobel said years later. "Even if they sat there and no one said a thing, it was going to be an amazing shot." Lobel rose to the occasion, however, and engaged the three superstars in a lively and entertaining discussion of their individual careers and achievements. But something curious happened when a video played of a leaping Orr scoring the series-winning goal in the 1970 Stanley Cup Finals, an iconic moment that has been immortalized in a larger-than-life bronze statue at the western entrance to Boston's TD Garden, the current home of the Bruins. Williams, never one for subtlety, could not resist needling

Orr about this career-defining act. "Jesus, I see that goal all the time!" he exclaimed. "Is that the only goal you ever scored?"

The Goal is emblematic of the uniquely talented Orr and the uniquely talented hockey club he played for—the Big Bad Bruins—which, according to one historian, "launched a thousand hockey rinks and sparked the explosion of the game in the United States." Indeed, most of the gold medal–winning 1980 "Miracle on Ice" U.S. men's Olympic hockey team—including Massachusetts-raised members Mike Eruzione, Jack O'Callahan, and Jim Craig—had grown up watching CBS network telecasts of their contests in the late 1960s and 1970s. At a time when the sport was dominated almost exclusively by Canadians, Eruzione, O'Callahan, and Craig were inspired to go out and elevate their games to a higher level. They were not the only ones. Such future NHL stars with local roots as Bobby Carpenter, Tom Barrasso, and Mike Milbury were similarly roused. "The city was in a Bruins fog," Milbury told author Fluto Shinzawa in *The Big 50: The Men and Moments That Made the Boston Bruins*.

> It's hard to describe. People—family and friends—would gather on a Thursday night to watch the game. The next day, that was the discussion. There was always something to discuss. They were one of the great entertaining teams of all time. . . . Cult-like is the best way to describe it. People were consumed with the Bruins.

The following pages tell their story and the amazing year they became champions.

I

1970

The nation appears to be coming apart at the seams and not even the sport of hockey can escape the tide of events.

"**H**ouston, we've had a problem." *Apollo 13* commander Jim Lovell uttered these famous words to Houston Mission Control two days after he and fellow astronauts Jack Swigert and Fred Haise blasted off in their Saturn 5 rocket from Cape Kennedy, Florida, on April 11, 1970. The crew's destination was the moon, but two hundred thousand miles into their journey, they heard a "loud bang" that set off an array of warning lights inside the cramped confines of their Odyssey command module. "It really was not until I looked out the window and saw the oxygen venting from the rear of my space craft that I knew we were in serious trouble," Lovell later said. Indeed, an attached oxygen fuel tank had exploded, draining the vessel's air supply and electrical power to critically low levels. *Apollo 13*'s scheduled landing on the moon, which was to be the third in history, had to be scratched. The mission now became one of life-or-death survival. "It seems almost more than human nerves [can] take," the *New York Times* commented. Only through the unruffled courage displayed by the crew and the brilliant technical assistance provided by the flight control team on the ground was disaster avoided. On April 17, Odyssey splashed down in the Pacific Ocean with everyone on board safe and unharmed. "One of the most beautiful sights we saw was the sight of the earth getting bigger as we came back," Swigert said.

The *Apollo 13* miracle provided one of the few bright spots in 1970, an otherwise bleak year that produced war, massive protests, political

scandal, and seething cultural unrest. And caught in its unforgiving, inex-
orable grasp was Richard M. Nixon. Elected by a narrow popular margin
in 1968, the dour, stooped-shouldered 37th president of the United States
had campaigned on the promise of ending the Vietnam War—an unpopular conflict he had inherited from his Democratic predecessor that was
being fought half a world away in Southeast Asia. The war, which pitted
a corrupt and hopelessly inept U.S.-backed regime in South Vietnam
against a stronger, Communist-led one in the north, had been raging for
several long years at the cost of tens of thousands young American lives.
Publicly, Nixon said he wanted to achieve a "peace with honor," but
privately the Republican conceded he wanted to cut U.S. losses and leave
Vietnam as soon as possible. To square this almost impossible political
circle, Nixon announced a policy of Vietnamization—a "plan in which
we will withdraw all our forces from Vietnam on a schedule in accor-
dance with our own program, as the South Vietnamese become strong
enough to defend their own freedom."

In covering for the phased withdrawal of U.S. troops, Nixon approved
of a targeted military strike against Cambodia, a weak neighboring neu-
tral country where the North Vietnamese had been funneling troops and
supplies to the south. Nixon announced the bold move during a nationally
televised address from the Oval Office on the evening of April 30. "This
is not an invasion of Cambodia," he claimed. "The areas in which these
attacks will be launched are completely occupied and controlled by North
Vietnamese forces. Our purpose is not to occupy the areas. Once enemy
forces are driven out of these sanctuaries and once their military supplies
are destroyed, we will withdraw." Indeed, the entire point of the exercise
was to put the North Vietnamese leadership on notice. "We will be patient in working for peace, we will be conciliatory at the conference table,
but we will not be humiliated. We will not be defeated. We will not allow
American men by the thousands to be killed by an enemy from privileged
sanctuaries." Nixon acknowledged his decision was bound to generate
controversy. Yet, he insisted there was no viable alternative, for in the
final analysis, he claimed, there was a higher purpose at stake. "If, when
the chips are down, the world's most powerful nation, the United States
of America, acts like a pitiful and helpless giant, the forces of totalitarian-
ism and anarchy will threaten free nations and free institutions throughout
the world."

Supreme Court chief justice Warren Burger surprised Nixon afterward by stopping by the White House to hand deliver a note praising the "sense of history and destiny" expressed in the speech. Nixon received a further unexpected boost the next morning when he was leaving the Pentagon after a briefing. A cheering, enthusiastic group of employees mobbed him in the lobby and told him how much they had appreciated his remarks. All the while, Nixon could not stop thinking about how markedly different the young men and women serving in uniform overseas were from the thousands of college students protesting the war at home, who, he claimed, "took advantage of their draft deferments and their privileged status in our society to bomb campuses, set fire and tyrannize their institutions." Nixon shared these feelings with the crowd of well-wishers. "You see, these bums, you know, blowing up the campuses," he told them. "Listen, the boys that are on the college campuses today are the luckiest people in the world, going to the greatest universities, and here they are burning up the books, storming around about this issue. . . . Then out there, we have kids who are just doing their duty. And I have seen them. They stand tall, and they are proud."

A wave of campus demonstrations broke out throughout the country protesting the Cambodian incursion. The most infamous occurred on the afternoon of May 4, when members of the Ohio National Guard fired approximately 67 rounds of live ammunition into a crowd of student antiwar protesters at Kent State University in Kent, Ohio. "The crackle of the rifle volley cut the suddenly still air," the *New York Times* reported in its next day's edition. "Some of the students dived to the ground, crawling on the grass in terror. Others stood shocked or half crouched, apparently believing the troops were firing into the air. Some of the rifle barrels were pointed upward." Four were killed and nine others seriously wounded during the melee, which lasted 13 seconds and forever came to be known as the "Kent State Massacre." "You know, I felt like I was in Vietnam," 21-year-old senior marketing major Yvonne Mitchell told a reporter. "Because all of a sudden the campus I had been on for over two years had become a battleground for a fight that was totally unnecessary." Two of the slain—William K. Schroeder and Sandra L. Scheuer—had not even taken part in the demonstration. They were walking between classes when they got caught in the hail of deadly bullets.

Other surviving protesters were awash in anger and disbelief. "Many of them clustered in small groups staring at the bodies," the *Times* said.

"A young man cradled one of the bleeding forms in his arms. Several girls began to cry. But many of the students who rushed to the scene seemed almost too shocked to react." Indeed, most refused to stand down when the Guardsmen issued a crowd dispersal order. "If they want to kill us all, let them do it now," a defiant student exclaimed. The latter seemed like a distinct possibility until a respected, mild-mannered geology professor named Glenn Frank stepped in to intervene. "I am begging you right now," Frank implored the gathering. "If you don't disperse right now, they're going to move in, and it can only be a slaughter. Would you please listen to me? Jesus Christ. I don't want to be a part of this." That did the trick. The students slowly retreated, and some semblance of calm was restored.

Mary Ann Veechio felt anything but serene, however. A 14-year-old runaway from Opa-locka, Florida, Veechio had been visiting the campus when she got coaxed into attending the demonstration. "I was kind of on the fringe of the crowd," she told author James A. Michener afterward. "I was walking slowly up with a guy, and I turned to ask him what was happening. I can't remember just what I said, I did ask him his name though, and he said, 'Jeff.'" That would be Jeffrey Miller, a 20-year-old transfer student from Michigan State University who was fatally gunned down once the shooting started. "There was blood coming out of his nose and mouth, and it looked like he had two apples in one cheek," Veechio said. It took her a few harrowing moments to process what she had just witnessed. Her first reaction was to flee, but then she had second thoughts.

> I saw a girl on the ground, and someone was trying to hold her head off the grass. So I went back to Jeff, and there was a big crowd around him and there was a whole lot of blood now. Some guy jumped up and down in it, yelling and screaming, and the blood was splattering all over us. I got some on my shirt and on my pants. I never saw this guy before. He just came out of nowhere, I guess.

Her anguish over Miller's shooting was vividly captured by campus student photographer John Filo, thereafter awarded the Pulitzer Prize for the image. The now-iconic photograph depicts a horrified Veechio kneeling beside Miller's bleeding body with her bent right arm extended outward in a pleading gesture.

The shootings shocked the nation and left many groping for answers. As *Life* magazine editorialized,

> The upheaval in Kent seemed at its outset to be merely another of the scores of student demonstrations that have rocked U.S. campuses. But before it ended, in senseless and brutal murder at point-blank range, Kent State had become a symbol of the fearful hazards latent in dissent, and in the policies that cause it.

The White House appeared disinclined to embrace this interpretation. In an official statement, Nixon lay full blame for the killings on the student antiwar protesters. "This should remind us all once again that when dissent turns to violence, it invites tragedy," he said.

> It is my hope this tragic and unfortunate incident will strengthen the determination of all the nation's campuses—administrators, faculty, and students alike—to stand firmly for the right which exists in this country of peaceful dissent and just as strongly against the resort to violence as a means of such expression.

Privately, Nixon confessed to taking a more nuanced view of the Ohio events, which he characterized as "among the darkest of my presidency." He wrote in his memoirs, "I could not help thinking about the families, suddenly receiving the news that their children were dead because they had been shot at a campus demonstration." Nixon felt even more "utterly dejected" a few days later when he read a newspaper quote from the father of one of the deceased victims. "My child is not a bum," the man said.

The incident at Kent State did not end the cycle of campus violence. Eleven days later at the predominantly black Jackson State University in Jackson, Mississippi, two students were killed when local and state police fired into a girls' dormitory on campus. A large group of concerned peers had earlier assembled near the front of the building in response to a false rumor that a popular local civil rights activist and his wife had been murdered. When law enforcement officers arrived in riot gear to break up the gathering, a bottle was angrily thrown in their direction. "So, the bottle is in the air, it's as if it's suspended like forever," remembered undergraduate Steve Vernon Weakly. "It floated down and came in from behind (the police), and it hit right in the middle of them and it burst. It was as if they just went crazy from there . . . they started shooting the guns immediately—immediately—and it was like all hell broke loose."

More than four hundred rounds of ammunition were used in the 28-second fusillade, which an investigative presidential commission later called an "unreasonable, unjustified overreaction." "The carnage . . . was just incredible," said Weakly, who suffered a gunshot wound to the leg. "Everybody was screaming, and all of a sudden everything got eerily quiet. Then it started back up again. It was like 10 times louder than it was before. People were screaming, girls were fainting, blood was everywhere." In Weakly's mind, there was no doubt about who bore responsibility for the violence. "Visualize, if you will, heavily armed policemen, primarily highway patrolmen and Jackson police, coming through our campus. Any campus in America that would have been a taboo. Of course kids are going to do what we did, which was scream and holler at them to get off campus."

The talk of revolution now filled the air as 364 colleges and universities nationwide shut down to avoid further bloodshed. Struggling to come to grips with the situation, Nixon made an unorthodox effort to engage with antiwar activists in the predawn hours of May 9. Accompanied by his personal valet, Manola Sanchez, and a contingent of Secret Service agents, he ventured to the steps of the Lincoln Memorial, where an estimated group of 50 protesting students had bedded down the previous evening. The latter were at the Capitol to attend a massive antiwar rally scheduled for the next day.

"I was trying to relate to them in a way that they could feel I understood their problems," Nixon wrote afterward. He told the students the Cambodian incursion was designed to get the country out of Vietnam rather than deeper into the war.

> I realize that most of them would not agree with my position, but I hoped they would not allow their disagreement on this issue to lead them to fail to give [the administration] a hearing on some issues where we might agree. And also particularly I hoped that their hatred of the war, which I could well understand, would not turn into a bitter hatred of our whole system, our country, and everything that it stood for.

Nixon's audience remained largely unimpressed, particularly when he bizarrely brought up the subjects of the Syracuse University football team and surfing. "He didn't look anyone in the eyes," remembered one student. "He was mumbling. When people asked him to speak up, he would boom one word and no more. As far as sentence structure, there was none." While Nixon described to a reporter afterward how the episode was "one of the most interesting experiences in my life," his White House chief of staff took a dimmer view. "The weirdest day so far," Bob Haldeman confided in his diary. "I am concerned about [the president's] condition . . . he has had very little sleep for a long time, and his judgment, temper, and mood suffer badly as a result."

The judgment and character of Nixon's greatest political rival was also coming under intense scrutiny. In the tragic aftermath of his brother Robert's 1968 assassination, U.S. senator Edward M. Kennedy of Massachusetts had become heir apparent to the most famous political dynasty in the United States. Indeed, expectations were high that the 37-year-old Democratic lawmaker would make a run for the presidency in 1972, and thwart Nixon's reelection chances. But a fatal late-night automobile accident on Chappaquiddick Island on July 18, 1969, threw these hopes in disarray. Kennedy was behind the wheel of a black Oldsmobile Delmont 88 that resulted in the death of his lone passenger—28-year-old Mary Jo Kopechne of New Jersey.

Kopechne, a veteran Washington political staffer who had risen to become a speechwriter for Robert F. Kennedy during his ill-fated 1968 presidential run, had earlier in the day attended a small cookout and reunion party at a rented cottage on the remote island off the southeastern coast of Massachusetts with a group of former campaign coworkers known as the "Boiler Room Girls." As the evening wore on, Kennedy, a married man, struck up a conversation with the single and strikingly attractive Kopechne. "I did not know her socially before that evening. Perhaps I had met her before but I did not recall it," Kennedy later wrote in his 2009 autobiography *True Compass*. Unsurprisingly, most of the Kopechne–Kennedy exchange focused on memories of Kennedy's slain older brother, which caused both to become emotional. Ted, in fact, felt a panic attack coming on. "I needed to get out of that party," he remembered. "I needed to get outside, to breathe some fresh air." Kopechne also experienced the need to depart the premises, giving Kennedy the opening he had been looking for. He offered to drive Kopechne to a local boat ferry that would take her to her hotel on nearby Martha's Vineyard. "I was grateful for the excuse to leave," he said.

Kopechne never reached the hotel. Kennedy made a wrong turn at a T-intersection and ended up on an unpaved road running in the opposite direction of the ferry. "It was very dark," Kennedy recounted. "I had not been to this part of the island before that day, when I had been a passenger in the car and not the driver." Kennedy became disoriented and was taken by surprise when a narrow wooden bridge suddenly came into view. "It had no guard rails and headed in a leftward angle from the road," he pointed out. The crucial seconds that followed would forever change his life. Kennedy plunged the black sedan off the side of the bridge and into a pond that flowed underneath. The car settled into the murky depths upside down. Kennedy was certain he was going to drown but somehow managed to break free and float to the surface. As for Kopechne, who he had felt struggling beside him in the submerged vehicle, Kennedy asserted he made several attempts to dive back into the water to save her. "I could not see her in the car," he claimed 40 years later. "I hoped she'd been able to escape, too. That's what I wanted to believe, even though I knew it was unlikely."

Kennedy eventually made his way back to the party to seek help. But it was too late. Kopechne had drowned. "The sad fact is that my flawed and wrongheaded actions had the opposite effect of having people link Mary Jo to me in a romantic way," Kennedy said. "I am deeply sorry about that."

His regrets notwithstanding, Kennedy waited an uncomprehendingly long nine hours before alerting police. Until the day he died, Kennedy offered no credible explanation for his puzzling behavior. "I was overcome, I'm frank to say, by a jumble of emotions: grief, fear, doubt, exhaustion, panic, confusion, and shock," he said. Kennedy did, however, manage to luxuriate in no small measure of self-pity. "I had suffered many losses during my life," he explained.

> I had lost all my brothers and my sister Kathleen [to violent deaths]. My father had been lost to me in many respects because of his debilitating stroke. And now this horrible accident. But again, the difference this time was that myself was responsible. I was driving. Yes, it was an accident. But that doesn't erase the fact that I had caused an innocent woman's death.

Kennedy pled guilty to leaving the scene of an accident and received a suspended two-month jail sentence with a year's probation. Yet, the verdict Kennedy cared most about was delivered by Massachusetts voters on Election Day the following November. Kennedy won reelection to the Senate by easily defeating Republican businessman Josiah H. Spaulding with 61 percent of the vote.

The year 1970 also marked a memorable time in popular culture. Americans flocked to movie theaters to see *Love Story*, a sentimental tearjerker about a happily married young couple played by Ali McGraw and Ryan O'Neill whose romance is tragically cut short when McGraw's character contracts a terminal illness. "Love means never having to say you're sorry," says McGraw in the film's oft-quoted [and mocked] line of dialogue. On television, the most watched program was *Rowan & Martin's Laugh-In*, a sketch comedy series that featured a talented ensemble cast headlined by Lily Tomlin, Arte Johnson, and future Academy Award winner Goldie Hawn. Known for its wacky unpredictability and irreverent attitude, the show made pointed satirical jabs at contemporary politics and society. As Hawn quipped in an early episode, "I don't see why there should be any question about capital punishment. I think everyone in the capital should be punished."

Despite the buzz generated by *Love Story* and *Laugh-In*, the biggest entertainment story concerned the Beatles. After a decade on top of the pop music world, the long-haired, trendsetting quartet of John Lennon, Paul McCartney, George Harrison, and Ringo Starr announced they were breaking up as a band in early April. "It's like they were saying, 'The 70s are starting, you're on your own,'" remembered one disappointed fan. Rumors had been thick for some time that intraband relations had grown toxic. Indeed, the recording sessions for their chart-topping *Abbey Road* album of the previous fall had been tense and acrimonious. "People would be walking out, banging instruments down, not turning up on time, and keeping the others waiting three to four hours, then blaming each other for not having rehearsed or not having played their bit right," remembered audio engineer Phil McDonald. Instead of the tight-knit musical unit they had always been, the group had dissolved into a discordant group of solo artists. "There was a tussle, an artistic tussle, and it was very difficult to hold them together in that way," confirmed Beatles producer and mentor George Martin. "There wasn't a cohesive feeling among them to do the same kind of music. They had to express themselves individually."

Lennon led the charge. Since leaving his first wife, the former Cynthia Powell, for Japanese avant-garde artist and peace activist Yoko Ono in 1968, Lennon had developed strong feelings about striking out on his own. "The Beatles had become a trap," he later explained.

> A tape loop. I had made previous short excursions on my own, writing books, helping convert them into a play. I'd even made a movie without the others, but I had made the movie more in reaction to the fact The Beatles had decided to stop touring then with real independence in mind—although even then my eye was on freedom.

Ono encouraged him to take bolder artistic risks, and together they formed *The Plastic Ono Band*, which produced the popular antiwar single "Give Peace a Chance." They also collaborated on several unorthodox film projects, one of which was a 42-minute feature on Lennon's penis titled *Self-Portrait*. "The critics wouldn't touch it," Ono said.

Lennon's behavior grew increasingly erratic, which added to the existing tensions within the group. Years of heavy drug use, including the ingestion of copious amounts of lysergic acid diethylamide [LSD], had taken a toll. "In a way, like psychiatry, acid could undo a lot—it was so powerful you could just see," Harrison said. "But I think we didn't realize the extent to which John was screwed up." Lennon further raised eyebrows when he and Ono started concealing themselves in a large white bag during joint public appearances. "If everyone went in a bag for a job there'd be no prejudice," Lennon said. "You'd have to judge people on their quality within. We call it total communication."

McCartney did make a desperate last-ditch attempt to keep the Beatles together. The singer-composer suggested they return to touring on the road at small club venues, something they had not done since the group's humble beginnings in the early 1960s. That way, McCartney argued, they could get back to their musical roots and become creatively reinvigorated. But this idea fell flat with the other band members. "I think you're daft," Lennon said. Still, the Beatles did manage to leave their legions of fans with a memorable final live performance on the rooftop of their Apple Corps headquarters in central London on January 30, 1969. They were finishing up what was to be their final released album, *Let It Be*, and spontaneously came up with the idea of recording some of the songs they had been rehearsing in an open, live setting. Remembered Harrison, "We went to the roof in order to resolve the live concert idea, because it was much simpler than going anywhere else; also, nobody had ever done that, so it would be interesting to see what happened when we started playing up there. It was a nice little social study."

Accompanied by a film crew that was capturing every moment for a future feature documentary, the Beatles played five songs, among them the soon-to-be hit singles "Get Back" and "Let It Be," in an infectiously entertaining 42-minute set. They would have performed longer but local police pulled the plug on the gathering due to public safety concerns. Starr became indignant at the intrusion: "I was playing away, and I thought, 'Oh great! I hope they drag me off.' I wanted the cops to drag me off—'Get off the drums!'—because we were being filmed, and it would have looked really great, kicking the cymbals and everything." The latter did not occur, but Lennon offered a fitting coda for the occasion and the tumultuous era in which the Beatles had catapulted to unprecedented fame and fortune. "I hope we passed the audition," he said.

In sports, events off the field dominated the headlines. All-Star St. Louis Cardinals outfielder Curt Flood rocked the legal and financial foundations of Major League Baseball when he refused to report to the Philadelphia Phillies after being traded there at the end of the 1969 season. "After 12 years in the major leagues, I do not feel that I am a piece of property to be bought and sold irrespective of my wishes," he solemnly informed baseball commissioner Bowie Kuhn in a letter. "I believe any system which produces that result violates my basic rights as a citizen and is inconsistent with the laws of the United States and of several other states." He added that even though the Phillies had tendered him a contract offer, he had the right to entertain offers from other teams. "I, therefore, request that you make known to all major-league clubs my feelings in this matter and advise them of my eligibility in this matter, and advise them of my availability for the 1970 season," he concluded.

Flood was challenging the way the game had been conducting business since the end of the nineteenth century. According to the reigning reserve clause system, players were contractually bound to the ballclub they had initially signed with for perpetuity or until said ball club decided to trade them or give them their unconditional release. Kuhn formally rejected Flood's request to become a free agent out of hand. "I certainly agree with you that you, as a human being, are not a piece of property to be bought and sold," Kuhn wrote the seven-time Gold Glove winner and two-time world champion. "This is fundamental to our society and I think obvious; however, I cannot see its application to the situation at hand." Undeterred, Flood sued on the grounds that Major League Baseball was acting as a business monopoly and therefore in violation of established federal statutory law. "I didn't doubt Curt's sincerity one bit," said former Cardinals teammate Tim McCarver, who was included in the Flood trade to Philadelphia. "What a courageous thing he did. The money he gave up. . . . I'm sure there were a lot of people who thought Curt was calling their bluff and that he would cave in for more money, but he didn't."

Flood took his case all the way to the U.S. Supreme Court, where, in a 5–3 decision, with one abstention, the high court upheld the sport's reserve clause system. "He struck out," wrote Larry Merchant of the *New York Post*, "but not before he fouled off so many pitches that he helped wear down the other side." Flood's trailblazing legal challenge emboldened other players to take on baseball's ruling powers in the coming years, the end result being the demise of the reserve clause. In 1975, an independent arbitrator named Peter Seitz ruled that owners had no right to retain a player's service beyond the renewal year in their contracts. Modern free agency had arrived in baseball, and Flood, who Pulitzer prize–winning commentator George F. Will once likened to "Dred Scott in spikes," was largely responsible, even though he had been forced to pay a steep price. Other than the 13 games with the lowly Washington Senators in 1971, he never again played in the big leagues. "Yes," Flood later conceded, "I sacrificed a lot—the money, maybe even the Hall of Fame—and you weigh that against all the things that are really important that are deep inside you, and I think I succeeded."

One of Flood's baseball contemporaries also raised an uproar that spring with the publication of a tell-all memoir chronicling his experiences in the game, especially what ballplayers said and did within the traditionally taboo confines of the locker room. In *Ball Four: My Life and Hard Times Throwing the Knuckleball in the Big Leagues*, author and veteran Houston Astros pitcher Jim Bouton openly talked about how players abused drugs, ogled young women in the stands, and belittled teammates for reading anything more intellectually challenging than the daily sports page. "There's pettiness in baseball, and meanness and stupidity beyond belief, and everything else bad that you'll find outside of baseball," Bouton wrote. His anecdotes about former New York Yankees teammate Mickey Mantle garnered the most attention. Bouton related how the popular sandy-haired slugger, who many held up as a moral exemplar to the nation's youth, was actually an uncouth, hard-drinking party animal. Indeed, Bouton claimed that Mantle had once hit a home run in a game while intoxicated. He also noted how Mantle was frequently dismissive of young autograph-seekers and journalists. "You'd think I had desecrated the flag," Bouton jokingly observed afterward.

A *New York Times* review called *Ball Four* a "gem of honest, good-naturedly biased reporting." Bouton's baseball peers were considerably less effusive. "Fuck you, Shakespeare!" Cincinnati Reds outfielder Pete Rose repeatedly screamed at him during a contest. Fiery Minnesota Twins manager Billy Martin said he had not bothered to read the book but claimed it was "horseshit" anyway. American League president and former Hall of Fame shortstop Joe Cronin simply called it the "worst thing for baseball I've ever seen." Bouton was unmoved by such criticism, for this "social leper," as reactionary *New York Daily News* sports columnist Dick Young described him, was selling too many copies to get upset.

Book sales got a further boost after Bowie Kuhn called Bouton into his office for a private closed-door meeting. During the course of the next three and a half hours, baseball's top executive demanded that Bouton sign a statement claiming *Ball Four* was a "bunch of lies." Bouton politely declined, and Kuhn, according to Bouton, "turned a color which went quite nicely with the wood paneling" on his walls. "I'm sure I would have been forgiven for writing *Ball Four* if I had just signed the statement, stood in the corner for a while, and kept my mouth shut," Bouton later wrote. Instead, Bouton settled for having written one of the most enduring sports classics of all-time.

In September, Judge Walter Mansfield of the U.S. District Court for the Southern District of New York ruled that banned former heavyweight boxing champion Muhammad Ali be allowed to fight again. After refusing induction into the U.S. Army on conscientious religious grounds in 1967—"I ain't got no quarrel with those Vietcong," he reportedly said—Ali, a convert to the Nation of Islam, was convicted of draft evasion and had his title stripped away by the World Boxing Authority. Due to the felony conviction, New York and other states barred him from competing for three and a half years. "I had seen promoters who were trying to end my exile turned down by 38 states," Ali later wrote in his autobiography. "And when the summer of '70 came, I faced the fact that not a promoter in America could get a fight for me legally." But thanks to Judge Mansfield's ruling, which argued Ali's ability to earn a living had been "irreparably" damaged by the ban, that was all about to change. "Wait long enough and some wrongs will be righted—or so most of us go on hoping, anyway," the *Boston Globe* editorialized. "The court's order does not reinstate the fighter as the world's heavyweight champion. It merely says he has the legal right to fight for the title in what experts so curiously call the squared circle—which is precisely where and how such matters should be decided, rather than by pols with wet fingers in the political wind."

Ali, whose draft-evasion conviction would be overturned a year later on appeal by the U.S. Supreme Court, wasted little time getting back into the ring. On October 26, he defeated top heavyweight contender Jerry Quarry on a technical knockout in front of a sold-out City Auditorium crowd in Atlanta, Georgia. Ali had opened a bloody cut above the pudgy Californian's left eye in the middle of the third round to force the decision. "It was not a [head] butt, and I don't want anybody saying that it was. It was a right hand," Quarry said afterward. Reviews on Ali's performance were mixed. *Sports Illustrated* claimed the bout marked the reemergence of a gifted fighter who "reclaimed his eminence and reputation." Others were skeptical. "The guy escaped with his life tonight," longtime boxing promoter Sam "Suitcase" Silverman said. "He wasn't in shape. His legs weren't going to take him more than seven rounds." Ali himself seemed less than satisfied. "I wish it had gone longer," he claimed. "I wanted to hit [Quarry] more to see how I could keep punching fast. I wanted to go 10 so I could find out more about myself. I haven't gone any distance even in training. I wanted to know more." Still, Ali had had absolutely no doubt about the outcome. "After the fight," event promoter Robert Kassel remembered,

> I'm in the middle of the ring—it's all kind of mayhem—and I'm standing next to Angelo Dundee [Ali's longtime trainer], who's cutting the gloves off of Ali. Inside the left-hand cuff, in the soft cotton part, it was written in ballpoint pen, "TKO, 3rd round." So help me God. That glove was taped on, so nobody could have slipped in there and written that.

This surfeit of confidence served Ali well in the coming years, as he was able to regain his heavyweight title and live up to his oft-repeated boast of being "The Greatest." "I'm the astronaut of boxing," he said. "I'm in a world of my own."

Meanwhile, the National Hockey League was experiencing major growing pains. Seeking to attract new fans and larger American television audiences, the league's Board of Governors approved a six-team, all-U.S. expansion in 1967, doubling the size of the existing "Original Six" operation. But the move raised concerns about competitive balance. Indeed, the California Seals, Los Angeles Kings, Minnesota North Stars, Pittsburgh Penguins, Philadelphia Flyers, and St. Louis Blues were composed of mostly unwanted castoffs from other established clubs and unproven younger players. In a clever stroke of creativity, however, the league came up with a fix. "All six expansion teams would be placed in the same [West Division] and play most of their games against each other, giving the new teams a chance to compete on equal footing while the traditional powerhouses did the same," wrote author Sean McIndoe in his informative and entertaining 2018 book *The Down Goes Brown History of the NHL*. Traditionalists cried foul, characterizing the new alignment as an ill-advised gimmick that gave a "black eye" to the sport. But fans in cities like St. Louis enthusiastically embraced the concept. Indeed, the Blues took full advantage and reached the Stanley Cup Finals in 1968 and 1969. That they were easily dispatched on both occasions was beside the point. "I went into this thing with the guarantee that the West Division champions would play the East Division champions for the Stanley Cup," Blues team executive Sid Solomon III said. "And if I have anything to say about it, it will remain that way."

Other newcomers were less fortunate. The Seals, for example, were a disappointment in the standings and at the box office. After a 1–13 start in their inaugural season, fans stayed away. The attendance situation grew so dire that when a woman inquired by phone about the starting time to a Seals game, a desperate team official on the other end responded by asking what time she could arrive at the arena. "It was the most rinky-dink setup you could imagine," former Seals general manager Bill Torrey later told ESPN.com. Flamboyant Major League Baseball owner Charlie O. Finley would later purchase the Seals and try to raise fan interest by decking out the club in white skates. Like everything else associated with the team, this promotion backfired. "When the skaters skated with their white skates on white ice," noted one observer, "it looked like they were skating on stems."

While the Seals provided a comic diversion, the main hockey story of 1970 involved a highly talented, if unorthodox, group of "kooks and degenerates" who captured the imagination of sports fans throughout the entire North American continent. They would add a colorful new chapter to the history of one of the NHL's oldest and most celebrated franchises.

2

HUB OF HOCKEY

Boston has long laid claim to being the "Hub of the Universe" when it comes to the vitality of its academic, financial, and cultural institutions. But this term of endearment—originally coined by celebrated nineteenth-century poet and physician Oliver Wendell Holmes—can just as easily apply to the city's abiding connection to ice hockey. For since the rapid growth and development of "hawkey" on these shores 140 years ago as a hybrid of traditional European and Native American stick-and-ball games, Boston has embraced the winter sport with an unbridled enthusiasm rivaling only that of their Canadian cousins to the north. As author and longtime *Boston Globe* sports columnist Bob Ryan once wrote, "Boston truly is the Hockey Capital of America."

Indeed, decades before Bobby Orr laced up a pair of skates for the local team, the city and the Greater New England region produced a slew of highly talented amateur players, notably the legendary Hobart Amory Hare "Hobey" Baker of St. Paul's School in Concord, New Hampshire. Baker, for whom college hockey's most prestigious award for the country's top player is named, was a star on the ice from the age of 14. Resembling a young Greek god, the golden-haired Hobey was an unusual amalgam of speed, grace, and power. He inspired awe in everyone who witnessed his hockey exploits, especially when he skated for the 1914 national champion Princeton University Tigers. "Men and women went hysterical when Baker flashed down the ice on one of his brilliant runs with the puck," one contemporary wrote. "I have never heard such spontaneous cheering for an athlete as greeted him a hundred times a night and never expect to again." Sadly, Baker died in a plane crash while serving with the U.S. Army Air Service in France at the end of World War I. But the overwhelming popular interest he and his hockey peers generated for the game back home left a lasting mark.

Small wonder then that the fledgling National Hockey League tapped Boston as the first U.S. entry into its previously all-Canadian operation in 1924. A local grocery magnate named Charles F. Adams had formally applied for league admission after he attended a 1924 Stanley Cup Finals game between the Montreal Canadians and the Calgary Tigers. "Those pros in the NHL can really play this game," Adams enthused. Grasping the mass entertainment value, the millionaire concluded that launching a new professional hockey franchise in Boston made perfect business sense. The city was already enamored with the game, and Adams saw the cross-marketing potential. His team would wear brown and yellow uniforms—the same colors his groceries used in their logo. But what to call the hockey club? A few ideas were tossed around before Adams finally settled on the name "Bruins." Legend has it that his office secretary made the winning suggestion when Adams said he wanted his team associated with the image of an "untamed animal whose name was synonymous with strength, ability, ferocity, and cunning."

These same competitive qualities were reflective of Art Ross, the storied coach and hockey pioneer Charles Adams hired to run the Bruins. Ross—a great defenseman in his playing days—is credited with developing the synthetic rubber puck and the first metal hockey sticks. But the future Hockey Hall of Famer did not suffer fools gladly and approached his coaching duties with an authoritarian brio. "Ross was not loved by his men, but he *was* feared," writer C. Michael Hiam maintained. "He was known to show his displeasure by walking into the dressing room before a game, throwing down a bunch of railway timetables to various places in Canada, and then walking out." The message delivered was that players were expendable and Ross could ship them back to their respective hometowns whenever he desired. For certain, Ross had precise ideas about how to do things, and when his players deviated from them—for example, preferring slap shots over more reliable wrist shots—he would not hesitate to impose stiff fines. His word was law, but at the same time Ross was smart enough to realize that players had the tendency to physically wear down as the long hockey season progressed. Thus, he held few team workouts and avoided exhibition games whenever possible. "We didn't

The indomitable Eddie Shore. *Le Studio du Hockey, HHOF Images*

practice a lot," one Bruin confirmed. "He'd say, 'Don't waste yourself in practice.'"

Ross's stern, if unorthodox, ways initially did not translate into many victories. The Bruins—playing their home games at the cramped Boston Arena, in the heart of the city's South End neighborhood—finished sixth in the six-team league during their inaugural 1924–1925 season. The dismal record was achieved in spite of Ross's frequent attempts to shake up the roster. "You actually had three teams then," Ross later joked. "That's right. One (playing), one coming, one going." There was scant improvement the next season, but the losing came to an end in 1926–1927, when the Bruins went 21–20–3, and made the playoffs. They were able to do so thanks to the arrival of a hard-nosed but electrifying player from the untamed wilds of western Canada—Eddie Shore. Shore would lift the team to perennial Stanley Cup contention in the decade ahead, while providing an unparalleled end-to-end ferocity on the ice. "If we hadn't secured Eddie Shore for the Bruins in 1926, I doubt the team would have survived," Ross said. "He was an exceptional defensive player, but his freewheeling style of carrying the puck and his ice-cold, methodical approach to everything caught the fans' attention. Before long, crowds were flocking to our games to watch him." Indeed, the team vaulted from a paltry average of 6,045 fans per game in Shore's debut season to a league-leading 14,096 three years later.

Shore "was the only player I ever saw who had the whole arena standing every time he rushed down the ice," remembered Bruins trainer Hammy Moore. "You see, when Shore carried the puck you were always sure something would happen. He would either end up bashing somebody, get into a fight, or score a goal." A wiry 5-foot-11, 190-pound defenseman with a face that resembled a clenched fist, Shore exhibited great speed, superior stickhandling ability, and a lethally accurate shot from the right side that frustrated many a goaltender. He relished physically mixing things up and slipping in the first punch in fights. He was equal parts mean, moody, and magnificent—in other words the NHL's version of ornery baseball superstar Ty Cobb.

"If ever a saga of hockey is written," noted one admirer, "Eddie Shore might well be its Achilles, Beowulf, Odysseus, or Hereward." A consummate showman or first-rate ham, depending on your point of view, Shore delighted Boston fans by donning a gold matador's cape before home games, as if to say he was "King of the Rink." Meanwhile, opponents seethed about what they regarded as an obnoxious attempt to show them up. "I hope you're going to wear that gown in the game tonight," Toronto defender Francis Michael "King" Clancy once taunted Shore. "You look so lovely in it. Trouble is, you'll probably get all tangled up in it, fall into the boards, and then start crying for a penalty." When Shore responded by offering to plant Clancy six feet under, the scrappy Ontarian informed him to think again. "You try it, Eddie," Clancy said, "if you don't mind taking a good licking right in front of your fans." In point of fact, Shore did not mind. The 978 stitches, 14 broken noses, 5 broken jaws, and busted hip he acquired during his spectacular 14-year NHL career attest to that.

"From the first time he put on skates," noted writer Frank Orr, "Eddie Shore was in the middle of trouble." Shore never disputed this assessment, as he lived for his next fight, usually dishing out more punishment than he received. "You either socked the other guy or the other guy socked you," he said. His legendary fistic skills had the effect of intimidating the opposition, but they also garnered unwanted scrutiny from game officials. "Shore was nasty and, as far as I was concerned, a threat to the life of other players, a real danger," claimed referee Cooper Smeaton. "He was a madman when he was out on the ice." "Old Blood and Guts" set a league record with 165 penalty minutes his sophomore year and was among the top 10 leaders in that category eight other times.

This behavior won him few friends outside of New England. "It's nice to know Eddie is still bad," quipped John Lardner of *Newsweek* near the end of his playing days.

> For 20 years, man and boy, this evil fellow has been punching people, hitting them over the head with his stick, chewing their ears, butting, gouging, shoving, and generally bedeviling his fellow men, and always for handsome fees. No one has ever made malevolence pay better money than E. Shore.

For sure, Shore became the highest-paid performer in the NHL, even when the Great Depression cast a bleak economic shadow over North America and most of the world in the early 1930s. He would not have it any other way, as he frequently threatened team management with holdouts if his salary demands were not met. "I figure that if I am to play 60 minutes a game and if I can save the Boston Club some money, due to the fact they do not have to employ another defenseman, then at least I should receive something extra for my time," he said.

Nevertheless, Shore could be a handful. In his third season, he got stuck in Boston traffic and missed a train that was carrying the team to Montreal for an away game. "Mr. Ross didn't know it, but I was running down the station platform, trying to jump on the last car of the train," Shore recalled. Since the contest wasn't scheduled until the following evening, Shore calculated he could easily make it in time for the puck dropping if he commissioned a taxi to make the 340-mile trek north. He also had a financial motive. The notoriously parsimonious Shore knew Ross would fine him several hundred dollars if he was a no-show in Montreal.

What Shore did not count on was a raging winter storm along the way that clogged the roads with heavy snow and slippery ice. The drive was slow going, and Shore became restive with his cabbie, who he felt was being overly cautious. He decided a change was needed. "Give me the wheel," Shore instructed. "I come from the Canadian West, and we're used to stuff like this." It was not the wisest move. Shore could barely see through the windshield as the snow began to pile up. At one point he even had to lean out of the side window on the driver's side to make out what lay ahead. The car eventually skidded off the main road and crashed. Undeterred, Shore trudged for a mile through the drifting snow to a nearby farm, where he rented a team of horses with a sleigh to allow him to complete the final leg of the journey. When he arrived at the Bruins hotel in Montreal just hours before game time, he resembled a broken-down journeyman boxer who had gone one too many rounds with the heavyweight champion of the world. Put another way, he was a mess. "He was in no condition for hockey," Art Ross said. "His eyes were bloodshot, his face frostbitten and wind burned, his fingers bent and set like claws after gripping the steering wheel so long. He couldn't walk straight. I figure his legs were almost paralyzed from hitting the brake and clutch." Shore had gone 22 hours without sleep, but he did manage to sneak in a 30-minute nap before teammates roused him from a deep slumber. They dumped several glasses of cold water over his battered and exhausted body.

Despite the adversity, the "blonde tiger of the Boston Bruins defense," as one awestruck Montreal writer described him, played most of the game that night and netted the winning goal. It was truly a performance for the ages. And while the insular Shore usually kept his teammates at arm's length, they could only shake their heads in amazement. "He was very cold and aloof, a real loner who stuck to himself all the time," a fellow Bruin later confirmed. "But I really admired the man's fortitude. Injuries which would have prevented most other men from playing never seemed to bother him." Art Ross was far less sentimental in his assessment after the Montreal game. He docked Shore for missing the team train. Still, Ross grudgingly gave credit where credit was due, rating Shore's Montreal showing "one of the greatest all-around games I've ever seen."

Hockey had never been Edward William Shore's favorite sport growing up as a farmer's son in Canada's remote Saskatchewan province. He preferred baseball and soccer, but when he enrolled at Manitoba Agricultural College in Winnipeg at 16, his interest in the game blossomed at the urging of his older brother. "Anybody can be a hockey player," he reasoned. Shore joined one of the college's three hockey squads and spent more hours obsessively practicing at the school's outdoor ice rink than tending to his studies. "Often we played at 30 to 40 below," Shore later recounted. "Our ears, noses, and cheeks used to freeze regularly, and we'd be playing a little while and you could scrape the hoarfrost off of our backs and our chests. I remember we once played a game when it was 55 below and our eyelashes froze so stiff we were almost blinded."

Shore became better and better at the sport, and by the time he hooked on with the Edmonton Eskimos of the Western Canada Hockey League in 1924, he had become a formidable hockey force. "Shore would roar up the ice like a human catapult, leading the two fastest forwards on the team," recalled *Sport* magazine editor Ed Fitzgerald. "Zooming toward the goal he would unleash a bullet-like drive—but *not* at the net. Instead, he would rifle the puck against the backboards and, head lowered like a vengeful bull, smash his way through the enemy defense as though it were so much paper." His blinding speed only made him more of an offensive threat. "Eddie was so fast that he could retrieve the puck as it came off the boards and pass it back to his forwards, and more often than not grin sardonically as his teammates angled it home for a goal."

Shore's athleticism, grit, and smarts drew the notice of Charles Adams, who seriously entertained purchasing the entire Western Canada Hockey League to obtain Shore's signing rights for the 1926–1927 season. As it turned out, that wasn't necessary, as the Bruins owner acquired Shore and six lesser talents for a then-princely sum of $50,000. "There was actually one key player I just had to have, because Eddie Shore was made for Boston," Adams later told writer Andy O'Brien. "Tough, scrappy, mean. A rushing defenseman who could take charge. The Boston fans didn't know hockey in those days, but you didn't have to know hockey to get delirious over Shore."

Shore made an immediate impression on his new Bruin teammates during an early season workout. He squared off against veteran defenseman Billy Coutu, whose reputation for violence and mayhem was the equal of Shore's. The former Montreal Canadians star viewed Shore's presence on the roster with growing alarm. He felt his job was on the line and was determined to chop the cocky rookie down to size. "It was a fight to the finish between that old-timer and myself," Shore remembered. Shore won the clash of wills when he sent Coutu flying several feet in the air with a vicious body check. Coutu wasn't able to get back up, but the force of the collision exacted a heavy toll on Shore. His left ear was left dangling by a thin strip of attached skin as blood came rushing out. The team doctor determined the ear could not be saved, but Shore stubbornly disagreed. After several unsuccessful medical inquiries throughout town, he eventually found a physician willing to reattach the organ. "[The doctor] asked me what type of anesthetic I wanted," Shore said. "I told him just to give me a small mirror. That way, I could watch the kind of stitching he did. I made him change the very last stitch. If I had not done that, he'd have left a scar. I told him I was just a farm boy who did not want his looks messed up." The surgery was a success, and Shore went on to have a standout rookie campaign, finishing fourth on the team in goals and leading the Bruins to the Stanley Cup Finals, which they dropped to the Ottawa Senators. "Shore showed that the aggressiveness he gave a game supplied more credits than debits for the Bruins," O'Brien wrote. "By obviously preferring to go through or over a checker he got the adrenalin flowing in the whole team."

The Bruins were an even better outfit in 1928–1929, when they stormed to their first Stanley Cup championship on the heels of a 26–13–5 regular season. In the playoffs, they swept the Montreal Canadians in the opening round and did the same to the New York Rangers in a best-of-three final that, for the first time, pitted two American teams against one another for hockey's highest prize. "There has never been a professional team where there has been less bickering, fewer jealousies, and better spirit," Art Ross claimed. "All season long that has been the case." Shore again was the straw that stirred the drink, finishing fourth in voting for the Hart Trophy as Most Valuable Player of the league. But he had plenty of help from a star-studded lineup that featured high scorers Harry Oliver, Cooney Weiland, James "Dutch" Gainor, and Aubrey Victor "Dit" Clapper. In terms of all-around hockey skills, however, Clapper was the cream of the crop.

A powerfully swift but graceful skater, Clapper was a tall, ruggedly handsome winger from Hastings, Ontario, who the Bruins had signed from the minor Canadian–American Hockey League the previous season. "In those days, the Bruins specialized in big, tough men," he said. Clapper—the first person to play 20 years in the NHL—fit the bill here, although his gifted biographers, Stewart Richardson and Richard LeBlanc, point out he was no Eddie Shore when it came to fighting: He did not actively seek out trouble. Nonetheless, "While Dit was rarely the aggressor," they wrote, "he was definitely a finisher when one of his teammates had been wronged." Clapper's legendary stamina and ability to endure great pain were equally unquestioned. As his son Don related,

> He [once] severed a tendon in a game, and it was a horrible injury. It required one hundred stitches inside and another one hundred stitches outside the wound. The doctors said he might never skate again, that he'd be lucky to be able to walk. Well, he was back on skates the following year.

That outcome is not surprising. Clapper understood before most of his peers the importance of keeping in-shape year-round. "If you want to stay in it you can't let yourself go during the offseason," he emphasized. "Conditioning and keeping in condition means everything. If you don't keep at it during the summer you might as well write finis to your career." He retired after the 1946–1947 season with 447 points in 835 games.

In goal the Bruins relied on rookie sensation Cecil "Tiny" Thompson, a former junior hockey standout from Calgary, Alberta. The 5-foot-11, 160-pound Thompson was not so diminutive, but he had been given the nickname as a joke when he was younger. "Tiny stood pretty tall in the nets because he played a stand-up style," hockey historian Lew Freedman wrote. "You didn't catch Thompson making saves on his knees." Thompson actually became the first goalie to popularize catching pucks with his hands rather than blocking them with his body, which had long been the accepted practice. He started all 44 games in 1928–1929, posting a miniscule 1.15 goals-against average. He also recorded 12 of the 81 shutouts he would accumulate during his impressive 13-year NHL career. In most seasons, Thompson would have been a shoe-in for the Vezina Trophy, which is awarded to the most outstanding goaltender in the league. But Montreal's George Hainsworth had an even better year, with 22 shutouts and an 0.92 goals-against average. Thompson—whose brother Paul played goal for the Rangers—would go on to win the Vezina the following season and on three separate occasions before leaving the game in 1941.

The championship season marked the debut of the Boston Garden, the team's impressive new home on Causeway and Nashua Streets. Built for $4 million by boxing promoter and former cowboy George L. "Tex" Richard, the Garden sat regally on North Station, a tangled cluster of railway lines that extended to the city's northern and western suburbs. In the years ahead, the handsome double-balconied arena would play host to an eclectic variety of athletic and nonathletic events, including traveling three-ring circuses, mass political rallies, music concerts, prizefights, cycling races, wrestling matches, rodeo competitions, and the National Basketball Association's Boston Celtics. But from the beginning, the building became most closely associated with professional hockey. "The lovers of the ice game surely have something in store for them, as the largest attendance that ever saw a game here is expected, judged by the demand for tickets," the *Boston Globe* reported on November 19, 1928, the eve of the Bruins' home opener against the Montreal Canadians.

Indeed, a rowdy, sold-out gathering was on hand at the "city's newest, grandest, and largest sports arena" to witness the Bruins drop a close 1–0 contest to the Habs. The real story, however, was what happened off the ice. "It was more than a hockey game," posited Stanley Woodward of the *Boston Herald*. "It was a riot, a mob-scene, a reenaction of the assault on the Bastille. It is estimated that 17,500 persons, 3,000 in excess of the supposed capacity at the Garden, saw the game." Lines of fans stretched around the corner of the building down nearby Beverly Street trying to gain entry. "The surplus were the shock troops who, in the front rank of a mob that swept before police lines, ushers, doors, and windows by force of numbers and tremendous pressure on the rear, came into the building ticketless, perhaps even against their will," Woodward wrote. "Five hundred standing-room admissions were sold in a few minutes more, and when the last legitimate space had been disposed of, the crowd still pressed forward, waving money, pleading for admissions, eventually demanding it."

The chaotic conditions were scarcely better inside. In some ways, they were worse. "The crowd spread like rushing waters to every corner of the Garden, blocking the aisles, overflowing in every direction. Seat holders who came late were walled out by packed humanity and had to go over the top or stay out." Still, the occasion proved the Bruins had established a loyal, even rabid following in only their fifth year of existence. Charles Adams's NHL investment had paid off. As the *Globe* noted, "Almost every hockey fan in Greater Boston and those from the suburban cities were present. The Bruins were favorites, and the big crowd gave each of the players a grand reception as they skated around the playing surface to get the feel of the ice."

The Bruins remained a top contender during the next several seasons, that is until Shore's penchant for generating controversy reached alarming new heights. On the night of December 12, 1933, he almost ended the life of Toronto Maple Leafs forward Irvine "Ace" Bailey when he delivered a savage hit on the Ontario native from behind during an early December home game. "I had many battles with Shore, but I never thought he was a vicious player," Bailey's Hall of Fame teammate King Clancy recalled. "He wasn't out there to maim anybody. But that night he certainly hit Bailey as hard as he could. It was a shocking thing to see." Leafs defenseman Red Horner inadvertently started the bloody fracas when he delivered a crushing body check on Shore in the Toronto end. Shore was momentarily dazed but spoiling to exact revenge on Horner. "Shore is sure mad," noted *Boston Globe* sports editor Victor Jones from his seat in the press box.

After regaining his bearings, Shore barreled down the ice at top speed, his sullen gaze focusing on the player he believed to be Horner. But he mistook Bailey for his Toronto antagonist, and things got out of hand fast. "It happened in the heat of the game," Clancy remembered. "Shore skated up to Bailey, jammed his knee behind Ace's leg, and with his own elbow across Bailey's forehead turned him upside down." Bailey hit his head hard on the Garden ice. "All of us in the press box could hear a crack you might compare to the sound you remember from boyhood days of cracking a pumpkin with a baseball bat," former Toronto assistant general manager Frank Selke said. "Bailey's knees were raised, his legs were twitching, and his head was turned sideways." Bailey fell into a coma and did not regain consciousness for another 15 days.

Shore's initial response to his bloody handiwork was to smile, which outraged Horner, who promptly lost any semblance of self-control. "The 'Ace' had an expression I'll never forget," Horner recounted afterward. "His mouth was hanging wide open, and his tongue was lolling. He was practically blue in the face, and my only thought was that Shore had pulled the dirtiest trick I had witnessed in my five years with the Maple Leafs. I figured Bailey might die." To rectify matters, Horner skated over to Shore for a face-to-face showdown. "[Shore] never spoke a word, just stood there with a vacant expression," Horner said. "So I . . . let him have it smack on the button. Sticks never entered the argument. My fist shows how hard he was hit." Shore collapsed in a heap. "[His] head struck the ice, splitting open," Selke said. "In an instant, he was circled by a pool of blood about three feet in diameter." Enraged by the incident, the Bruins bench collectively vaulted over the boards to confront Horner. But with brawny 6–1 Toronto teammate Charlie "The Big Bomber" Comacher at his side, a stick-waving Horner managed to hold off the crush of angry Bruins. "Which one of you is going to be the first to get it?" Comacher asked menacingly.

Bailey was rushed to City Hospital in Boston's South End, where attending physicians held little hope. "We have rummies brought here with fewer complications, and they are dead in 12 hours," a hospital staff member told a reporter. An obituary was duly prepared in the *Toronto Star* to announce Bailey's expected death. Maple Leafs owner Conn Smythe—who had earlier gotten into a dustup with a Boston fan that resulted in the latter's eye glasses being shattered—had an even grimmer task in mind for Selke. "I understand it means a lot of red tape to get a body across the [Canadian border]," Smythe told his top assistant, "so you better start getting things ready." Yet, Bailey somehow managed to pull through. "A blood clot formed between my brain and the skull, and they had to drill a hole deep into the side of my head and probe for the clot before they could take it out," Bailey said. "The operation took three hours."

Meanwhile, Bailey's father rushed to Boston to be with his stricken son. He also had something else planned, as he brought along a .45-caliber pistol. Sitting in the ornate lobby of the Copley Plaza Hotel, where he checked in as a guest, the elder Bailey openly revealed his intentions. "He was telling everybody, in no uncertain terms, that he intended to use the gun on the man who had put his boy in the hospital," Selke recalled.

Fearing the worst, Selke contacted an old acquaintance on the Boston police force named Bob Huddy to handle the situation. Huddy complied, locating Bailey and escorting him to a nearby bar. "They must have slipped dad a couple of mickeys," Ace Bailey later speculated, because his father soon found himself disarmed and half-conscious on a train heading out of North Station. "To the conductor, [Huddy] simply showed his badge and gave the order that Mr. Bailey should not be let off the train until he was safely back in Toronto," Selke said. His gun was later returned to him in the mail.

Sporting a nasty three-inch cut on his scalp from Horner's blow, Shore was universally condemned for his assault on Bailey. "The Bailey–Shore incident has aroused the ire of all fair-minded hockey fans," the *Boston Evening American* maintained. "There is no place for such actions in any sport, and unless immediate steps are taken to eradicate the parties responsible the game will not survive." Although Shore was absolved of any criminal wrongdoing after a short police investigation, he was not so fortunate with the NHL. Embarrassed by the adverse publicity generated by the incident and motivated by the public outcry to do something about Shore, the league's managing director—former Hall of Fame player Frank Patrick—announced a 16-game suspension for the Boston star. Patrick claimed Shore's life-threatening hit on Bailey was unintentional and therefore did not require a harsher punishment.

Unsurprisingly, the sentence did not go down well with Torontonians. They were expecting an outcome more along the lines of a full year ban and cried foul. "To us the leniency of the suspension can be attributed to dollars and cents," the *Globe and Mail* said. "The Bruins are not drawing without Shore, either at home or abroad, and the result is poorer gates than usual." Regardless of the reason, Shore—who took an extended vacation to Bermuda with his wife during the suspension—was nonplussed. He sincerely believed he had done nothing wrong. If anything, he felt the aggrieved party. As Shore complained to a Boston newspaper, "This reputation as the 'bad boy' of hockey who specializes in rough play is something that has been thrust upon me since this affair happened."

Bailey—a solid goal scorer, with 192 points during his eight-year Toronto career—miraculously recovered from his injuries, but his days of playing hockey were over. To help defray the costs of his mounting medical bills, an exhibition game was arranged in his honor at Maple Leaf Gardens on February 14, 1934, with all proceeds going to Bailey.

The match pitted the Maple Leafs against a group of the league's best players, one of whom was Eddie Shore. "A crowd of 14,074 paid $20,909 to see the wide-open contest, which set an all-time high for the number of famous players assembled on one rink," the Associated Press reported. A thinner but healthy-looking Bailey was on hand for the event, which provided a template for the first official NHL All-Star game in 1947. "There was a big table with sweaters, and Ace presented every one of the All-Stars with a sweater before the game," noted one observer. "When Ace gave Eddie his jersey, the two shook hands and the building just shook [with applause]." "I'm sorry, Ace, I didn't mean to hurt you," Shore reportedly told his rival.

Bailey slipped seamlessly into a successful college coaching career with the University of Toronto and remained an avid fan of the pro game until his death in 1992, at the age of 88. "I watch hockey on TV all the time," he said in retirement. "Sometimes I wonder whether these guys are getting paid to play hockey or to fight. Maybe the owners think they need those brawls to fill their buildings, but I don't think they do." Bailey claimed to bare no lingering animosity toward Shore, although he pointedly added, "He ended my career as a player." As for Shore, the curmudgeonly hockey great remained unrepentant. "I wouldn't be telling the truth if I said I've had to live with this thing throughout the years," he later told writer Stan Fischler. "I never let it affect me. It was an accident—nothing else."

With Shore missing a substantial portion of the 1933–1934 season, the Bruins collapsed to last place and were out of the playoffs. The team needed retooling, and by the end of the decade they were once again able to drink champagne from Lord Stanley's Cup. "The team we had in 1938–1939 was the best we ever had," Art Ross told Lee Greene of *Sport* magazine in 1963. "Every player was a major leaguer." The old Boston coach was not exaggerating. The club, which won or tied 38 of the 48 games it played that season, was loaded with young talent, starting with the legendary "Kraut Line." Composed of center Milt Schmidt, left winger Clarence "Woody" Dumart, and right winger Bobby Bauer—who grew up together in Kitchener, Ontario—the explosive unit produced a little more than a third of the team's goals, with 46. The line—earning its culturally insensitive nickname from the common German ancestry each of its members shared—had first come together in the minors. "We didn't have much experience, of course, but we worked well together because each of us had something to offer the others," Schmidt said. Bauer represented the "brains of the line," while Dumart provided muscle and defensive prowess. Dumart "could battle around that cage, and he had a great hard shot," Schmidt said. "Off the ice he was a very quiet person who minded his own business." As for Schmidt himself, the future Bruins general manager and five-time All-Star was a scoring beast, tallying 229 goals in 776 career games. "Milt Schmidt was the greatest competitor I ever played against," claimed former Detroit Red Wings forward Ted Lindsay.

> And tough! Why, he would come down on the right side, and if he didn't make it through he would turn and come down on the left side. And if you stopped him there, he'd grab the puck again, and this time he'd come down the middle and skate right on top of you. And he would hurt you. There were some jarring collisions when he did that. It took a brave person to stand in his way.

Complementing the Kraut Line were the standout offensive contributions of teammates Roy Conacher (a league-leading 26 goals), Bill Cowley (eight goals and 34 assists), and Dit Clapper (13 goals and 13 assists).

The extensive scoring detracted from the reality that the Bruins were a gifted defensive outfit that wore down opposing teams with superior speed and brawn. "In fact," Ross said,

> our defense was so strong we used to do something that would be suicidal today. I used to order my forwards to play outside when backchecking against the opposing wings. In other words, instead of driving the play toward the outside, which is normal, I had them driving it inside *toward* the goal and not away from it.

There was a degree of logic to this unconventional approach. "That way," Ross argued, "my forwards could be looking at their defensemen at all times and be ready for a pass or loose puck. You had to have a great defense to play like that, and we had it. They were the best team I ever saw in my life."

Handling duties between the pipes was rookie newcomer Frank "Mr. Zero" Brimsek. A surprise starter when the popular Tiny Thompson was traded to Detroit at the start of the season, the Eveleth, Minnesota, product was initially not warmly received. "The team took [the trade] pretty

All-time Bruins great Milt Schmidt in his prime. *Le Studio du Hockey, HHOF Images*

badly," Schmidt confessed. "Dit Clapper was Tiny's roommate, and he was ready to quit. We just couldn't understand why Mr. Ross was replacing a sure thing with a rookie." They found out soon enough, as Brimsek kept enemy scorers stymied—hence the Mr. Zero nickname—with a combination of lightning-quick moves and mind games. "I tried to make the opposition player do what I wanted him to," Brimsek once said. "I always felt that the glove side was the strongest for a goaltender. And I would make the shooter believe this, too. In that way, I would make most shooters fire the puck to my stick side, which is what I wanted them to do in the first place." Brimsek ended up leading all goalies that season with 33 victories, a 1.56 goals-against average, and 10 shutouts. He also played a decisive role in the Bruins' six-game triumph against the Maple Leafs in the Stanley Cup Finals. Thus, he was an easy choice for the Vezina Trophy and the Calder Trophy for the league's Rookie of the Year.

The Bruins—whose uniforms now sported a striking black and gold color scheme—failed to repeat in 1939–1940, despite winning one more regular-season game than the year before. They fell to the eventual champion New York Rangers in the first round of the playoffs—not that hockey or any form of mass entertainment much mattered at the time. In September, German tanks rolled into Poland to inaugurate the start of World War II. By the spring, France had fallen to Adolf Hitler's marauding armies, while Great Britain's Expeditionary Force barely escaped annihilation through a massive naval evacuation from the beaches of Dunkirk near the Belgian border. The future looked bleak for the Western Allies, notably Canada, which had declared war on Germany on September 10. The United States had yet to formally engage in the hostilities, but the likelihood of that happening increased as time passed. "There can be no reasoning with an incendiary bomb," President Franklin Roosevelt warned his fellow countrymen. "We now know that a nation can have peace with the Nazis only at the price of total surrender." Bostonians could be forgiven for not feeling too disappointed about the Bruins' early playoff exit.

Yet, there was an air of distinct melancholy surrounding Eddie Shore's abrupt departure from the team in late January. The "Edmonton Express" had been traded to the last-place New York Americans for veteran forward Edward Wiseman and undisclosed cash. "For a man to receive such bitter medicine in return for what he has given to hockey is entirely unwarranted, and to see his name in another N.H. League lineup is unthinkable," wrote a devastated fan to the *Boston Globe*. Advancing years and a litany of injuries had diminished Shore's hockey skills, but that was hardly the reason why the Bruins sent their cantankerous star packing. In the offseason, Shore had spent $40,000 of his own money to purchase the Springfield Indians of the International-American Hockey League, later the American Hockey League. He not only intended to run the floundering western Massachusetts minor-league franchise, but also planned on being the team's player-coach. As for the Bruins, Shore worked out a deal to continue playing for them but only on a part-time basis.

Art Ross and Weston A. Adams—an Ivy Leaguer who had taken over the presidency of the team from his father Charles in 1936—quickly soured on the agreement. Performing in two professional leagues simultaneously placed too much of a physical strain on Shore, as the 38-year-old could manage only two goals in limited action for the Bruins. The unique arrangement also wreaked havoc on Shore's home life. He had practically no time for his wife and young son. "I was only nine years old when my father started playing for the Indians," Eddie Jr. later remembered, "but I can remember him being at the rink all day, coming home for a nap at 3:30, then having [a quick meal], before heading back to play in a game." In the end, Shore and the Bruins decided it was best for both parties to part ways. "Deal with Americans satisfactory to me," Shore wired Ross.

Although some jaundiced observers likened Shore to a museum piece on skates, most hailed the two-time Hart Memorial Trophy winner as a conquering hero when he arrived in the Big Apple. "Maybe Very Good Eddie, the erstwhile Bad Man of the Bruins—the Bad Man of the League, for that matter—isn't quite what he was a couple of seasons ago," *New York Times* columnist John Kieran wrote. "But unless this innocent by-stander is wrong again, he is still the biggest drawing card on the big-league hockey circuit." But Shore had little left in the tank. He played in only 10 games for the Americans, amassing five points on two goals and three assists. The end of the line had arrived for Shore. He retired from the NHL at the conclusion of the season to devote his full energies to overseeing the Springfield operation. His competitive fires still burned brightly. According to one contemporary newspaper account, Shore as-saulted a referee named Eddie Kuntz during a 1942 game in New Haven, Connecticut. He attempted to "detach [Kuntz's] ears and ram them down his throat two a breast." Having failed to accomplish this, Shore pro-ceeded to follow Kuntz into the dressing room afterward for a second round of bullying behavior. "Ultimate word says that Mr. Shore has been hurled out of the American Hockey League on one bounce, 'pending further notice,'" the report said.

Shore's antics seemed to produce results. Springfield became a yearly contender under his watch, winning three consecutive AHL champion-ships from 1960 to 1962. But Shore exercised authority like a petty third-world dictator. He brooked no dissent and often subjected his players to withering criticism. He nicknamed future Bruins coach and television hockey commentator Don Cherry "The Madagascar Kid" because, in Cherry's words, "that's where he would have sent me, if given the oppor-tunity." "You could never figure the man out," complained another vic-tim. "The team would win a game, and Shore would be angry because we hadn't played the game to his orders or some players had skated with their feet too far apart. Then we'd lose by a big score, and he'd be happy because we'd played exactly the style of hockey he wanted." Nor was Shore shy about injecting himself into intimate personal matters. "The club is not doing too well, and there's a very good reason for this state of affairs," he once admonished a room full of players' wives. "You ladies are giving your husbands too much sex!" His eccentric notions did not end there. On another occasion, Shore told defenseman Don Johns he knew the underlying reason why he wasn't playing up to his potential. "You're not combing your hair right," he said. If this wasn't bizarre enough, Shore also fancied himself a skilled chiropractor. He thought nothing of twisting a player's head into a series of painful contortions if the latter unwisely complained of a stiff neck. "Eddie," asked a bemused observer, "did you ever have one of those things come off in your hands?"

Shore was at his worst when it came to financial matters. Always looking to squeeze out a profit, he thought nothing of shutting off the arena lights when his players practiced at home. That way he was ensured of saving a few extra dollars on the monthly electricity bill. "We were on strict budgets with him," forward Billy McCreary later told *Sports Illustrated*. "He never allowed us to tip taxi drivers more than 15 cents. After a while, we got so well known around the league none of the cabbies wanted to pick us up." Other cost-saving moves involved saddling his players with cheap, inferior equipment. "He would make his goalies use skates so small they would lose toenails," revealed a team insider. Shore was even stingier with salaries, often finding creative new ways to deprive players of promised performance bonuses in their contracts. "If they got, say, 20 goals, they'd get more money," McCreary explained. "So a guy would be comin' close to 20 near the end of the season. Does he make it? Hell, Shore would sit him out of the late-season games so he couldn't score anymore. And you think I'm joking, just ask anyone who skated for Shore." "You couldn't top the Old Man," Cherry said.

In 1967, the entire squad tried to push for change. "We decided that things were so bad that we had to do something and that a strike couldn't be any worse for us than playing for the team," said defenseman Larry Johnston. The walkout lasted just a few days, as the players caved to Shore's threats of replacing each and every one of them. "I'll bring in enough players to man two more clubs," he boasted. But Shore had experienced enough, stepping away from the team's presidency a short time later. His personal health had gone into a tailspin, thanks to several heart attacks. "Everybody agreed that that was the right thing to do," his son recalled. Although Shore briefly returned to the franchise's helm in 1975—winning yet another league championship—he retired for good the following season after the team was sold.

Shore died from liver cancer in 1985, at age 82, leaving behind a complicated legacy. Shore "was the most determined man I ever encountered," Art Ross once observed.

> When he got an idea in his head, there was no changing it. He gave everything he had on every shift in every game he ever played. Eddie had a quick temper, but much of his trouble was produced by his low frustration point, plus the fact that once he made up his mind on something, no one could change him even when he was obviously wrong.

It was an apt description for a man whose actions created great disruption both on and off the ice.

Shore's departure did not prevent the Bruins from recapturing the Stanley Cup in 1940–1941. "A good year or a bad year is mainly a matter of breaks," philosophized team captain Dit Clapper before the start of the season. Yet, luck had nothing to do with the stellar way Boston played. The team finished 27–8–13, with a 23-game winning streak from late December into February. They were somewhat less dominant in the playoffs, barely squeaking by the Maple Leafs in the opening round. But they regrouped and swept the Detroit Red Wings, 4–0, in the best-of-seven finals. The Kraut Line of Milt Schmidt, Woody Dumart, and Bobby Bauer once again led the way. Briefly rebranded the "Kitchener Kids"—due to the then-strong public animus against Adolf Hitler and all things German—the remarkable trio accrued 111 points, with 48 goals and 63 assists in 48 games. Such was the degree of their personal closeness that they now felt comfortable negotiating their contracts collectively with Art Ross. "We felt that if we went to see him together, asked exactly for the same salary for each, and took a united stand in our dealings, we'd be a lot better off," Schmidt said. "It generally worked pretty well, although in 1940, we were all holdouts when Mr. Ross turned down our bids for a $500 raise—after we'd finish one-two-three in the league scoring, too." Frank Brimsek was in fine form, too, proving his sensational rookie year was no fluke. Mr. Zero posted 27 wins in goal, along with six shutouts.

"He's as quick as a cat," praised one rival. "Trying to get him to make the first move is like pushing over the Washington Monument."

With their second Cup victory in three seasons, the Bruins appeared on the cusp of winning several more. Alas, hopes for a Beantown hockey dynasty were crushed, thanks to the surprise Japanese attack on U.S. naval and air installations at Pearl Harbor, Hawaii, on December 7, 1941. The team roster was decimated, as subsequent military draft calls compelled many players—including Brimsek and the entire Kraut Line—to depart for the conflict. "You just get established in a business like hockey and you have to give it all up," Brimsek lamented. "The ---- Japs bomb Pearl Harbor and a damned war comes along." The development did lead to a memorable sendoff for the Kraut Line on February 10, 1942. At the conclusion of their last game together before entering the service—an 8–1 home victory over the Montreal Canadians—they were dramatically carried off the ice by their rivals to the deafening roar of a packed Garden audience. "When they grabbed Bobby, Woody, and myself, we felt like saying, 'What are they doing?'" Schmidt revealed to an interviewer decades later. "Well, we found out in a hurry that they all grabbed us and carried us off the ice." The high emotion of the moment never left the Bruins center. Schmidt said, "That goes to show you that you have friends, although they are bitter enemies. You had friends in the [NHL], not necessarily on the ice, but off the ice."

When the fighting ended overseas in 1945, the Bruins veterans returned, but they were unable to recapture the magic of the prewar years. The Bruins were still a playoff-caliber team, but they were no longer great, as three years in the service had robbed the key players of their hockey prime and eroded their skills. In the case of Frank Brimsek, who had seen significant action in the South Pacific, he had trouble of a different sort; he could not put his wartime experience behind him. "I came back too soon after being in the service," Brimsek later confessed. "My nerves were jumpy. I should have taken a rest before coming back, but I needed the money." He played three more seasons in a Bruins uniform but did not part on good terms. He had earlier informed Art Ross that he wanted to be traded to Chicago to join a promising business venture his brother had started there. Ross initially gave his assent but then withdrew it. Brimsek exploded in anger. "If that's the way you feel," he informed Ross, "I'll quit altogether!" Given the ultimatum, the chastised Bruins GM backed down. Brimsek played one last season for the Black Hawks before quitting for good.

By the mid-1950s, Brimsek's old championship teammates had departed as well, including the Kraut Line. But these longtime comrades-in-arms managed to share one last magical moment together. On March 18, 1952, a retired Bobby Bauer was persuaded by team management to sign a special one-day contract and rejoin Milt Schmidt and Woody Dumart for a final go-round against the Chicago Black Hawks at home. The contest was billed as a special night to honor Schmidt and Dumart for their banner service to the Bruins throughout the years. Despite being away from the game for five years, a physically fit Bauer was more than up for the occasion. In fact, the winger, who was now 37 years old, helped set up Schmidt for his 200th career goal in the second period. "Milt's tally was a typical Kraut production," Tom Fitzgerald of the *Boston Globe* wrote. "Schmidty himself sent the plug out of the right corner, and Bauer took a swipe as it went across the front of the cage. The disc went over to Woody Dumart on the left. He passed it to Schmidt, set up in a fine spot for a certain six-foot smash." "It was a night that comes only once in a lifetime," an emotional Schmidt declared to reporters afterward. "Mr. Bruin" would end his NHL playing career in 1955, outlasting Woody Dumart by a season.

While no championship banners were raised to the Garden rafters during these years, the Bruins still managed to break new historic ground. On January 18, 1958, the team erased the long-standing NHL color line by playing Willie O'Ree—a 22-year-old black forward from the Quebec Aces of the AHL—in a road game against the Canadiens. "He was received quietly," said Bruins general manager Lynn Patrick, a former New York Rangers star who oversaw the team from 1954 to 1964. "Ninety-eight percent of the players were Canadian, and Willie was a Canadian. Some had played against him in junior hockey. It was no big deal because by that time many blacks were in baseball and basketball." The move came as no surprise for O'Ree—the product of a prominent black family from Fredericton, New Brunswick.

Willie Eldon O'Ree had always known he possessed the talent to play in the NHL. A speedy skater with an intuitive feel for the game, he had played organized hockey since age five and scored 22 goals with 12 assists in his first professional season with the Aces. "All I needed was a break," he explained. That came when O'Ree received an invitation to attend Bruins training camp before the start of the 1957–1958 season. Although he failed to make the final cut, team officials were impressed enough by his overall performance to tell him he needed only a "little more seasoning" to reach the big time. "They knew what I could do," O'Ree later recalled in his 2000 memoir, *The Autobiography of Willie O'Ree: Hockey's Black Pioneer*.

When it came time to make history against the Habs, O'Ree could barely control his excitement. "I could see fans pointing, 'There's that black kid. He's up with the Bruins,'" O'Ree said. Despite the butterflies, he did nothing to embarrass himself during a rare 3–0 Boston shutout against their archrivals. "O'Ree is not only fast, but he's a strong skater," Montreal coach Frank Selke praised afterward. "He looks as if he could go all night." The compact, 5-foot-10, 185-pound O'Ree further distinguished himself by almost scoring a goal against the formidable Jacques Plante in net. "I got the puck, and I should have shot," he later recalled. "I hesitated. I wanted to make a shift, and just as I did, I was hooked. But I should have shot." O'Ree suited up for only one more game as a Bruin that season before returning to the minors. "I knew from the beginning that I wasn't going to be up for long because the Bruins had an injured player who would return to the lineup," O'Ree noted. Still, he was hardly crestfallen. "I'm just happy to get a chance up here, that's about all I can say," he told the *Boston Globe*.

O'Ree returned to the Bruins in 1960–1961, notching four goals and 10 assists in 43 games. His first NHL goal—a game-winner against Montreal at the Boston Garden on New Year's Day 1961—proved memorable. "I was playing left wing that night, and we were leading the Canadians 2–1 in the third period," O'Ree later recounted to hockey analyst and author Mike Brophy.

> Both teams were down a man because of penalties, so we were playing four-on-four. I broke away from my check, and I was busting down the left wing when [teammate] Leo Boivin hit me with just a perfect pass. I didn't have to break stride, and I had the afterburners on. I went into the Montreal end and skated past their defensemen, Tom Johnson and Jean-Guy Talbot.

Montreal goaltender Charlie Hodge was unable to adjust. O'Ree let fly a shot along the ice that slid under Hodge's glove hand. "That made the score 3–1 for us," O'Ree said. The Canadians narrowed the Boston lead three minutes later on a goal by center Henri Richard, but O'Ree and the Bruins were able to hold on for a hard-earned 3–2 victory. For his standout effort, O'Ree received a rousing standing ovation from the home crowd that lasted several minutes. "I knew the fans in Boston were on my side, but I didn't realize how much," he said.

O'Ree was not so well received at other NHL venues. At New York City's venerable Madison Square Garden, fans showered him with vile racial insults before he even stepped onto the ice. "Racist remarks from fans were much worse in the U.S cities than in Toronto and Montreal," O'Ree said. "The fans would yell, 'Go back to the south' and 'How come you're not picking cotton.' Things like that. It didn't bother me. Hell, I'd been called names most of my life. I just wanted to be a hockey player, and if they couldn't accept that fact, that was their problem, not mine." Teammates and Bruins management could not help but admire his stoic attitude. "He had a good personality for it," Milt Schmidt observed. "It didn't take him long to make friends. He wasn't real quiet. Somebody could have called him all the names in the world and he could have accepted it."

O'Ree's remarkable forbearance was not without limits, especially when he was targeted for abuse by bruising Black Hawks forward Eric "Elbows" Nesterenko at the start of a contest in Chicago. After calling O'Ree the n-word, Nesterenko took the butt-end of his stick and rammed it into O'Ree's unsuspecting face. A broken nose and two missing front teeth later, O'Ree had had endured enough. Nesterenko "just stood there and laughed, like, 'What's this guy gonna do? He's probably not gonna do anything,'" O'Ree said later. "Well, I had to make a choice right there. Either turn and skate away or fight." O'Ree chose the latter. "I hit him over the head with my stick. Cut his head open. Broke [my] stick in half. Soon as I did that, I dropped [my] gloves, because I knew we were gonna fight. And he dropped his gloves and grabbed me—he was strong—and hit me a couple [of] times. So I grabbed him and tried to get a couple in." O'Ree's teammates came rushing to his aid as both benches emptied. What followed was a classic hockey donnybrook that resulted in O'Ree being sent to the Bruins locker room for medical treatment. It was there that O'Ree seriously contemplated quitting. "Willie, you don't need this," he told himself. But almost as quickly, O'Ree developed second thoughts. "If I'm gonna leave the league," he reasoned, "I'm gonna leave because I don't have the ability and skills to play anymore. I'm not gonna leave it because some guy's trying to get me out."

O'Ree—an equally talented athlete on the baseball diamond—had first been exposed to this kind of rough treatment when he tried out for the Milwaukee Braves at their major-league training camp in Waycross, Georgia, in 1956. "This was the first time I had ever been to the South, and I flew into Atlanta," O'Ree remembered. "I walked into the airport terminal, and the first thing I saw was 'White Only' and 'Colored Only' washrooms. I couldn't believe it, but since I had to use the washroom, I walked into the colored one. I wasn't going to cause a revolution during my first few minutes in town." Things grew progressively worse when he was told to sit in the back of a bus en route to Waycross. "Why am I here?" O'Ree asked. While he survived several rounds of player cuts, he was eventually told there was no place for him on the club's big-league roster. Instead of bitter disappointment, O'Ree only felt relief. The extended tryout convinced him that his path for career success lay in becoming a professional hockey player. "I was happy as I could be," he said.

But O'Ree's dream of hockey glory was almost cut tragically short. While playing in a junior-league game in Guelph, Ontario, he lost most of the sight in his right eye after a deflected slap shot struck his face. Recalled O'Ree, "I was in the hospital about four or five days, and when I opened my eyes, I could see just a light out of my good eye, and I couldn't see anything out of my right eye. And I thought I was blind." O'Ree ignored his doctor's advice to hang up his skates and continued to play despite being at an obvious competitive disadvantage. "I was a left shot, and I was playing left wing, but I had no right eye," O'Ree said. "This meant that I had to turn my head quite a bit so my left eye could see what was happening. I was having to slow down, and guys who could never touch me before were hitting me now." O'Ree tried hard not to let others know of his handicap as it probably would have scared teams away from employing him. "It was my secret," he said.

The Bruins traded O'Ree to the Montreal Canadians before the start of the 1961–1962 season. O'Ree was personally devastated. "Considering the talent Montreal had, I knew I had no chance of making their squad," he said. O'Ree spent the remainder of his career playing on a number of minor-league clubs, notably the Los Angeles Blades of the Western Hockey League. He was a major standout for Los Angeles, scoring a career-high 38 goals in 1964–1965. But the NHL never gave him a second look. "It was probably the eyesight that held him back," Milt Schmidt later speculated. O'Ree did serve as an inspiration to future NHL players of color, for example, Jarome Iginla and Mike Greer. "I'm in awe knowing what he went through," Iginla told Jack Gruber of *USA Today* in 2008. "There is a lot of trash-talking going on [in the game], and I can't imagine what he must have gone through." For his part, O'Ree never voiced any regrets. He had, after all, defied the odds by becoming the "Jackie Robinson of hockey."

The Bruins were a hockey club in steep decline as the somnolent 1950s gave way to the uncertain 1960s. Art Ross had long since departed, and the team deteriorated to the point where it failed to make the playoffs the first eight years of the new decade. Once a flagship franchise for the NHL, the Bruins had become a laughingstock. "We just didn't have enough talent in those days," forward Johnny Bucyk later wrote in his 1972 memoir *Hockey in My Blood*. "It seemed as though no matter who they put together on a line, nothing worked. It was discouraging to keep losing and losing and losing. I can remember that 'down' feeling all too well. It was hard to get the morale of the team up then." If there was any bright spot during these "dark days," it was the continued loyalty of the Garden fans. "It was very unusual not to fill the place," Bucyk recalled. "The only time there weren't big crowds occurred when there would be a snowstorm and people couldn't get in."

Weston Adams, who had repurchased the team in 1964, after relinquishing majority control to Garden president Walter A. Brown in the early 1950s, began a painstaking rebuilding process. One of his most important moves involved naming Milt Schmidt to head the team's front office. Schmidt—the former Kraut Liner and club coach from 1955 to 1966—had a sharp eye for talent. Through skillful drafting and shrewd trades—particularly a blockbuster deal that brought future Hall of Famer Phil Esposito to Boston from the Chicago Black Hawks—Schmidt was able to turn the team's fortunes around. The Bruins returned to the playoffs in 1967–1968, and advanced to the East Division semifinals of the newly expanded 12-team league the following season. They fell to Montreal in six games. "We all thought we could take them," recalled Derek Sanderson, a promising third-year center who notched 26 goals and 22 assists on the regular season. "But the Canadians got lucky. Although we outplayed them in the first two games, they came from behind twice to beat us in sudden-death overtime. Then we took the next two games, and it looked like we had them in a corner." Unfortunately, fate and Montreal's notoriously brutish enforcer, John Ferguson, intervened. "[He] caught me with a dirty check—I'd do the same thing to him if I got the chance—and knocked me out of the series," Sanderson revealed. Montreal captured the next two games en route to winning their 16th Stanley Cup championship in franchise history.

Heartbreaking although the loss to the Canadians was, there were no tears shed in the Boston locker room afterward. As Bobby Orr—the team's outstanding 21-year-old defenseman—later wrote, "We were disappointed yet determined, and most of us couldn't wait to get to camp the next year and do something that hadn't happened in Boston in a very long time. We had our eyes on Lord Stanley."

The Big Bad Bruins were ready to roar.

3

BREAKING BAD

Ancient Chinese military strategist and philosopher Sun Tzu once wrote in *The Art of War* that every battle is won before it is ever fought. While it is unknown whether Harry Sinden was familiar with the influential text, a similar thought must have crossed the mind of the laconic 38-year-old coach when the Bruins opened training camp for their upcoming National Hockey League season in London, Ontario, on September 12, 1969. After three years of presiding over a challenging rebuild, which saw the Bruins rise from last place to the playoffs, Sinden finally had a roster at his disposal that had the talent to go all the way. "At last we were ready to make it all work," he later recounted. To say the club was loaded was a little like saying the late, great New York Yankees slugger George Herman "Babe" Ruth had pretty decent home run power. The Bruins were that good.

Everything began with Bobby Orr. Entering his fourth NHL season, the precocious, baby-faced All-Star defenseman was already being discussed in the same breath as the great Eddie Shore. Sinden found such a comparison ridiculous, not because he felt Orr did not measure up to the "Edmonton Express," but because he felt Orr surpassed him. "Remember," Sinden said, "when Shore was playing, no forechecking was allowed. When Eddie got the puck he had plenty of time to start a rush. But the rules were changed, Bobby does get checked in his defensive zone." Not that the latter slowed him down. Orr's lightning speed allowed him to weave around defenders with the ease of someone changing a television channel with a clicker. An indication of Orr's superior talent was his plus/

minus rating, a hockey statistic that measures a player's overall impact on a game by the number of times his team scores a nonpower-play goal when they are on the ice. In 1968–1969, in only his third season in the league, Orr tied Phil Esposito with a NHL-best 55, a mark he would either equal or improve on five more times during the course of his Hall of Fame career. "Orr can do everything," Milt Schmidt said. "The fact is that we have to find anything he can't do. You watch him every game and you say, 'That's the best play he' s ever made.' Then you look again, and he's doing something better." Indeed, Harry Howell of the New York Rangers spoke for many of his peers after he won the 1967 Norris Trophy as the NHL's top defenseman. "I'm glad I won it now," he said, "because Bobby Orr is going to win it for the next 10 years."

Joining Orr on the blue line was Ted Green, an All-Star performer and a tenacious competitor who was feared throughout the league for his ability to floor an opponent with a single punch. He was easily the most respected player in the Bruins clubhouse. "Green always has been the unofficial team leader of the Bruins," Sinden observed. "He inspires players to be more courageous than they are. They simply don't want Teddy to think they don't want to mix it. They don't want him to say, 'That S.O.B. is chicken.' So they make sure they're not." For his part, Green downplayed his reputation as a fighter. "Sure, I play tough," he said, "but there are other players a lot tougher than I am, and you don't hear about them. They do sneaky things like sticking you with an elbow in the rib. Everything I do is out in the open, and everyone sees it." Apart from Orr and Green, the Bruins looked to get quality minutes from a rotating core of talented defenders like Don Awrey, Rick Smith, Gary Doak, and Dallas Smith. Dallas Smith—a native of central Canada who signed with the Bruins as a teenager—appeared the most promising. He had an unusually high hockey IQ and was especially effective when paired with Orr. "I can't put my finger on it or explain it," Sinden told *Hockey News*.

> But . . . there are few players in the league who can work with Orr as efficiently as Dallas. He just seems to sense what Bobby is going to do. How I don't know, because Bobby certainly doesn't play orthodox defense. But Dallas seems to know how to get out of Bobby's way, and they go together like corn beef on rye.

Up front, the Bruins were blessed with three solid lines. Reigning NHL scoring champ Phil Esposito anchored the top unit at center. Esposito lived to shoot, but no one could ever argue with the results. After all, he ended up having a record-shattering 126 points in 1968–1969, on 49 goals and 77 assists. "It was an ideal situation," Esposito later said. "The Bruins were a young and hungry team, and we were becoming a force. Bobby was already this incredible player, and we needed scoring. I was going to do my best to score as much as I could, and they encouraged me to shoot whenever I had the opportunity."

Esposito's wingmen were Ken Hodge and Wayne Cashman. Hodge had been a throw-in from the earlier Chicago deal that had brought Esposito to Boston. A one-time highly touted prospect, the hulking 6-foot-2, 210-pound Toronto native had become something of a bust for Chicago; he had an underwhelming 16 goals during his two-year stint there. His numbers would greatly improve with the Bruins. The same season Esposito tore up the league in scoring, Hodge cranked out 45 goals and 45 assists, good for 90 points and a fifth-place ranking among NHL players. Hodge credited the advice he received from Bruins general manager Milt Schmidt for the turnaround. Schmidt suggested Hodge use a less angular blade on his hockey stick to achieve better control of his shots. "It has worked," Hodge said. "My shots seem to go where I want them now, and they are lower and usually just off the ice. This way, the goalie cannot catch the puck and . . . Phil may get the rebound."

Cashman—a rough-and-tumble skater from Kingston, Ontario—was less concerned about the scoring end of things than he was with keeping opponents off-balance with his highly aggressive style of play. "I'm really a nice guy," he said, "but frequently when an opponent, the puck, and I are in the corner at the same time, unusual things happen. There's no malice involved. I just want the puck." Cashman also earned himself a reputation for being one of the league's most notorious pranksters. In a road game against the Los Angeles Kings, he once took a pair of scissors and cut the wires to the public address system as a singer was attempting to belt out "God Bless America" during a pregame ceremony. Stadium officials "tried to locate the source of the electrical malfunction," *Sports Illustrated* reported, "but in time they gave up." Cashman never gave up.

The second line featured Fred Stanfield at center and grizzled veterans John "Pie" McKenzie and Johnny "Chief" Bucyk on the wings. The son of a Toronto police inspector, Stanfield was a superb playmaker with excellent speed and stickhandling skills. He made sure the puck went where it needed to go. "I can make soft passes or hard ones," he said. "With guys like Chief and Pie, I throw it to them real hard. They can reach them, and it gives them more time to make the play. We keep the passes off the ice, and that's to our advantage because the puck doesn't get blocked by anybody's stick that way."

While Stanfield went about his business in a quiet and unassuming way, McKenzie was the opposite. He was loud, irreverent, and confrontational. "I like to take a run at somebody on my first shift just to stir things up and plant the idea that if a squirt like me [he was 5-foot-9, 175-pounds] can go after 'em—particularly if my target is a big star—then why not everybody?" he said. A one-time rodeo rider nicknamed "Pie" because of the shape of his face, McKenzie accumulated his share of bumps and bruises throughout the years. But nothing compared to the misfortune he experienced in 1963, while playing for the Black Hawks. He ruptured his spleen after accidentally impaling himself on his own stick. "I was lucky," he said afterward, "the body compensates for the loss of a spleen." McKenzie also played with a fractured skull. "It wasn't much as skull fractures go," he joked. "Just a little bone where the nose is hooked to the forehead. It was unhooked."

While not as fearless or quick-witted as McKenzie, Bucyk was a dependable scorer—the Bruins' career record holder in that department, with 545 goals in 21 seasons—and a steady leader by example. It was no accident that he had been given team captain honors. "You couldn't have had a finer person as captain than [Bucyk]," Orr later wrote in his autobiography *Orr: My Story*. "He was not a big speechmaker, but he came to work every day and set the standard with his level of play." Bucyk had made a point of looking out for Orr when the callow young superstar entered the NHL with high expectations and a huge publicity buildup. He became Orr's roommate in training camp and schooled him on the ins and outs of the professional game, while also easing the pressure he faced. "It was my job to take any rookie under my wing . . . and make them feel welcome," Bucyk explained. Orr appreciated the effort. "Rooming with Bucyk . . . was unbelievable," he said. "You don't feel nervous around him. He makes you feel like you're one of the guys right away, and it doesn't matter who you are. Rich or poor, great or not great, he's like that with everybody."

Derek Sanderson and Eddie Westfall were the standouts on the third line, otherwise known as the checking line. On most hockey clubs, such units were primarily used for defensive purposes against another team's top line. But on this explosive Bruins club, they could also put the puck in the net, as evidenced by Sanderson and Westfall accounting for seven of the team's 13 shorthanded goals in 1968–1969. Similar to Cashman and McKenzie, Sanderson carried a reputation for being an agitator. The future television broadcaster and best-selling author liked to rile up opponents to the point of distraction. "He says things to get you mad. Like, 'We're going to put that puck right between your eyes tonight,'" said New York Rangers goaltender Eddie Giacomin, a favorite personal target. Nor did Sanderson mind paying a physical price when other teams inevitably retaliated against his provocations. "I've taken my lickings," he said. "I've had my head smashed, my nose broken. I've been speared. My arm has been broken twice, my knees messed up, all from fighting and hitting. . . . I don't care how many lickings I take."

Sanderson's escapades too often eclipsed the crucial team role performed by Westfall, the tall, fun-loving forward from Belleville, Ontario, who first arrived on the Boston scene in 1961. Westfall was tasked with carrying out the toughest defensive assignments. "The thing about Eddie is that he has a knack of covering the big scorers like [Bobby Hull of the Chicago Black Hawks] without throwing his arms around them," Milt Schmidt said. "Eddie plays squarely and fairly, he doesn't hook and hold like some of those other shadow-men." Westfall was so adept at the job Hull once complained he saw Westfall's reflection staring back at him in a hotel bathroom mirror the morning after a particularly frustrating on-ice encounter.

In goal, the Bruins were relying on the puck-stopping abilities of cagey 29-year-old veteran Gerry Cheevers. A professional since 1956, Cheevers had cemented his position as the team's starter in 1967–1968, with a 17–5 record, with three shutouts and a 2.83 goals-against average. More importantly, he was seen as a dependable performer when games were on the line. "As far as I'm concerned," Sinden said, "Gerry is one of the best money players in the game. He's never bothered by pressure. He just goes out there and does his thing." Cheevers was ably backed up by Eddie Johnston, a tough-as-nails Montreal native who had been called up to the Bruins in 1962, after spending six years in the minors. He once had his nose broken three times in a 10-day stretch and the unfortunate luck of having a portion of his ear sheared off in the middle of a game. "Happened right in Boston," he told the *Boston Herald-Traveler* in a 1971 interview. "The ear was just hanging, and they sewed it back on. I went back [into the contest]."

In sum, the Bruins had the necessary elements in place to produce a winner. And no one was more thrilled by this prospect than Johnny Bucyk, the only skating team member who could claim to have been a Bruin when John F. Kennedy was still a nondescript back-bencher in the U.S. Senate. Bucyk experienced firsthand the depressing downward trajectory the franchise had taken in the first half of the decade. It was not a pretty sight. "We never once made the playoffs, and I felt like sending up smoke signals it was so agonizing," he maintained. But the arrival of Orr and Esposito changed everything. Bucyk now waited anxiously like an over-eager child waiting to open his presents on Christmas Eve to see if his most fervid dream of becoming a Stanley Cup champion would come true.

The story of John Paul Bucyk is one of hard work, pluck, and an uncanny determination to succeed. Born to Unkrainian immigrant par-

Veteran winger Johnny Bucyk: the heart and soul of the Big Bad Bruins. *Lewis Portnoy, HHOF Images*

ents, Bucyk learned about adversity at a young age while growing up poor in Edmonton, Alberta, after World War II. "My father died when I was 11," he told writer Stan Fischler, "which meant that my mother had to work at more than one job to keep us going." Johnny did his best to help out by delivering newspapers and performing odd jobs for a local pharmacy. The latter activity, however, was not without its dangers. "I remember the time [Bucyk] picked up a big jar of sulfuric acid," said Dick Hoelton, the pharmacy manager. "The jar was cracked, and when Johnny lifted it, it broke and all the acid went all over his lower legs and feet. It ate away at his shoes, socks, his pants, and he was jumping around screaming something awful. He was burning up." Fortunately, Hoelton had the presence of mind to reach for some bicarbonate of soda and douse Bucyk with it. "It neutralized the acid, and we finally got him out. Luckily, he wasn't seriously hurt."

Hoelton's quick thinking probably saved Bucyk's hockey career, which had begun years earlier on a makeshift outdoor rink in his own backyard. "We didn't have hockey sticks so we'd use old broomsticks, and for pucks we'd use old tennis balls or stones or frozen balls of manure from the milk wagon horses," said Bucyk's older brother Bill, who went on to have a long hockey career of his own as a minor-league defenseman. "I remember later when some of us did get hockey sticks, they'd sometimes break so we'd get old tin cans, flatten them, and wrap them around the broken part of the stick to hold it together and then string around that."

Young Johnny graduated to pee-wee hockey, where he spent most of his time as a goaltender. He quickly tired of the position, however. "I didn't like it because I found out I didn't get enough space in the local newspaper," Bucyk wrote in his autobiography. "All I ever read about was the guys scoring goals. So then I played defense for a little while, but it was the same thing all over again. All I read in the newspaper was about a few players who were scoring all the goals. It made me wonder if anybody was watching me at all." After some additional trial and error, Bucyk settled on left wing, where he would play for the rest of his hockey career. Yet, finding a position was one thing and performing well at it was another. "Johnny had so much desire," recalled his pee-wee coach, Bob Magee. "But his skating wasn't too good." To work on this deficiency, Magee made Bucyk skate between periods of every game. "I remember telling him to keep his head up too—I'd yell at him to keep it up because sometimes he'd get nailed. His skating [got better] some, but he was still down on his ankles a lot when he left me. But he had a great big heart and would do anything you told him."

It was not until Bucyk reached the junior hockey level and came under the tutelage of a former New York Rangers goalie named Ken McCauley that his skating markedly improved. McCauley instructed him to enroll in a figure skating school. "He didn't like it, thought it would be sissy, but I told him he *had* to learn to skate if he wanted to play pro hockey some-day," McCauley said. "He couldn't turn right, see. He'd coast. Turn left and not right. He'd fall down." Bucyk acceded to McCauley's wishes but only after extracting a promise from him that the lessons would be private. "Just him and the instructor so nobody would laugh at him," McCauley said. Satisfied with the results—Bucyk could now skate backward and sideways effectively—McCauley next moved on to improving Bucyk's grasp of such hockey fundamentals as checking and passing. "I would harp, harp, and harp until he got it right," McCauley said. "Then— bingo—it suddenly comes. I can remember whacking him on the butt with a stick to get him to move up to forecheck. Kept whacking him. Takes patience, but they finally learn. He *loved* hockey. He even played some goal for us and was great."

The new and improved Bucyk signed with the Detroit Red Wings in 1955, but he became disillusioned when he first cast his eyes on his competition at training camp. The Red Wings, who had won four of the previous six Stanley Cups, were stacked at left wing with such established players as Ted Lindsay, and Bucyk knew he had no realistic shot at cracking the starting lineup and seeing meaningful minutes. "Like most rookies who come and sit and get discouraged on the bench, I wasn't any different," he confessed. "I always liked to be on the ice playing, and I just didn't get the ice time." In fact, the only action Bucyk saw was at the end of games when the Red Wings were hopelessly down by several goals. "I never got on when things were close," he said. "By that time it would be late in the third period, and your legs would be all stiff, the circulation would be sluggish, and you didn't feel up to your best." Bucyk scored only one goal that rookie year and did only marginally better the next season, with 10 goals and 11 assists. But the former string bean had physically filled out, at six feet, 215 pounds, and developed into a good forechecker. He still had a lot of maturing to do, however. When Detroit coach Jimmy Skinner told him late in a blowout loss to New York that it was his turn to go out on the ice, Bucyk quipped, "All right coach what do you want? A win or a tie?" While his teammates on the bench chuckled at the insolence, Skinner did not crack a smile.

Whether related or not, Bucyk found himself traded to Boston that offseason for All-Star goaltender Terry Sawchuk. He welcomed the move, however, as he figured it would mean more regular ice time and reunite him with Rudolph "Bronco" Horvath and Vic Stasiuk—former junior line mates who the Bruins had also acquired. "I was thrilled," he recalled. Bucyk was further pleased when Bruins coach Milt Schmidt phoned him unexpectedly and predicted he would become a valuable club contributor. "We think your rugged hockey style will go better with the Bruins than any other club; report in good shape in September and your best season will lie ahead, believe me," Schmidt said. Bucyk would reward his new boss's faith in him by averaging 21 goals and 33 assists in the next six seasons and becoming a feared intimidator. "The guy is deceptive," an impressed opponent said. "He's much heavier than he looks, and he hits low, with his hip. The thing you have to remember whenever he's on the ice is that you can never afford to stand admiring your passes. Not the way Bucyk hits."

With fellow winger Horvath and center Stasiuk, Bucyk also formed one of the most prolific scoring trios in the league—the "Uke Line." Dubbed in honor of Bucyk and Stasiuk's ethnic Ukrainian roots, the line made the Bruins a playoff contender in the late 1950s with their crisp puck movement, clutch scoring, and precision-like teamwork. "The three of us worked well together," Bucyk said. "Each of us knew where the other two fellows would be. Bronco and Vic turned out to be the big scorers, whereas my job was to get the puck out of the corner." Injuries and trades broke up the line in the early1960s, forcing Bucyk to become the last Uke standing. Now officially known as "Chief" due to what one magazine called a "dark complexion" that many mistook for being Native-American, Bucyk remained a productive, if somewhat disenchanted, club staple during a bleak stretch in Bruins history. For sure, it often became a chore for Bucyk to "get up" for opponents he knew the team had no chance of beating. "It was very frustrating," he wrote. "A lot of the players went up to the front office and asked to be traded, and quite a few times they were traded." Bucyk pointedly did not include himself in this group. "I never asked to be traded and never wanted to be traded," he maintained. Indeed, it would have been to both his and Boston's detriment if he had been.

The good karma established in Bruins training camp came crashing down on the night of September 21. In an otherwise meaningless exhibition game against the St. Louis Blues at the Civic Center in Ottawa, Ontario, star defenseman and all-purpose tough guy Ted Green experienced a close brush with death. At the 13:06 mark of the first period, Green got embroiled in an ugly stick fight with Blues forward Wayne Maki that resulted in Green lying half-paralyzed on the ice with a fractured skull. "I could see right away that Green was badly hurt," St. Louis play-by-play announcer Dan Kelly later told writer Brian McFarlane. "When he tried to get up, his face was contorted, and his legs began to buckle under him. It was dreadful. I almost became physically ill watching him struggle because I knew this was very, very serious."

Green had no feeling on his left side, and alarmed teammates rushing to his side could barely make out the slurred words coming out of his mouth. "I'm gonna get that sonofabitch," he said. "I'll kill him—I'll kill him." Meanwhile, a "bewildered and vulnerable" Maki was swinging his stick like a scythe at a cluster of enraged Bruins players spoiling for revenge. "We all went after Maki," Phil Esposito later recounted. "Johnny McKenzie tried hard to get him. Pie would have speared him, because he was mean with a stick." Maki—the raw-boned younger brother of veteran right winger Ronald "Chico" Maki of the Chicago Blackhawks—managed to beat a hasty retreat. "They opened the door behind the net that they used to bring in the Zamboni and escorted Maki off the ice and out of the arena," Esposito said.

The incident began when Maki hit Green from behind while the latter was chasing down a loose puck in the Bruins defensive end. Angered by the cheap shot, Green made a point of getting even once he cleared the puck. He skated up to Maki and delivered a sharp blow to the face with his left glove hand. Maki dropped to the ice. But the 5-foot-11, 198-pound winger wasn't out for the count. Maki bounced back up and speared Green in the testicles with the blade of his stick. Maki admitted afterward he was afraid of acquiring a "scaredy cat" reputation if he had allowed Green's affront to go unanswered. "If you skate away from a person like that, it could drive you out of the league," he explained.

The situation rapidly deteriorated from there. "Where at first I had just been annoyed, now I was sore as hell," Green said. He slashed wildly at

Maki with his stick, landing a thrust to Maki's shoulder just below the biceps. Then came the retaliatory blow that would forever alter the lives of both players. "Maki . . . let go a two-handed swinging of his stick—certainly not the way Teddy had swung—hitting Green on the head," said Milt Schmidt, who witnessed the event firsthand. Green crumpled to the ice like a marionette having its strings clipped. Green later claimed he had momentarily taken his eyes off Maki when the Ontario native appeared to backpedal. "I sort of felt [the fight] was all over," Green said. "It was my mistake. . . . I took [Maki's blow] really good on the side of the head, and . . . after that I was so much scrambled eggs. People say that my stick was up and [Maki's] glanced off mine before it hit. I say I wish it had because but it wouldn't have hit me so hard. But as far I know it was a direct blow and felled me like a ton of potatoes."

Bruins head trainer Dan Canney confirmed the severity of the injury. "[Green] went down with his knees buckling, and then his head kept thrashing around," Canney said. Maki later denied having any intent on hurting Green. "I just swung in desperation," he claimed. "To protect myself. Not at any particular area of Mr. Green's anatomy. It all happened so fast." But the damage had been done. "Teddy's face was all bashed to one side," Sanderson observed. "Just like it had collapsed. There was blood all over the ice. It was the worst thing I ever saw."

Veteran linesman Ron Finn—the first game official to arrive on the scene—said there was little he could have done to prevent the violence. "I put up my hands [as a warning to both players to stop], but they had their sticks up in the air above my head and I stepped back," he said. "You are taught to never step into a fight or altercation alone. If you moved in and grabbed one player, you might give the other player an advantage. He would be free to do whatever he wanted." Finn did step in after Maki flattened Green. He was concerned Maki would attempt another lethal swing. "I figured the other linesman would cover Green," he said. "[Maki] reacted like he didn't want to go back at him. I didn't have to grab him. All I did was stand in front of him."

Green had entertained thoughts of not playing that night. He had been a holdout throughout most of training camp, and although he had verbally agreed to terms with Bruins management shortly before the incident, he still had not signed a contract. "Ted said he wanted to hold [the finished draft] for a couple of days, just to look it over, for no special reason," his agent, Bob Woolf, said. Derek Sanderson thought the exhibition game was a bad idea. Strolling with Green through the Parliament section of Ottawa before the game, Sanderson reminded his older friend that he ran the risk of ending up with no money or job security if he got hurt. Green demurred. "Nah, we agreed to terms, and I'll play," he said. "I've got to hit a few players and get my timing before the season starts. And this is a good organization, so even if something happens, they'll still pay."

After Maki delivered his shattering hit, a barely conscious Green was moved onto a stretcher to the clubhouse underneath the stands. "Looking at him on the stretcher was the most depressing sight in the world," Sanderson recalled. "It looked as if his eyes were in the back of his head. He was absolutely motionless." Green was carefully placed on a table inside as teammates and two local doctors hovered anxiously around him. "Considering his condition, he was astonishingly lucid," remembered Dr. Rudy Gittens, one of the attending physicians. Green called him a "SOB" after Gittens initially got his name wrong. Nonplussed, Gittens apologized and asked Green to squeeze his fingers with both his hands. The results were not encouraging. "His right was strong, but the left was weak," said Gittens, who diagnosed a depressed skull fracture. "That was a polite way of putting it," Green later said. "What I had, in fact, was a big hole in the head. The skull splintered, and they had to find the bits and pieces floating around inside."

An ambulance soon arrived to transport Green to nearby Ottawa General Hospital, where Green—a Catholic—requested the Last Rites of the church. He was wheeled into the operating room for two and a half hours of emergency surgery. "He had a fairly significant amount of bruising to the scalp and muscles because it was a blunt, low-velocity injury," said Dr. Michael Richard, who performed the surgery. "When you have a blunt injury you get a lot of bruising, not like a gunshot wound, where all you have is a small hole for an injury. In a case like Green's, what you do after all the bone fragments are removed is close the cover of the brain and put the skull flap back in, leaving the hole there for the present."

The hole was eventually sealed with an inserted plastic plate. But Green had a major setback when he suffered a cerebral hemorrhage only days after the first operation. "I was alone [in my hospital recovery room] when I started hemorrhaging and blacked out," he said. "Somehow, before losing consciousness, I'd managed to flick down the switch [in his bed] that tells the nurse at her desk that you need attention. But for that . . ." Green was again rushed into emergency surgery, and while it looked "touch and go" in the days that followed, he improved, albeit with a limp left arm he said resembled a "strand of spaghetti." Green slowly got feeling back in his appendage when he awoke in his hospital bed one morning. "I lifted my limp left arm over with my good right hand and moved it straight over my head," he recalled. "When I then tried to move my left arm [by itself], the strangest feeling came over me, and I thought, 'It's going to work!'" Green was not mistaken. He felt a faint flicker of life surge back into the arm, as he was able to move it a few short but crucial inches. Green was overcome with emotion. "Y'know I started to cry," he confessed. "I was so damned happy." He shouted his good fortune to a neighboring patient. "I can move my arm," he said. "See . . . it moves. Somebody must love me."

Edward Joseph Green had never received much love from opposing players or fans. When he entered an enemy rink, he was singled out as public enemy number one due to his combative style of play. "There were a lot of fights and a lot of stick fights that I got into that I certainly haven't enjoyed, and I wish I had never gotten into them," Green said. "But I was brought up this way through hockey, and in my formative years in the National Hockey League, they said the only way I would make it was by using my dukes. And that's the way I played." Green had first become acquainted with the fistic elements of the game growing up in St. Boniface, a tight-knit French-speaking community in Canada's south-central Manitoba province. Green remembered,

> The town had a booster weekend where they would have a hockey game and prizes for speed skating and fancy skating, and the whole community was there to watch. And they had to call our hockey game in the middle of the second period because all of it was a big scrap. It was ridiculous. In the team picture that year, almost everybody had a bandage on his head.

Nonetheless life was good. Ted and his friends wiled away their youthful days playing whatever sport was in season. But hockey always took center stage. "We did everything for ourselves," Green recalled.

> We flooded our rink and scraped it when it snowed. It was natural ice, outdoor ice, and we skated in weather when it was—well, I can tell you how cold it was. We had this one guy on one of our kid teams and he was dripping from the nose with a cold, and in no time at all he had

an icicle hanging from his nose. We used to skate outside when it was
30, sometimes 40 degrees below zero. In those days everybody did
that.

Initially signed by the Montreal Canadiens at the age of 18, Green was
snatched up by the Bruins in 1960, after the Habs failed to keep him on
their protective list for the pro draft. This became an especially bitter pill
for Green to swallow, as Montreal had always been his favorite team. No
matter, because Bruins GM Lester Patrick had been keeping close tabs on
him and came away impressed with his aggressiveness. Following a year
of seasoning in the minors, Green was promoted to the Bruins active
roster at the start of the 1961–1962 season. He had sipped a brief cup of
coffee with Boston the previous campaign, and although his ice time had
been limited to a few uneventful minutes, Green still managed to pick up
a penalty. "It was the first of many," he later joked.

Green had no problem sticking around in his second go-round with the
Bruins. He made an immediate impression as both a rugged defender and
team enforcer. "I play defense," he explained,

> and I own the front of my net, and I own one corner in our end, and I
> have to be the boss in front of the net. I have to be the boss in the
> corner. If I'm not the boss in the front of the net, I'm not worth my salt
> because that's where they stand to score goals. And you have to for-
> cibly move almost everybody from in front of the net, and you have to
> let them know you're boss. Otherwise they're going to be standing
> there all night, trying to tip pucks into the net or get clean shots or
> something.

Green racked up a massive number of penalty minutes in his first five
NHL seasons, including 156 in 1964–1965. Green later said he was proud
of his record then, but hard-earned experience and wisdom forced him to
revise this view. "It's pretty stupid to get banished by the referee for
breaking the rules, although sometimes you can't help it," Green later
admitted. "In any contact game, you'll break some rule, intentionally or
otherwise, but hockey is so fast you'll often get away with it. I think I
picked up a good deal of penalty time because of my reputation. Since the
officials watched me closely, they naturally caught me more often."

None of this pleased his wife—the former Patricia Mascarin—who
grew up a street over from Green's family in St. Boniface and had no

interest in her husband's livelihood. Her preference trended toward art and music. "She knew nothing about sports," Green confirmed. "I doubt if she could tell a hockey stick from a baseball bat." Still, she cared enough to ask him why he had such a "Bad Boy" reputation in the game. Green offered a pragmatic assessment. "This is the only way I'm going to stay up [with the parent club]," he said. "Right now I'm the team policeman. If somebody gets hit, it's up to me to go after the guy. This helps attract attention to the Bruins, because we're not winning." Eventually Green believed he would develop a more polished game where he would not have to rely exclusively on his brute strength. "The more I learn, the more they'll depend on my ability instead of my roughness," he said. Interestingly, Green never thought of himself as a dirty player. "Hockey is not like most other team sports, say, football where it's stop and start, and the players have a chance to cool down," he once explained. "Much of the retaliation in hockey is instinctive because of the pace. You have to expect these things to happen. Many of the fouls are accidental."

Accidental or not, Green's notoriety as one of the league's premier hatchet men was cemented when he speared New York Rangers center Phil Coyette during a game at Madison Square Garden in 1965. "He'd do those things to anybody that was around him," Coyette later told writer Jay Moran. "If you were around the net or anything, he made sure you didn't stick around. We had some players, some defensemen, maybe do the same to make sure that the front of the net was clear." Yet, this incident occurred away from the net in the corner, causing the unsuspecting Coyette to collapse in a heap. "The move so lacked finesse that Green drew a five-minute penalty for deliberately attempting to injure Coyette, who has about as many enemies around the league as your elderly Aunt Nellie," sports columnist Hal Bock maintained. Coyette said he did not think Green was out to intentionally harm him. "But it did happen," he added. After the game, Coyette ended up going to the hospital, where fluid was drained from his lung. He was out of action for a month and later diagnosed with pleurisy—an inflammation of the lining surrounding the lungs. Green's hit "could've, you know, caused the reaction," Coyette said.

The spearing was not Green's only infraction during the contest. "He collected seven separate penalties—three minors, two majors and two misconducts—sprinkled liberally throughout the game," Bock noted. "That tied a NHL single-game record." Little wonder then that Rangers president Bill Jennings became unhinged in his comments about the Boston defenseman afterward. "I think the Bruins have wild animals on their team," he roared to the assembled media. "When a bear runs wild in Maine, the state declares a bounty for shooting the bear. I declare a bounty on Green." While nothing came of the threat, angry Rangers fans henceforward held up "Kill Green, Kill Green" signs whenever the Bruins visited the Big Apple. "Green wasn't an angel," Chico Maki said. "He was a mean SOB. Don't let anyone tell you any different."

Green disagreed. "I've never really had any intention of really hurting anybody bad, no, never in my life," he claimed. "I really wanted to cream somebody, I really wanted to maybe hit somebody with a real solid check and let him feel it, but other than that I never wanted to hurt somebody so bad that they'd have trouble thinking or playing after it, no. No way." Still, Green was shrewd enough to realize his extreme physicality provided certain ancillary benefits to his game. "Take yourself," he once told an interviewer.

> If you were playing against me and you knew you weren't going to get hit, you'd freewheel and fancy-dan all over the place. But if you knew I was out there waiting for the right opportunity to crank you, you'd be worried about getting hit, right? Maybe a guy figures that if he hits me, I'm going to turn around and rap him with the stick. I probably won't but . . . he doesn't know that.

For all of Green's calculated thuggishness, few appreciated the fact that he had developed into one of the league's top defensemen, demonstrating superb skating skills and notching a career-best 46 points in 1968–1969. His 34 assists that season broke the league mark for defensemen set by one-time Boston teammate Doug Mohns a decade earlier. "When I first started there were a lot of Ted Greens in this league," Bruins scout Tom Johnson said. "But now he is one of the few real tough guys left. So he stands out, and people overlook his hockey in favor of his fighting."

Green was lucky to be alive after his encounter with Wayne Maki, but the real challenge for him would come during a lengthy and arduous recuperation process. His speech remained impaired, and he experienced difficulty walking. He had other complications as well, including a low humming sound in his head that he first mistook for a ringing telephone. His own small children reeled at the sight of his bald postoperative head and diminished appearance. Green tried to keep up a brave front and not

Ted Green was a feared and much-respected All-Star defenseman before his tragic injury. *Graphic Artists, HHOF Images*

give in to self-pity. "What does Ted Green got to complain of?" he asked a Toronto reporter.

> I was [undergoing physical therapy] just now, and they've got a poor kid [in the hospital] who was in a car accident. His skull wasn't even fractured. All that happened was his brain was jammed against his skull in the crash. There's not too much left for that kid. It would break your heart.

His thoughts turned to Maki. "It could just as easily have been him in here," he told Bob Pennington of the *Toronto Telegram*. "What happened in the end was that I zigged when I should have zagged. I'm certain [Maki] didn't intend to hit me so hard. It's just that nobody really knows what damage a hockey stick can cause until it happens." Green said he didn't want Maki to suffer any kind of official sanction from the NHL for the incident. "He should not be punished any more than Ted Green," he said. "I hold no malice against him."

To make good on this point, Green wrote a letter to Maki with the assistance of his wife, absolving the Blues player of any blame. "When I was lying paralyzed in the hospital," Green related, "I was praying, and my family was praying, and my teammates were praying, and I got letters from people all over Boston saying they were praying and having Masses said for me. If at the same time I was thinking that when I got better I was going after that SOB Maki, I would really have been a hypocrite. I couldn't generate any hate for the guy." Indeed, Green had been on the other end of a similar stick-fighting incident two years before with Doug Mohns of Chicago. Green had struck the former Bruins forward/defenseman with a powerful two-hander that landed directly on Mohns's head. "[Mohns] was wearing a helmet, but he still sank to his knees," Green said. "If he hadn't been wearing a helmet I would have killed him. I know that now. I understand a lot more now. I also know how I would have felt if Mohns had been badly hurt."

Green became increasingly more philosophical in his outlook on life. "I was kind of a helter-skelter guy before," he said. "Well, I'm not that guy anymore. I have a different set of values, right? Off the ice and on the ice, I know I'll be a changed person now. I don't think I'll ever be as carefree as I was before." He did not rule out a comeback but cited his family and his own physical recovery as his chief concerns moving forward. "My health is more important than making a few extra bucks playing hockey, although it's still always nice to have the money," he said. But before he could do anything, Green first had to contend with the law, namely the Ottawa police, who belatedly charged him and Maki with aggravated assault. "This was the first time in the history of professional sports that police authorities had issued a complaint against players because of an incident that occurred in a game," legal historian and author Roger I. Abrams noted. "It would not be the last." Green and Maki ended up receiving acquittals in short separate criminal trials. In Green's case, presiding provincial judge Michael J. Fitzpatrick found no compelling reason to throw the book at him given the violent nature of his sport.

"When a player enters an arena, he is consenting to a great number of what otherwise might be regarded as assaults," he stated. "The game of hockey could not possibly be played unless those engaging in it were willing to accept these assaults." Green heaved a sigh of relief. "I'm only glad it's over at last," he told reporters.

Not quite. Given the swirling negative publicity the incident produced—the respected *Ottawa Journal* referred to it as "Carnage on the Ice"—the NHL felt compelled to act. League president Clarence Campbell held a brief hearing and suspended Green for 13 games and Maki for 30 days. Aside from the official reprimand, however, Maki faced punishment of a more visceral sort. Although Green had passed on word to his teammates that he didn't wish to see any retribution directed against Maki, many Bruins players pretended not to hear. When the St. Louis forward skated against them in an early regular-season game at Boston Garden for the first time since that fateful evening in Ottawa, Maki was on the receiving end of a barrage of cheap shots. "It was really uncalled for," complained Maki's coach, Scotty Bowman. "But that's the kind of team they are." Harry Sinden took offense at this comment. "Scotty Bowman is a crybaby," the Bruins coach said. "We kept the sticks down. We just put a lot of good solid checks on him."

At about this time, Green also managed to make a surprise appearance in the Bruins locker room. It turned out to be a memorable reunion. Outside of Bobby Orr, Eddie Johnston, and Eddie Westfall, who had impersonated a doctor to gain entry into Green's hospital recovery room, few of Green's teammates had been in direct contact with him since the injury. "We were getting ready to practice," Bobby Orr remembered.

> Teddy walked into the room and sat down . . . where he used to dress. His head was shaved from the operation and everything, and he didn't say a word. He just sat down, undressed, and started to put on his long underwear—as if he were getting ready to practice. As the guys came in, he'd look up and swear at them or give them a shot—just like the old Greenie, like nothing had happened.

Despite the loss of Green, most hockey writers and prognosticators were bullish on Boston's chances entering the 1969–1970 season. The team was seen as the crème de la crème of the NHL, with the possible exception of the defending Stanley Cup champion Montreal Canadiens. "Barring medical catastrophe, the Bruins can again press Montreal, and if they can contrive to win some 'big games' they could dethrone the Canadiens," wrote Gary Ronberg of *Sports Illustrated*. *Hockey News* agreed with this analysis, arguing that Montreal's aging roster, led by 38-year-old center Jean Beliveau, would be highly vulnerable to Boston's youth and physicality. "They have Bobby Orr, the nonpareil defenseman who controls a game better than anyone else in the league today," the publication said. "They have Phil Esposito, the super point man of 1968–1969, who is proving that last season was no fluke. And they have muscle." Indeed, public expectations for the Bruins were sky high, and this concerned the normally unflappable Harry Sinden, who staunchly disagreed with the so-called experts. He believed Green's injury represented a potentially serious blow to the team's title hopes. "I know a lot of our players felt then that this would cost us the Stanley Cup," he later confessed. Sinden also thoroughly understood the consequences if his club came up short. He would most likely be out of a job. "This is a dangerous year for us," the coach said. "We could be awfully good or . . ."

Harry James Sinden never took anything for granted. The son of immigrant parents from the United Kingdom who settled in the Toronto

The proverbial straw that stirred the drink: head coach Harry Sinden. *Hockey Hall of Fame, HHOF Images*

area, Sinden gravitated toward ice hockey at a young age. "Across the street from our house were two large cushions—that's what we called them—outdoor natural ice surfaces surrounded by boards," he recalled. He would spend every free moment of his time there, playing the game when he was not listening to Maple Leafs contests broadcast on the radio by legendary local play-by-play man Foster Hewitt. Sinden's father—a talented former multiple-sport athlete who worked three jobs to support his family during the Great Depression—encouraged his son's burgeoning love for the game by buying him his first pair of skates at the age of six. Sinden would later accessorize his hockey wardrobe by rolling up old magazines and taping them under his socks for use as shin pads. "By the end of winter, I had played so much with my stick that the blade was worn as thin as a toothpick," he claimed.

Sinden became a good enough player as a teenager to be invited to a tryout camp with the Montreal Canadiens in 1948. "I was very proud," he later wrote. "I had never been outside of Ontario before, so the train ride to Montreal was extra special for a kid who [fancied] himself well on the way to a Hall of Fame career." The Canadiens signed him to a contract and assigned him to an underperforming junior-league team in the Ontario Hockey Association. He languished there for the next four years before coming to the reluctant conclusion at age 20, that playing in the NHL was an unrealistic reach, especially since he was now married and starting a family. He decided to go a more secure route and take a well-paying job as a stationary engineer at a General Motors plant in Toronto. But he still could not bring himself to wash his hands of hockey. He spent his evenings skating for the Whitby Dunlops, an amateur team that was sponsored by the Dunlop Tire Company. The Dunlops, which Sinden believed ranked "just below an expansion team when the NHL went to 12 teams," would go on to win a world amateur title in 1958. Sinden played a crucial role in their success. "Harry was a smart defenseman, always the league leader in points among defensemen," former teammate Bob Attersley told the *Globe and Mail* in a 1998 interview. "The knock against him was his skating." Indeed, this perceived shortcoming prevented Sinden from competing at the highest pro level. "In those days, if just one guy upstairs [in a club front office] didn't like you, you didn't make it," Attersley said. "Someone upstairs thought Harry didn't skate well enough. There were NHL teams that could have used Harry, but he couldn't get a fair shot."

Sinden capped off his amateur hockey career by earning a spot on the Canadian national team, which went to the 1960 Winter Olympics in Squaw Valley, California. Canada was expected to take the gold medal that year but ran into a brick wall in the final round when U.S. goaltender Jack McCartan stymied them in net for an unlikely 2–1 American victory. It was Canada's only loss the entire year. "You know, in many ways we were poor losers, and I say 'we' because I'm not going to say whom," Sinden said.

> We cried about bad luck. I remember a management person on our team wanting to challenge the Maple Leafs after we had lost, because everybody in Canada was saying we were no good. We had every right to feel down, because the gold medal game was against the U.S. and we were all over them—it was something like four-to-one in shots.

Sinden characterized the loss as the worst of his hockey career, at either the professional or amateur level. "The silver medal was tough to take," he said.

Sinden still had a job waiting for him at GM in Toronto, but he received an intriguing offer from Bruins general manager Lynn Patrick to be a player-coach of the team's Eastern Pro League affiliate in Kingston, Ontario. "I got a lot of advice—most of it to turn down the offer," Sinden recalled, "but the chance to coach was what made the proposal attractive." After considerable soul-searching, Sinden decided to take the plunge. "That turned out to be the break I needed in my hockey career," he said. Sinden won a league championship during his two-year stint in Kingston and then made additional minor-league stops in Minneapolis and Oklahoma City during the next five seasons. All the while, he was gaining valuable on-the-job experience and impressing his superiors in the Boston front office.

Sinden could sense he was being groomed for the Bruins head coaching job, but he had reservations. "Silly as it seems, part of me didn't want that job," he later revealed. "I had a chip on my shoulder against the National Hockey League. I thought I should have been playing in it a few years earlier. When I was with Kingston I was leading all defensemen in scoring and winning the league's Most Valuable Player Award." Yet, to Sinden's everlasting consternation, the Bruins did not seem to show an iota of interest in his demonstrated playing ability. He continued,

Cellar dwellers every year, [the club] kept taking guys up from our Kingston team who weren't any better than I was. But I was dumb. I should have spoken up. In those days no one talked back. You got up in the morning, did your job, and kept your mouth shut. It's ridiculous that I never got a chance, and I will always be bitter about that.

Nevertheless, Sinden did not turn down the opportunity to lead the Bruins when the call finally came in 1966. Although the team wasn't very good, there were unmistakable signs of better times on the way, as stellar rookie Bobby Orr lived up to the advance hype. Sinden just wished he could have lived up to his own expectations. "I made plenty of coaching mistakes that first year, no doubt about it," he admitted.

For some reason I tried to play a strong forechecking game when I did not have the talent to do so. Little guys generally are not good fore-checkers. What I should have done is play an opportunistic, waiting game. . . . But I learned that a 34-year-old coach doesn't know every-thing about the NHL.

The fans reminded him of this fact at every opportunity. "Hey Sinden," one of them shouted from the stands, "there's a bus leaving for Oklahoma City in the morning. Be under it."

Sinden's position was further complicated by new Bruins GM Hap Emms. "Emms never liked the way I did things," Sinden maintained.

He wanted to run the show himself. He wanted to come on the ice when I was coaching; he wanted to come into the locker room during and after games to address the team; and he was always finding fault with the way I did things. I really resented it at the time. He was using me as a crutch for the problems of the organization.

Sinden, in particular, clashed with Emms on the issue of discipline. Emms, a hardcore traditionalist, wanted to employ a hammer at all times on the players, monitoring their every movement both on and off the ice. Sinden took a more nuanced view, believing discipline should be applied sparingly and only when a clear violation of team rules took place. "The important thing is shared trust and confidence," Sinden said.

I wanted my players to give me a decent shake the night before a game, and I, in turn, would be out of sight when the game was over. A coach can't spy on his players having a few beers after a game and say, "Gosh, are you guys drinking?" That type of coach does not last very long in any professional sport.

The situation vastly improved in Sinden's second and third years after Emms was replaced by Milt Schmidt. Sinden could now focus his energies solely on the roster, which had added Phil Esposito, Ken Hodge, Fred Stanfield, and talented rookie Derek Sanderson to the mix. Suddenly the entire club started to gel. "The Bruins became a real team rather than a collection of individuals," Sinden said. "The players began to establish personal rapport with one another. They understood they might be the butt of joke at any time. When a player did protest about a joke or got mad on the ice, Johnny McKenzie would kid him, lying down and kicking his feet in a mock tantrum." Orr also stepped up to provide important leadership. When two of his teammates got into a bitter spat with one another, Orr diffused the situation by employing a creative diplomatic tactic. "He called them to the center of the dressing room before a game and offered them their choice of weapons—a miniature cannon, a rubber knife, or a water pistol," Sinden recalled. "Suddenly the feud was over. This was in line with the old Vince Lombardi notion that your teammate is all-important." Sanderson believed Sinden's influence was crucial here. "He pulled the team together," he said. "We're a strange bunch of guys, let's face it. A lot of us don't think alike. But he was the one guy who could overlook a lot of things and get us working together." Whether this low-key approach could produce a Stanley Cup moving forward, however, remained to be seen.

4

SPELLING POWER

The Bruins started their season on October 12, against the New York Rangers. Performing in front of a crowd of 14,831, at an unseasonably warm Boston Garden—where the reported game-time temperature of 88 degrees made the ice soft and slushy—the Bruins prevailed, 2–1, against their Big Apple visitors on first period power play goals by Fred Stanfield and Pie McKenzie. "You can bet it was like a steam bath out there," Sinden said. "The players were wiped out by the third period. The air was very heavy. We earned those points tonight. People had to really push themselves." Eddie Johnston, who received a surprise nod in net over Gerry Cheevers, counted himself in the latter category. "It was hot, really brutal out there," he said. "But it was doubly worse for me because I must have caught a virus or the flu yesterday. It's taken a lot out of me. The mask made it hot, too. But I wanted to play. This was my best training camp in years, and it was good to get the two points. That's a pair we won't have to chase later on."

Stanfield got the Bruins out to a 1–0 lead just 65 seconds into the contest when he drove a low rising shot by Rangers goalie Eddie Giacomin. "All I really tried to do was shoot on the cage," Stanfield told the *Boston Globe*. "That's the first thing I think of when playing the point on the power play. Even if your shot is stopped, you have that extra man in front to possibly knock in the rebound." The Bruins added to their lead six minutes later on a freak goal by McKenzie. The diminutive forward had found himself with little maneuvering room behind the New York net and decided to flip the puck out front for a teammate. But the disk somehow managed to deflect off Giacomin's back and into the goalmouth. "Yeah, it was one of those crazy shots," McKenzie said afterward. The Rangers cut the Boston lead in half late in the period, but a superlative performance by Johnston, who registered 37 saves, kept the New Yorkers at bay the rest of the evening.

The Bruins remained undefeated through their first seven games, good for first place in the rugged Eastern Division, where they had to compete against all of their long-standing Original Six rivals. Interestingly, the team achieved this enviable mark with only modest help from Phil Esposito. The National Hockey League's reigning scoring champion had got-

A familiar sight: Phil Esposito scoring in front of the net. *Graphic Artists, HHOF Images*

ten off to a slow start offensively and appeared to be pressing. "There might be a little pressure subconsciously, I don't know," Esposito said of his scoring difficulties. "I'm missing the pass out from the corner when I'm in the slot. I'm rushing that shot a bit, and it's all timing. But there is pressure on everyone on this team." Esposito would break out of his slump in the weeks to follow, but not before receiving a "pretty good verbal roasting" from a disapproving Garden faithful. "I heard them," he said. "It made me feel terrible. I didn't deserve it."

Nothing ever came easy for Phillip Anthony Esposito, who looked better suited wearing a hard hat on a construction site than playing in the NHL. His goals were never flashy or considered works of art like those of Bobby Orr or Wayne Gretzky, of a later generation. Rather, they had a more mundane, utilitarian quality about them, due to the fact that Esposito's offensive game was centered around basic positioning and opportunism. He made sure to plant his stout 6-foot-1, 205-pound frame in front of the enemy net and wait for the right moment to drive home a rebound or stray puck that would inevitably find his stick like an unfortunate fly in a spider's web. "He was the ultimate garbage man, of course, refining his job, sanitizing it, delivering goals at a tidy, Hefty-bag pace that never had been dreamed possible, but he still was a garbage man," noted *Boston Globe* columnist Leigh Montville. "His average goal traveled anywhere from one to eight feet. It was about as exciting as the click of a turnstile, the flutter of a middle-aged eyelash. . . . His goal was the goal 'that should have been scored.' The difference was that he scored it." Esposito always laughed that others viewed his goals as "cheap" or pedestrian. "Who cares what they call them—they all look like slap shots in the next morning's papers," he said. "Who cares how they go in, as long as they count?" A popular local bumper sticker said it best at the time: "Jesus Saves, but Esposito Scores on the Rebound."

For Esposito, the game was not that complicated. "I just get the puck and fire at the net, and I just figure the net hasn't moved in 50 years so I'm bound to be on target," he said. "The rest will take care of itself. It's like being a baseball pitcher; he should never aim the ball, just rear back and throw it." This scoring philosophy did not preclude using a bit of circumvention. Esposito loved lulling unsuspecting opponents into believing he had the quickness of a tortoise and then leaving them gasping for breath. "Espo's moving nice and slow," Eddie Westfall related. "The next thing the other guy knows, Phil is by him. Espo may look cumbersome and slow, but he's deceiving. He's so strong that many times he'll beat the other guy by four or five feet. The only other guy on the club who can do these kinds of things is Bobby Orr." Speaking of Orr, the Bruins' brilliant playmaker always kept his eyes open for Esposito when he was making one of his patented rushes down the ice and needing to dish off. "Espy's long arms, they're what make him so effective around the net," Orr explained. "With that long reach he can stay out maybe 25 feet from the cage. The defensemen can't come out to guard him because they'd leave the rear open. Yet, with his long arms Phil can stop a pass 15 or so feet in front of the cage, something most centermen can't do."

The speed of Esposito's shots was nothing to sneeze at either. While no comparisons were ever made to a Nolan Ryan fastball, they nevertheless got the job done thanks to an unusually quick release. "I'd rather see Orr with the puck on the point than Esposito with the puck in the slot," posited veteran All-Star goaltender Rogie Vachon. "It comes out off his stick so fast you can't see it until it's behind you." Of course, Esposito was never averse to teeing it up. "He's good because he shoots so much," another opponent said. "I'll bet he shoots as much as his two wingers combined, and I'm certain he shoots more than any other center in the league." For the record, Esposito had the second most attempted shots (351) of any NHL player in 1968–1969. He would, however, go on to become the undisputed league leader in this category from 1971 to 1974. "Phil was always a great player," insisted Bobby Hull, his former high-scoring line mate on the Chicago Black Hawks in the mid-1960s. "The big thing is that he has reached maturity in the game. He was an unselfish partner for me, and I know he does better now because he has more chances to do things himself instead of passing off to me so much."

Esposito was not without faults. Like so many of his NHL contemporaries, he drank too much and was often far from being in peak physical condition. Nor did his active night life make him a candidate for Father of the Year. "My family didn't come first," he later admitted to Stu Cowan of the *Montreal Gazette*. "Hockey always came first. I loved hockey more than anything else." Esposito additionally possessed a superstitious bent. He regularly consulted Ouija boards to predict future game performances and was a firm believer in good luck charms and set routines. Before each game he made sure to have a stick of chewing gum placed at his locker while putting on a black turtleneck underneath his uniform jersey. His equipment also had to be arranged according to his exact specifications with gloves palm up on either side of his hockey stick. "If he doesn't get a new set of playing underwear every third game, there's hell to play," Bruins assistant trainer John "Frosty" Forrestal said. "The worst, however, is if he sees crossed hockey sticks. . . . That's when he goes ape." Indeed, Esposito thought such an occurrence represented a bad omen. "I hate that," he said. "I remember my first year in the league. One day there were crossed sticks in our dressing room. [A teammate] said, 'Look at the crossed sticks. Somebody's going to get hurt.' And somebody broke his leg." Esposito even claimed he had once been traded as the result of someone putting the "Evil Eye" on him. Esposito's dead seriousness on the subject did not prevent his teammates from poking fun at him. They would, on occasion, deliberately place crossed sticks in front of his locker to provoke his wrath. "I never knew a guy so superstitious," Derek Sanderson said. "When we were on a winning streak . . . he wouldn't let me change the cotton in my shin pads as long as the streak lasted. By the time we finally lost a game, those pads wouldn't stop anything. Me, I'm not superstitious. But it seems to work for him." It sure did.

Esposito had come to the Bruins in 1967, by dint of what *Toronto Daily Star* reporter Jim Proudfoot called the "worst trade in the history of the sport." For sure, the transaction became the hockey equivalent of a bank heist. The Chicago Black Hawks shipped Esposito, along with future All-Stars Ken Hodge and Fred Stanfield, to Beantown for a physical young defenseman named Giles Marotte and two marginal players. "We all hated to give up Marotte, but you have to give up something to get something," Harry Sinden told the *Boston Globe.* "I'm happy with the trade. It gives us strength as center ice, and that's where we needed to strengthen ourselves and we did." That was for public consumption. Privately, the Bruins were in full celebration. Esposito "was one guy, when [Chicago] mentioned his name, I almost fell through the floor," Milt Schmidt later said. In truth, the deal was so one-sided that many hockey insiders automatically assumed Esposito was seriously injured. When Red Fisher of the *Montreal Star* was approached by the Bruins to quietly investigate whether such suspicions were true, he came up empty. "Tell the fuckers there's nothing wrong with Espo," Chicago forward Stan Mikita told Fisher. Esposito had learned of the trade himself while attending an offseason sports banquet in his hometown. "I got a call from my wife," he remembered.

She told me Don Murphy, the Black Hawks press guy, had phoned and told her I was traded to Boston. It wasn't the coach or the general manager, just the press guy. I was so surprised I just said, "Yeah, thanks," and I hung up. Then I said to myself, "What did she say?" and I had to phone back. When I got off the phone I was white.

Esposito had good reason to be upset. "I remember thinking at the time, 'Jeez, there goes all the playoff money down the drain,'" he said. At the time, Boston was considered a hopeless NHL backwater, and it was one of only two teams to which Esposito had prayed he would never be traded. The New York Rangers happened to be the other. "I didn't like the idea of New York City because of my wife and kids. And I didn't like Boston because they were always in last place," he lamented. It also stung that the Black Hawks had given up on him. "Guys talk about trades being part of the game," he later wrote. "I suppose it's always in the back of your mind if you're a professional athlete. But when it happens—pow. It's a slap in the face. What it means to a guy is that someone doesn't think enough of him to keep him around. That was my reaction, anyway." Once the news had sunk in, Esposito did something that had never occurred in professional sports. Decades before NBA superstar Lebron James and the Decision, Esposito publicly announced his change in teams via the airwaves of his own sports telecast on CJIC-TV in Ontario. "Hi sports fans," he said, "This is Phil Esposito. Yours truly has been traded to Boston. . . . This is no hoax."

It was also no hoax why the Black Hawks decided to deal him. Despite posting 21 goals and 40 assists the previous season, Esposito had vastly underperformed in the playoffs. He had been held scoreless when the top-seeded Hawks were ousted by the Toronto Maple Leafs in the first round. "There's no doubt Toronto stole the Cup from us that year," Hawks president Bill Wirtz said. "We had the best team in hockey, but they got the Cup." Esposito was blamed for the postseason loss. The tall, sad-faced center had further undercut his status with his off-hours barhopping with Bobby Hull and open contempt for club general manager Tommy Ivan and coach Billy Reay. "We've got a great team here. You could almost have a dynasty, but you two are going to screw it up," Esposito told them. Unsurprisingly, neither Ivan nor Reay appreciated the unfiltered criticism. When Esposito stopped by Ivan's office at season's end to pick up his expense money, an indignant Ivan refused to offer the standard courtesies. "You tell that son of a bitch I don't want to see him,"

Ivan instructed his secretary. "I don't care about him. Just give him whatever he wants and tell him to get out of my sight. If I ever see him again, it'll be too soon."

Esposito had a history of wearing out his welcome. As a rebellious teenager, he got into trouble at his all-boys Catholic high school for his stubborn refusal to take an English essay exam. He had been up late the previous evening playing hockey and was in no mood for scholarly activity. He instead placed his head on his desk and fell asleep. When his teacher woke him up and ordered him to begin writing, Esposito got annoyed. "I don't know nothing," he scrawled on his exam and then abruptly left the classroom. He was equally unapologetic when he was hauled into the principal's office the next day to explain his behavior. He told the presiding Mother Superior, who had expressed open concerns about allowing "hockey bums" into the school, that he considered himself a hockey player first and a student second. "So you can stick your school," he said.

Esposito learned such directness from his father, a broad-shouldered no-nonsense welder at a local steel plant in Sault Sainte Marie, Ontario. Pat Esposito believed in hard work, personal loyalty, and no excuses. When Phil's younger brother and future NHL goalie Tony once complained about being served spaghetti at a family dinner, the elder Esposito hurled a fork at him that lodged in the boy's head. "If you ever, ever push food away again, that will be the end of you, pal," the stern paterfamilias warned. Fortunately, such angry outbursts were rare. Pat genuinely loved his family and was an indefatigable supporter of Phil and Tony's hockey careers despite his early doubts. "To be honest," he said, "I never thought they'd make the majors." He was especially unimpressed with young Phil. "Phil grew big and tall, but he was weak in the ankles and slow and awkward, and wasn't a good skater. I just didn't see anything special about him as a player. But he loved it and kept playing. And he kept leading his leagues, but I never felt certain he'd make it as he moved up." Yet, Phil, who one coach nicknamed "fatso" for his generous girth, did make it, thanks to his own driving ambition and willingness to put in the necessary long hours at the rink to improve his game. "It's all I ever wanted to be—a hockey player," he said. "I can remember early in my school years the guidance counselor would come around and ask each kid what they wanted to be. I'd tell her, 'a hockey player,' and she'd look at me and say, 'No, I mean a vocation in your future life,' and I'd tell her again, 'a hockey player.'"

After toiling for two years with Chicago's minor-league affiliate in St. Louis, Esposito made his NHL debut in a contest against the Montreal Canadiens midway through the 1963–1964 season. "I was too nervous to eat on the flight to Montreal," he remembered.

> I was too nervous to eat before the game. I was scared sick. For a Canadian kid the Forum in Montreal is a special place. Just going into the building was a big deal. Going into the dressing room as a player was out of this world. You play pro because you expect to make the majors, but down deep I guess you wonder if it will ever really happen. When it happens, it's really something.

Esposito received a reality check once he entered the game. "I felt lost out there," he said.

> I didn't think there'd be much difference between the majors and the minors as there was. The pace was a lot quicker. The players skated faster and shot faster. They made fast moves. They didn't hesitate. As slow as I was, it showed. I was only out a couple of shifts, maybe three or four minutes. I didn't get a single shot on goal, and I was dumped by body checks that all but shook my fillings out.

Things improved when Esposito scored his first goal against the Detroit Red Wings four games later. He noticed in warm-ups that Detroit goaltender Terry Sawchuk bent down on his right knee whenever he made a save. He filed this knowledge away for use later in the game when he was assigned to a line with Bobby Hull. As he later recounted to author Mike Brophy, "We have a breakout from our zone, and I end up with the puck. I split the Detroit defense. I have a breakaway from their blue line in. I give Sawchuk a little fake, and he goes down on his right knee, so I fire it up over his right shoulder."

The noteworthy performance notwithstanding, Esposito would always remember that first year as the time he got to meet his favorite television star while visiting Paramount Studios in Hollywood, California, with Bobby Hull. The Black Hawks were in town to play an exhibition game, and he and Hull decided to kill some time by watching a taping of *Bewitched*, the popular long-running sitcom about a married suburban witch. Once on the set, the married Esposito wasted no time making moves on an attractive supporting cast member. "Man, I got to get a piece of that one, I'll tell you that!" he told Hull. Rebuffed, a disappointed Esposito had to settle for watching Elizabeth Montgomery—the show's lead actress, nominated for both an Emmy and a Golden Globe—go through her paces in a scene wearing a revealing negligee. "Elizabeth was tall and beautiful," he gushed. "There was a glow around her. She was one really gorgeous woman. And for years after that I watched *Bewitched*, because she turned me on. I still watch the reruns." Equally memorable was what Esposito did when he got back to his hotel room. Discovering that he had developed a painful charley horse that made it difficult to walk, let alone skate, Esposito unwisely decided to notify his coach after consuming a few beers. "Hey, Bill, Phil Esposito here," he told Billy Reay over the phone. "I got a pretty bad fucking leg here!" Such histrionics only served to hasten his eventual departure to Boston.

The Bruins cooled down after their blistering start. But as 1969 gave way to 1970, they still found themselves among the NHL's elite in the standings. Bobby Orr was the primary reason. "Childe Bobby," as one local columnist called him, would rewrite the record books for defensemen that season, leading the league in scoring, with 120 points on 33 goals, and 87 assists. Phil Esposito, fully recovered from his earlier scoring woes, would finish in second place, with 99 points. More than a half-century later, Orr remains the only backliner in history to accomplish such a feat, although he personally managed to pull off the same trick again four years later. Wrote Jack Olsen of *Sports Illustrated*,

> Let it be said and done with: By acclamation Bobby Orr is the greatest player ever to don skates. Not the greatest defenseman, the greatest defenseman, the greatest player at either end of the ice. . . . To comprehend what it means to be the best both defensively and offensively in the brutal game of ice hockey, the fan must imagine a combination of Dick Butkus and Leroy Kelly, Boog Powell and Bob Gibson, of Bill Russell and Oscar Robertson. Because of Orr, there are fewer arguments in the big hockey towns about "the good old days." He has brought a sheen to every skater, a gloss to the whole league and the whole sport.

Olsen was not just spouting hyperbole. With Orr on board, NHL attendance figures and network television viewership for hockey soared. In the Boston area alone, Bruins regular-season game broadcasts on the small independent UHF station WSBK-TV 38 attracted an average of one in four viewing households for an incredible 25 rating share. "All New England was clamoring to see Bobby Orr," noted longtime Bruins radio and television play-by-play announcer Fred Cusick. "When [he] was on TV38, it would cause a 25 percent decline in viewers of the three network affiliates, who had the market all to themselves before the arrival [of Orr and Channel 38]."

Of course, Orr had a colorful and appealing supporting cast, for these were the "Big Bad Bruins," hockey's answer to Major League Baseball's Gashouse Gang" from the 1930s. They slugged first and asked questions later. "When they drop the puck to start the game," Philadelphia Flyers general manager Bud Polie said, "the Bruins think it is a piece of raw meat. Do they go after it! I'm afraid my guys will desert the place some night." *Boston Globe* columnist Kevin Paul Dupont did not dispute the point. The Bruins *were* intimidating. "Was this really a team," he later wrote,

> or some type of brotherhood that had come together years after signing a blood oath in the backwoods of Canada? From afar, one had to wonder. They could be seen partying at [a popular Italian food restaurant] down the street from the Garden or the Elbow Lounge on the Boston/Brookline line. The next night, they would line up, five across, pummeling any Canadien, Red Wing, Black Hawk, or Maple Leaf who rubbed them the wrong way.

Brad Park was a case in point. The New York Rangers' high-scoring defenseman was targeted because he had the temerity to publicly accuse Orr and company of being "bloodthirsty animals" specializing in cheap shots and mayhem. He may have had a point. "They were the most penalized team in the NHL and richly deserved to be such," noted the *Toronto Telegram*'s Paul Dumage.

> Had their aggression been penalized at a rate equal that applied to other clubs, the Bruins might have had to play the entire season without ever getting a sixth man on the ice. One referee cannot possibly see everything, nor can he call it. The Bruins give you the stick, the trip, the elbow, and the shove away from the play. They hunt heads.

Harry Sinden always had a ready response to counter such critics. "Listen," he said, "for nine years the Bruins have been the laughingstock of the NHL. Now, for the past few years we've come up with some tough young players, and we're trying to win back our self-respect. No one laughs at the Bruins anymore, do they?"

If anything, the Bruins were the ones doing the laughing. They were "two parts Agincourt, one part Marx Brothers," pointed out historian and current New England Sports Museum curator Richard Johnson. Put another way, they took the game seriously but never themselves too seriously. Esposito set the tone with his self-deprecating humor and impulsive behavior. For example, it was not uncommon for the future Hall of Famer to make like a cut-rate Las Vegas lounge singer and spontaneously break into song on team charter flights. "O, sole mio," Esposito would bellow as his fellow Bruins egged him on. "He keeps everyone relaxed and loosey," Orr said. "When he came here, he came with a winning spirit that he brought from a winning club. He brought us all together and made us believe we could win." Indeed, nothing or no one was off-limits within the boisterous confines of the Bruins dressing room. When informed by a *Sport* magazine feature writer that Orr had been on the cover of the publication, Esposito turned to Derek Sanderson and feigned disgust. "You hear, Turk, you hear?" "You're chopped liver, like me," Sanderson replied. Not willing to let the matter drop, Esposito hollered across the room to Orr, calling him a "cover boy." Orr shook off the good-natured jest as easily as he would an opposing defender in a game. "Aw, shaddup, Espy," he said.

Esposito would just as frequently find himself a target. Johnny Bucyk would mischievously cut the suspenders holding up his pants before Esposito ventured out onto the ice, leaving him exposed and red-faced. Esposito also drew pointed comments concerning his pudgy, nonathletic physique. "Look at that body," Gerry Cheevers chortled. "Can you imagine that body scoring more than 100 points?" "We had characters," Esposito said. "You never knew what any of 'em might do." And that was the point. One came to expect the unexpected from these Bruins, whether it was Pie McKenzie stealing a police motorcycle and driving it into a bar, Derek Sanderson interrupting some strangers' poker game by diving through an open hotel window, or Wayne Cashman doing an impromptu striptease at Boston City Hall. "They were viewed as modern-day Vikings, a collection of athletes with the ethics of a motorcycle gang," Boston sports authority and Purdue University professor Randy Roberts wrote.

Even the usually polite, mild-mannered Orr got caught up in the hi-jinks. Stephen Brunt, in *Searching for Bobby Orr*, wrote that Orr had a unique way of picking "dates" to spend late evenings with at Daisy Bu-chanan's, a popular local tavern and after-hours team hangout owned by Derek Sanderson. Usually fortified by a few drinks, Orr would stand at the bar with his right arm extended outward toward a line of women "all giggles and miniskirts and open minds," and allow himself to be spun around "like a crazy top." "Whichever way the finger was pointing, that was Bobby's girl," Brunt wrote. "The other guys would fight over the rest." Orr also became both a victim and a participant in a bizarre team hazing ritual involving first-year players being bundled into a blanket on the clubhouse floor and having most of their body hair shaved off. Vete-rans usually performed the honors with a straightedge razor, but it was not exactly an enjoyable experience for the initiates. Sanderson could attest to that. "It hurt like hell," he said. "They lacerate you some, and then, while you're bleeding, they throw shaving cream on the wounds. I mean this really is no fun."

What was fun was the time Orr and several of his teammates kid-napped Esposito from Massachusetts General Hospital to attend a season-ending club breakup party. Esposito had undergone a surgical procedure on his leg a couple of days prior and was recuperating quietly in a cast that extended from his groin to his toes. Then things got wildly out of hand. As Esposito recounted to NHL.com in 2009, "Well, about 7:30 that night, the door slams open in my room, and Bobby comes in. He had a surgical gown on, a hat, and a mask. And he says, 'Ok, we are going.' And I said, 'What are you talking about,' and he says, 'Come on. We are going.'" Esposito was wheeled away on a gurney to the elevator, while "Dr. Orr" informed nurses and other shocked onlookers who recognized him that there was a medical emergency in process. By the time the Black and Gold contingent exited the building and reached the street, Orr had a strange request to make of his friend. "There's a car coming behind us, Espo, signal a left turn," he said. The night ended with Esposito having the time of his life at the Branding Iron Steak House, a short-lived neigh-borhood restaurant Orr opened in 1970. Esposito would be sheepishly returned to Massachusetts General the following day, but this time the hospital staff took no chances. They put him in full lockdown. "Let's face it," Eddie Johnston declared, "we're just a bunch of kooks and degener-ates who get along."

If so, Derek Sanderson was truly in a league of his own. Known for his quick temper, explosive offense, and wildly unpredictable ways, the long-haired Bruins center intrigued hockey fans everywhere with his hard-nosed approach to the game and brash, unconventional attitude. When he appeared on the popular late-night television talk show the *Tonight Show* and was asked about his posthockey career plans by host Johnny Carson, Sanderson pulled no punches. "Your seat doesn't look too bad," he responded. Unsurprisingly, Sanderson was never invited back. On other occasions, he did not hesitate to share his definition of an ideal soulmate: ["The type of girl who can fit into a dinner at the Waldorf or a draft beer down at the beach"] or offer unsolicited style tips to high profile teammates like Orr ["Bobby, the brush cut, forget it"]. It was all a day in the life for the colorful Sanderson. As he once said,

> Some people act as though I was a freak. All I am is my own man. I think my own way, say what I think. The writers love me because I'm outspoken. What's so freaky about that? Why shouldn't a person be outspoken? Why shouldn't a person say what he thinks? Isn't it more freaky to hold things in, to say all the right things even if they're lies?

Derek Michael Sanderson had always followed the beat of his own drummer. The product of a struggling working-class family in Niagara Falls, Ontario, Sanderson had been raised to think for himself. "It's your life, kid," his father told him. "I've brought you up to make your own decisions. Just be prepared to back up whatever you do." For sure, Harold Sanderson—a decorated World War II veteran who twice had been wounded in battle—was the central figure in young Derek's life. He worked the night shift at a local factory sweeping floors and wanted his only son to have a better future. "I don't want you to end up like me," Harold said. "I want you to have a shot at everything. . . . Whatever you do, be something—a surgeon, lawyer, dentist, or writer. But preferably, be a hockey player." He had come to this latter conclusion after reading a magazine article ranking the most respected professions in Canada. And performing in the NHL topped the list. "My boy's gonna be a hockey player," he triumphantly informed his wife afterward. Derek did not need much coaxing. "I came up in a dead-end neighborhood," he said. "I came up where you scratched and fought all your life. It was dog-eat-dog. If you wanted a cigarette, you'd say, 'Gimme a weed,' and that was it. You

A man of his times: the colorful and always controversial Derek Sanderson. *Lewis Portnoy, HHOF Images*

didn't say, 'May I please have a cigarette?'" Hockey seemed like a way out, especially since his studies at school held no appeal to him.

Still, the lure of the streets exerted a powerful hold on Sanderson. As a teenager, he got into the habit of stealing from local business establishments. He started out absconding cheap jewelry for friends but then graduated to cigarettes. "I'd go into the supermarket or grocery store and stake out the cigarette area," he recalled. "Actually, it was very easy to steal cigarettes because they were kept near the checkout counters. They were in big barrels and were almost never watched by anybody. I'd slip in the door, take two or three cartons, and then slip out." Sanderson's mini crime spree only came to an end when a fellow partner in crime ratted him out to his father. "You're nothing but a filthy, low-life thief," Harold yelled, before punching his wayward progeny in the stomach, neck, and chest. "I'd punch you in the mouth, but I'd have to pay the dentist bills." The beating only ceased when an emotional Harold broke down in tears. "Suddenly my defenses wilted," Sanderson said. "The sight of him got to me as deeply as it was possible, and right then and there I made up my mind that I'd never steal again."

Sanderson doubled down on hockey instead and became a certifiable rink rat, spending countless hours scrimmaging with friends or competing in organized leagues. "We'd keep playing even without lights," he recounted. "It wasn't easy, and it was dangerous. I'd run into people and the boards, as well as the nets. I mean, you just didn't know where you were going. Yet, it was a lot of fun. And it really taught me how to stickhandle without looking at the puck, which is very important in the NHL." Sanderson also developed a well-earned reputation for being able to take hits and deliver them, too. "One theory I go on," he said, "I don't care who [an opponent] is; his face will bleed just like mine, right? That stick is a great equalizer. I cut people so often I can't remember who or when." Such an attitude made him an unpopular figure on the ice, but no one had ever confused him with a Boy Scout. As his father told him, "If you have talent, that's great, but if you've got talent and toughness, that's unbeatable." Sanderson needed no reminding. He took a certain perverse pride in the number of times his face needed to be sewn up following run-ins with opponents. "Dad used to cut out the stitches and put 'em in a little box," he said. The practice halted when the figure reached one hundred. "I've got 18 friends in the world, and they are the guys I play with," Sanderson maintained. "As for anyone else, I couldn't care less what happens to him. If I have to hit a guy and hurt him to win again, I'll hit him and hurt him. If a guy is afraid of being hurt. I'll give him the stick all night long."

Sanderson carried this aggressive attitude with him when he quit high school at 17 and played four seasons of junior hockey with the Niagara Falls Flyers of the Ontario Hockey Association. He became a bona fide star with the Flyers, leading the league in scoring, with 41 goals and 60 assists, in 1966–1967. But there were few fans rooting for him outside of his hometown arena. That's because his roughhouse play, which earned him 431 penalty minutes in his first two seasons, made him a marked man. "Every punk rookie in the league took a shot at me," he complained. "I had 24 fights in 48 games. In some rinks people tossed hot coffee on me as I skated along the boards. Other people would spit at me." Sanderson had particularly raised hackles the previous season when he made a run at the rising young star of the Oshawa Generals—Bobby Orr. "From the moment I first saw him, I hated his guts," said Sanderson of his future best friend.

> He was the all-Canadian boy, the clean-cut, baby-faced, humble, wholesome kid who was going to knock the NHL on its butt. He made everything look so easy, and everybody raved about what a sweet kid he was. It was enough to make a guy throw up. Me, anyway, I was another breed of cat. And it's no wonder the fans loved him and hated me.

Sanderson, a highly skilled fighter with a long reach and quick hands, pummeled the daylights out of Orr at the blue line. Onlookers, particularly Bruins team management, were horrified, but there was a method to Sanderson's madness. "Look," he said afterward, "I came into this game knowing there was going to be a lot of important people in the stands. I was having a bad night around the net so I had to do something to be noticed. What better person was there for me to pick on than him? I figured it might work in my favor in the long run."

It did, as Sanderson received an invitation to Bruins training camp in the fall of 1967. "I wouldn't be here if I didn't think I had a good chance of making the club," he told reporters. "And if I make the club, I don't want to spend the season on the end of the bench. I came here to play." Such unbridled confidence annoyed many of the squad's veterans. He came off as a wise-ass punk who needed to be taught a lesson. "I guess my junior reputation had preceded me, and they all tried to test me a little," he said. Sanderson did not back down from the challenge. He was too close to making hockey's big time to go half-throttle now. "Anytime anyone came near me—smack!—I tried to hit him," he recalled. "I went after every guy on the team." And that included the meanest, baddest of them all—Ted Green. "Listen, kid," Green snarled during a practice, "I hit you, you *don't* hit me! You got that straight? You don't ever hit me or you won't be playing in this league very long." Sanderson was unrepentant. "The next time you do that, I'm gonna crush your face," he replied. That got Green's attention. Green was unaccustomed to anyone—opponent or teammate—talking back to him. He menacingly grabbed Sanderson by the arm in the dressing room afterward and instructed the brash newcomer to meet him later. "This was it," a suddenly concerned Sanderson thought, "I was going to leave pro hockey in sections." Then Green surprised him. He leaned over with a grin on his face and told Sanderson how much he admired his grit and determination. "You're a cocky little bastard, but I like your guts," Green said. "I'm fed up with doing all the fighting on this team. This year, any guy who backs away is going to have to answer to me. You keep doing what you're doing. Don't take crap from anyone, because I'll be right there at your elbow."

Green was not the only Bruin to take a shine to Sanderson. The recently acquired Phil Esposito also issued his own personal stamp of approval. "I've been around a while and you are going to be on this team," the fellow center said. Esposito was dead-on with his prediction. Sanderson made the squad and went on to win the Calder Trophy as NHL Rookie of the Year, with 24 goals and 49 points. His rugged, physical play was also instrumental in helping the Bruins secure their first postseason berth in almost a decade. "When I took over this job," apprised new team GM Milt Schmidt, "I said we'd have to hold our own against the bigger clubs if we were to make the playoffs. Derek is the perfect example. He doesn't take a back seat to anyone." Well, almost anyone. Sanderson was reluctant to tangle with Chicago's bruising superstar forward, Bobby Hull. "He's too strong for me," Sanderson confessed. "Man, he's got muscles like you wouldn't believe. Once, we nearly came to blows, but I told him, 'Bobby, you're a good lookin' fella and a credit to the game. Don't ever change.' I trip him a lot, though." Apart from the "Golden Jet," however, Sanderson had few qualms about throwing his weight around. He served notice of this fact in his very first game, when he took on Montreal

Canadien defenseman Ted Harris, a former Eddie Shore protégé who was one of the fiercest competitors in the league. "Harris was in a fight with Orr, and Bobby was giving him a licking," Sanderson remembered. "I could tell Bobby was tired, so I stepped in and said, 'Try me.' Harris took a swing—he's got a lot of guts—but I got the jump on him." Sanderson made no bones about the kind of performer he was. "Sure, I'm a dirty player," he said. "I like playing dirty. Anyway, that's the way the game should be played. I like fighting. Maybe I'll get beat up a lot, but I'll get the guy eventually."

This propensity for violence earned him the nicknames "Dirty Derek" and "The Terrible Turk," but it also obscured the vital contributions he made to the team, as Sanderson was a clutch scorer and excellent face-off specialist who quickly developed into one of the NHL's best penalty killers. "There's a bit of a pattern in every team's power play," he once observed.

> I watch them very closely until I find it, then I make moves accordingly. Of course, I have to guard against falling into a pattern myself, especially in making a big commitment to going into their zone after the puck. If I get trapped there and they break out, then we're really two men short, not one.

Yet, Sanderson quickly came to realize that such skills, important as they were in helping the Bruins win, were not flashy enough to command him a lot of money come contract time. And the former "Dead-End Kid" wanted to make a lot of money. That's why he decided to add some old-fashioned show business pizzazz to the equation. "I figure a guy needs three things to succeed in hockey," he said. "One is points, the second is talent, and the third is color. On this team, Phil Esposito has the points. Bobby Orr has the talent. But, the kid here [gesturing to himself] is the one who's goin' to have the color."

Sanderson was as good as his word. This "Elvis of the ice lanes" sported long sideburns; dressed in Edwardian suits; hosted a local television talk show called *Everybody's Talkin' at Me*; and generally made the scene with such A-list celebrities as Super Bowl–winning quarterback Joe Namath of the New York Jets, who he briefly teamed up with as a nightclub owner. "Joe Willy lined me up some dates in New York," he said. "They were great, man. He's good people, that Joe Willy. He's on to Playmate-of-the-Year stuff now." Sanderson was so taken by Namath's flamboyant lifestyle that he tried to mimic the football legend's choice of footwear. Namath famously donned white cleats in games, and Sanderson believed wearing skates of a similar hue would make him a distinct presence on the ice. Milt Schmidt thought otherwise. "Listen," the old-school Bruins executive told him,

> you've got two things to face if you're planning to wear white skates: First of all, they're going to try to run at you till you're silly. Every tough guy, every fringe player, is going to take a run at you because you're trying to be a big shot with the white skates. Second, you've never looked down at your feet and seen white skates. You'll be taking a face-off and look down, and when you see white skates you might get sick.

Sanderson reluctantly agreed to shelve the idea, but not before complaining about the "squareness" of team management. "They're a little stuffy," he said, "they figure it's 'Americanizing' the game and that the players, who are nearly all Canadians, might take offense."

Sanderson's most outrageous act occurred a few years later, when he attempted to make his film-acting debut in a picture being shot in Montreal. "I reviewed Derek's portion of the script and found it harmless, if not exactly the kind of material that would make the world forget Laurence Olivier," Sanderson's agent, Bob Woolf, said in *Behind Closed Doors*, a racy tell-all memoir he published in 1976. Sanderson was cast in a bit part as a hockey coach who has a romantic encounter with the film's lead actress. But after attending a private preview screening of the film with Sanderson, Woolf grew alarmed. "We were not very far into the movie before my heart sank and my stomach grew queasy," Woolf wrote. "*It was a porno flick.* I couldn't believe my eyes. While Derek's scene was clean, nothing else in the movie was. The scene in which he met his 'love interest' was preceded by one in which she slept with 10 or 11 guys—forgive me but I lost count." Luckily, Woolf was able to persuade the film's producers to drop the offending sequence after some deft negotiating. "I had an escape clause in the contract," Woolf explained. Sanderson thus avoided what could have been an embarrassing public relations nightmare, but the episode would not deter him from getting tangled up in future controversies. Life was supposed to be a wild roller coaster ride anyway, right? As Sanderson told an interviewer in 1970, "I'm young and I want to have fun. I don't hurt anyone. Not off the ice, anyway. I like nice things. I like luxury. I like pretty girls. I like to swing. Most people do. Maybe they don't get the chance to do these things I do."

Just the same, the "Gallery Gods" ate it up. These mostly white, male, working-class fans of the Bruins, who hailed from such surrounding hard-scrabble communities as South Boston, Somerville, Charlestown, Lynn, Revere, Worcester, Fall River, and Quincy, lived vicariously through their beloved Bs. They would plunk down their hard-earned money from jobs working as bartenders, longshoremen, and truck drivers for tickets to see roughneck favorites like Sanderson or Ted Green battle it out on center ice at Boston Garden, a now-shabby, rat-infested edifice from a bygone era. The building is a "dark, cold, concrete tomb," wrote celebrated author Pat Jordan in a 1970 piece for *Sport* magazine.

> Its echoing corridors smell of cigar smoke and stale beer. It is the kind of arena where people instinctively reach to their back pockets when jostled in a crowd. The Garden's shadowy runways are patrolled by sour-faced ushers in stiff red uniforms who seem to get more pleasure from pushing people out of the aisles than leading them to their seats. But no matter how gruff the ushers might be, and no matter how much dampness is seeping up through the seats, you could not sell even your soul for a seat in that Garden when the Bruins are playing hockey.

For sure, the Bruins had always banged out the place, even during the lean years of the early 1960s, when the hope of making the playoffs was about as realistic as Barry Goldwater winning the presidency. This painful truth annoyed a top team executive from the "other" winter sport tenant at the Garden—Arnold "Red" Auerbach of the National Basketball Association's Boston Celtics. "It seems unbelievable to me that the Celtics, after winning 10 world championships and two division titles during the past 12 years, have failed to gain the recognition of the city's fathers," fumed Auerbach in a speech at the Boston Chamber of Commerce in 1968. "Here is a team that has brought so much pride and honor to the city of Boston while achieving unprecedented feats but still fails to gain the recognition of lesser competitors." The problem was Boston lacked the kind of local basketball tradition the Bruins could draw on with hockey. The Celtics, after all, did not begin as a professional sports franchise until 1946, whereas the Bruins opened their doors for business in 1924, the same year former Massachusetts governor and Boston mayor Calvin Coolidge was elected to his only full term in the White House. As author and journalist Michael Connelly wrote, "Boston sports fans had already committed their attention, discretionary income, and time to the established franchise in the city; they had little interest in a team playing a sport that was unproven and confusing to the post–World War II sports fan."

It also did not hurt that the Bruins' marquee player was the white, apolitical Bobby Orr, while the Celtics had built their dynasty around brooding, goatee-wearing African American center Bill Russell. Russell had not been shy in talking about the many social, political, and economic injustices people of his skin color faced on a daily basis in a racially divided country like the United States. He openly seethed at the memory of a 1962 car trip he took with his children to visit their grandfather in the Jim Crow South. "I was a world champion," he said to biographer William McSweeny in the controversial 1966 best seller *Go Up for Glory.*

> I was a man. Yet, from Washington, D.C., to Louisiana, my children could not stop to eat [due to segregated facilities]. My children could not stop to sleep. They rode in the back seat of the car driven by their

Home ice: the Boston Garden in the late 1960s. *Frank Prazak, HHOF Images*

father, who was their father and a man and a world champion, and we could not stop because we were black. Were I the lowest white trash in the world, I would have been able to stop. But I was black. And I had to keep going. My children had to keep going with the wonder in their eyes that things could change, with the not understanding pleas from the back seat: "Daddy, can't we stop? Daddy, I'm hungry."

Nor did Russell spare Boston from criticism. He bristled at what he saw as the demeaning treatment most black athletes received from the biased white media establishment in town, as well as the extreme tribalism that permeated everyday life. "You know," he once revealed to the *Boston Globe*,

> I remember when [Carl] Yastrzemski was a rookie [for the Red Sox]. One of the writers said, "Too bad he ain't one of us." This is what made Boston different for me. It really went past black and white. They would be into, "Is he a Jew?" "Is he Irish?" "Is he Polish?" "Is he Italian?" And it seemed all the ethnic groups were contemptuous of each other. It wasn't just the whites were contemptuous of the blacks or vice versa. You know, when I came to Boston as a 22-year-old I didn't know what a Jew was. But I became aware of it here, because people here make a distinction based on ethnic background, race, religion, or whatever.

The times were about to dramatically change, however. The tipping point came during the 1967 Boston mayoral race, which pitted progressive Democrat Kevin Hagan White against former city school committee member Louise Day Hicks. Hicks was a reactionary political firebrand from South Boston who was a staunch opponent of efforts to desegregate the public schools. "Boston for Bostonians" became Hicks's campaign rallying cry, and by Bostonians she meant to infer "whites only." "I have guarded your children well," she told voters, "I will continue to defend the neighborhood school as long as I have a breath left in my body." White, meanwhile, offered a more inclusionary vision of the future, one that favored the building of broad, community-based partnerships across diverse racial and ethnic lines. It was a close race, but White was able to pull off a narrow victory on Election Day after the influential *Boston Globe* broke an almost century-old tradition of withholding editorial endorsements for political candidates and came out in favor of the earnest 38-year-old. "There is a principle at stake in this election," the paper said.

In a city which once led the nation in public education and in calling for the end of slavery, it is now the principle of equal treatment of all people. And because principle rather than politics dictates this decision, the *Globe* today departs from its tradition and endorses Kevin White for mayor, and hopes that Boston voters will support him.

While years of intense racial strife still awaited the city due to the federal court-ordered desegregation of Boston schools in the mid-1970s, White's election marked a defining moment for the city. The emerging "New Boston" he would help create would gradually shed its narrow provincialism and become a more dynamic urban metropolitan area where people from a diverse array of different racial and cultural backgrounds would come together to live, work, and play in the early twenty-first century. Boston, in effect, became a true Hub.

But that development was still several decades into the future when the Bruins wrapped up their long NHL regular season with a 3–1 home victory against the Toronto Maple Leafs on April 5, 1970. While boasting a final record of 40–17–19, the team had been unable to establish a firm grip on the East Division, despite the fact that the Montreal Canadiens— their strongest expected competition heading into the campaign—experienced an uncharacteristic off-year. The Habs would fail to make the playoffs for the first time since 1948. "A year of frustration," Canadiens coach Claude Ruel said. "A year of frustration from start to finish. I never thought that one day I would live through such a disappointment." The Bruins instead ended up tying a surprising Chicago Black Hawks squad for first place with a league-best 99 points. Yet, by virtue of chalking up five more victories than their Beantown rivals, the Hawks were able to secure the division title on a tiebreaker and earn important home-ice advantage throughout the postseason. Curiously, none of this seemed to bother the confident Bruins, who demonstrated all the concern of a squirrel trapped in a nut processing plant. They had treated the entire season as a mere warm-up for the playoffs. "We're still number one, in our opinion," Ken Hodge told the *Boston Herald-Traveler*. "We still have a club which spells power."

Now all they had to do was go out and prove it.

5

BRAWLING AND SWEEPING

The opening round of the 1970 Stanley Cup playoffs saw the Bruins square off against the New York Rangers, who finished with a 32–11–11 season record. Coached by the stern but fatherly Emile "Cat" Francis—a former backstop credited with developing the first modern goaltending glove from a baseball first baseman's mitt—the team was a hard-hitting collection of gamers. They could put the puck in the net and drop gloves with anyone. Their undisputed star was a 6-foot, 200-pound sophomore defenseman named Brad Park, who was already being talked about as the best blue liner in franchise history. "A Brad Park comes just every so often," Francis said. "I think he has about 15 to 20 years more to play in the National Hockey League, and he should be improving for the next half-dozen or so."

Park's value to the club was demonstrated when he suffered a broken ankle in a game against Detroit in February and was out for 16 games. The Rangers went on a woeful 3–10–3 skid during that stretch, losing nine straight games and seemingly ending whatever hopes they had of making the postseason. It was a frustrating and painful time for Park. "During the rehab process I would be skating just fine and without pain, and then all of a sudden, I would do something that my ankle didn't agree with and the discomfort would return," Park recalled. Although he had been medically advised to sit out the rest of the season, Park ignored the warnings. He returned to the Rangers lineup in late March and promptly scored a power play goal against Montreal in a crucial victory his second game back. Park said he "damn near cried" when the puck found net.

"That kid is to our club what Bobby Orr is to the Boston Bruins," Emile Francis said afterward. "He makes things go out there. He can change the tempo of the game, and he's aggressive."

With Park back in the fold, the Rangers were able to pull out of their nosedive in the standings and secure the last playoff spot in the East. He also made the first of nine career NHL All-Star Game appearances. "It's a little hard to believe," he told Bill Libby of *Hockey News*.

> Here I am, 21 years old, two years out of the amateurs, playing with and against the best players in hockey. Guys I was only reading about just the other day it seems like, and holding my own, sort of, and reading how good I am in the newspapers and magazines, and trying to keep my head from swelling up like a balloon.

Douglas Bradford Park never lacked confidence. The son of an insurance executive and a former Royal Canadian Air Force physical education instructor, Park experienced a relatively normal postwar childhood in Uniondale, Ontario, a middle-class suburb just north of Toronto. At age six, he got into his first organized hockey game when the goalie for his older brother Ron's team failed to show up. Things did not begin auspiciously for the chubby, moon-faced lad. "No sooner did I take my position when a player came charging down the wing and fired the puck at me," Park remembered. "I grabbed the goalpost for support, but the puck sailed into the corner of the net on the far side. I'd given up a goal on my very first shot." He began to cry, and his mother rushed to his side for comfort. "What's the matter?" Betty Park asked. "Why are you crying?" Park held nothing back. "That guy wasn't supposed to shoot the puck where he did," the future Hall of Famer said. "He was supposed to shoot it *at* me." Needless to say, Park did not remain a goalie for long. Under the tutelage of his father Bob, who spent most of his free time laboring as a highly respected local coach and referee, young Brad quickly picked up the fundamentals of the game. "Skate, shoot, check," Park later wrote in his 1972 autobiography *Play the Man*.

> Those were [my father's] favorite words. He insisted I engage in a lot of body contact and learn to take an opponent out of the play. This wasn't easy because I was one of the shortest kids around. I didn't reach five feet until I was 14 years old. I couldn't knock down the big fellows, so I'd fall in front of them.

New York's Brad Park was Bobby Orr's great rival on the backline. *Lewis Portnoy, HHOF Images*

Park's slow physical development dissuaded the nearby Toronto Maple Leafs—his favorite team growing up—from drafting him. A disappointed Park instead went to the Rangers as the second overall pick in the 1966 NHL Amateur Draft. "The idea of being picked up by any other team than the Leafs never occurred to me," he told *Sporting News.* "The Leafs . . . had some fellows I really idolized. But, on the other hand, I had heard a lot about New York as a city, and the more I thought about playing there, the more I got intrigued—although my folks weren't crazy about my leaving Toronto." Park arrived in Kitchener, Ontario, for his first official training camp with the Rangers in 1968. To say he instilled awe in his new teammates is a vast overstatement. "He looked like the sports editor of a high school newspaper bent on a story about Ed Giacomin," author and journalist Stan Fischler wrote. "But he talked with the mustard tongue of a Derek Sanderson. We all laughed at him. He was a nice kid . . . but he seemed to have delusions of grandeur above and beyond the call of duty."

No one was laughing when Park made the team after a brief minor-league stint when the season began. His advanced shooting and defensive skills soon earned him starting minutes. "He knew how to play the game," said teammate and fellow blue liner Harry Howell. "He was a good power play specialist because he could handle the puck as well as any other defenseman in the league. That was a big thing for him." Park received additional raves for being unafraid of going toe-to-toe with more physically imposing players, for instance, Gordie Howe of the Detroit Red Wings. In one game, Howe whipped an elbow at Park for having the temerity of stepping in his way while pursuing a puck in front of the New York net. "I don't know how the referee didn't throw him out for deliberate attempt to injure," Park said. "I ducked under the elbow, and sure enough [Howe] knicked me with his stick in the Adam's apple. I was down for the count and couldn't swallow for two days." Still, Howe's cheap shot did not prevent Park from seeking out the Hall of Fame winger once the Rangers trainer revived him with smelling salts. Park informed Howe in no uncertain terms that if he pulled something like that again, he would personally end his career. "I remember when that happened, and Brad just stood up for himself," Howell said. "Of course, he went up against the best player in the NHL in Gordie Howe, who was a tough player as well. When Brad stood up to Gordie, that showed me a lot about Brad's character and told me he wasn't going to be pushed around."

Indeed, Park averaged seven hits per game, while collecting 70 penalty minutes that first season. "Nobody goes into a corner with him without getting hit," Emile Francis said admiringly. Dana Mozley of *New York Daily News* was even more effusive. "The boy is a beautiful brute," Mozley wrote. "He loves to hang 'em on the glass."

Park's toughness and obvious talent did not make him a household name in the Big Apple, however. As Mark Mulvoy of *Sports Illustrated* observed,

> Stop people on the streets of New York and ask them about Brad Park, and the answers will sometimes be confusing. Brad Park is a playground in the Bronx. Brad Park is a botanical garden over in Brooklyn. Brad Park is a garage near the 59th Street Bridge. But mention that name on Ste. Catherine Street in Montreal or on Boylston Street in Boston. "Brad Park," goes the response, "is Bobby Orr disguised as a New York Ranger."

Park accepted the situation with a heavy shrug. "New York always has been a basketball town," he said. "Look at the newspapers. Willis Reed this. The Knicks that. Basketball is spread across the top of the sports pages. Heck, all hockey ever gets is a little space down at the bottom." What he cared most about was how his hockey peers viewed him, especially when some began comparing him to Orr. Park never took such talk seriously. "Bobby's the greatest hockey player I've ever seen," he later maintained.

> I never said I was as good as he was, others did. But people kept saying, "Hey Park, who are you kidding? You're no Bobby Orr." And I've got to admit that I have a lot of [determination] and enjoy a challenge. I was influenced by Bobby. Sometimes I'd find myself trying to rush end-to-end like he did, and I'd have to remind myself to stop it.

As good as Park was, he could not prevent his team from being manhandled by the Bruins, 8–2, in Game 1 of the East Division quarterfinal playoff series. A Phil Esposito hat trick paced the Boston attack, as the Bruins never trailed in the contest, to the delight of the 14,835 Garden fans in attendance. "One game don't make a series—not by a long shot," Emile Francis said. "You still have to win four games." But the coach could not have been happy with the ease by which the Bruins dominated play. Two of Boston's goals embarrassingly came in shorthanded situations. By any objective measure, the Rangers received an old-fashioned butt kicking. And no one was happier with the outcome than Esposito. "That's what we've been talking about all year," he said. "We know we have to skate. We know we have to hit. We did it. But it was more than that. We were high for the game, higher than any game I can remember since I came here." In fact, Esposito was so excited that he almost caused serious harm to himself after celebrating his first goal early in the first period. "I threw my hands up in the air and belted myself in the jaw," he said. "I never even felt it, although I had a bump on my jaw after the game."

Bobby Orr had two goals, while Derek Sanderson, Wayne Cashman, and Fred Stanfield also cracked the scoring list. Yet, only one Bruins player received a standing ovation. That would be seldom-used 5-foot-11, 200-pound stay-at-home defenseman Billy Speer. Speer—a barber's son who recorded only six career NHL goals in 130 games—saw a lot of action in this contest because Harry Sinden decided his burly size would be useful in physically wearing down the Rangers. "Giving a fine impersonation of a Sherman tank," noted one newspaper account, "Billy jolted eight or nine of the Rangers. All of these were quite legal with one exception which drew a cross check penalty." A frustrated Francis did not dispute the analysis. "The night belonged to [Speer]," he said. "He hit a few people out there." Speer was far from the only player getting his licks in. Four fights broke out during the game, notably an ugly tussle between Sanderson and Park, which the former easily won. "I pulled his shirt over his head, and it was no contest after that," Sanderson boasted. "My father had taught me that one. And once I got the shirt up I had a real advantage, and I really gave it to him."

Although not as dominant as they had been in the opener, the Bruins still managed to cruise to a 5–3 victory in Game 2. Ken Hodge was credited with the game-winner at 1:24 in the third period. He stripped Rangers defenseman Ab DeMarco of the puck at the New York blue line and broke toward the net. "I had [Esposito] going in with me," Hodge said. "It was really a two-on-one, and before the goalie had time to think about a pass, I just got it by him." Apart from Hodge, four other Bruins registered goals, including Ed Westfall, Johnny Bucyk, Pie McKenzie, and rookie center Jim Lorentz, who later became a radio and television color analyst for the Buffalo Sabres. If there was any kind of silver lining for the Rangers, now staring at a 2–0 series hole, it was their ability to hold Orr scoreless. "They keyed on Bobby all night, particularly their centermen," Sinden said. Orr did manage to elude his Rangers defenders long enough to set up the Westfall and Bucyk goals, which earned him an impressive five points in two games. But what really got people in the Garden stands scratching their heads was the absence of a serious brawl. "A Bruins game without a fight is like a Polish wedding without beer," wrote *Boston Globe* columnist Bud Collins in a culturally insensitive tone common for the time. "But the crowd was fairly understanding. Nobody asked for a ticket refund. Although there was grumbling, the faithful knew that the playoffs will be with us at least until Memorial Day." That was certainly the case with Maine resident Shirley Taylor, a rabid follower of the Black and Gold in section 3. She proudly sported a head-to-toe bear's costume that stood out in the unusually subdued crowd. "I'm not taking off the bearskin until the Bruins win the Stanley Cup," she said. Tellingly, her husband, sitting nearby, was less than enthused. "He looked mad enough to fight," Collins observed, "but he was the only guy in the joint who felt that way."

The Bruins were a self-assured team, some might even say cocky, when they traveled to New York City's Madison Square Garden for Game 3—and for good reason. The Rangers had been as competitive in the previous two contests as the Washington Generals were in their famously staged basketball exhibitions with the Harlem Globetrotters. That was about to change. In what became the most penalty-ridden playoff game in NHL history—a whopping 174 minutes were assessed to both teams—the Bruins got edged by the Rangers, 4–3, in front of a boisterous capacity crowd of 17,250 fans. "It was a nightmarish situation," Gerry Cheevers said. Indeed, the Bruins sensed there would be trouble even before the puck dropped. "The fans booed and gave us the finger as we skated out," Sanderson recalled. "They pelted Cheevers with eggs. All the while, the organist played 'Talk to the Animals.'"

The best was yet to come. Before a face-off in the New York end at the start of the first period, veteran Rangers goalie Eddie Giacomin skated over to teammate Walt Tkaczuk and told him not to let Sanderson get a shot off from the draw. Overhearing this, Sanderson angrily shouted at Giacomin to get back in his net. "Fuck you," Giacomin responded. The exchange fired up the Rangers, who were already smarting from earlier disparaging comments Sanderson had made about the team being "dead" in the playoff hunt. What followed was a wild donnybrook. Sanderson got into a fistfight with Rangers forward Dave Balon that led to both team benches emptying and more brawls breaking out. "Punches were flying all over the place," Esposito remembered. "It was the roughest playoff game in history. There were 24 penalties called for a total of 132 in the first period alone." By the time things had settled down, Sanderson had been ejected from the game. "It's different in New York, isn't it?" he told reporters afterward. "Sure, we know what the Stanley Cup does to you. You'll do anything to win. You expect that. But we don't expect it this way. As I said, we've got 22 guys who can fight. They'll be running out of bodies soon." Sanderson did not stop there. He also claimed Giacomin had told him the Rangers were out to get him and that their coach had placed a bounty on his head. "I thought Emile Francis had class," Sanderson said. "I thought the Rangers had class. They're just as bad as New York fans, they're the animals, not us." The only problem was that Sanderson had made up the entire story to give the media something sensational to write about. "So they printed it," he later confessed.

Lost in the bedlam was a pretty good hockey game. After the Rangers had gone ahead, 4–1, the Bruins mounted a furious comeback in the third period. Orr narrowed the New York lead to 4–2, with a shorthanded goal at the six-minute mark. Fred Stanfield followed a few minutes later, netting a deflection off Dallas Smith's stick. But the Blueshirts managed to hold on for the victory when a promising Esposito bid to tie the game fell short with two minutes remaining. His blazing 15-footer struck the post. Emotions were still running high after the final buzzer sounded. "A lot of Boston players kept telling me they were going to cut my head off," Giacomin complained.

> Sanderson was one of them. He'd been yelling things at me all season. He'd skate by me and say, "We're going to shoot for your eyes tonight, Giacomin. You're going to get the puck shoved down your throat." Things like that. I knew what he was trying to do: shake me up, get my mind off the game.

Orr was equally upset. "The Rangers started as many fights as we did," he said. "But I haven't read anything about the big, bad Rangers. . . . Look how bad Madison Square Garden was. What they did to Derek was incredible."

Incredible does not begin to describe how poorly the Bruins played in Game 4. They fell again to their Big Apple hosts, 4–2, to even the playoff series at two games apiece. "We lost the puck too much in our end," Sinden said. "We got beat fair and square. I expected it would be a long series. I said it before the series started." The Bruins, who had 29 shots on goal to New York's 27, were in the game until the midway point of the second period. Sanderson had a shorthanded breakaway opportunity, but at the last second Giacomin flicked the puck away with his stick. "I had him beat, and I didn't get [the shot] up," Sanderson said. "It was strictly Dec. 25 for him. He never dreamed of making that save. . . . It was all luck for him." Luck or not, the spectacular stop seemed to let the wind out of Boston's sails. New York scored twice more to put the game out of reach. "It hurt a lot," Harry Sinden said. For sure, not even individual goals by Orr and Bucyk could remove the pessimistic gloom that had settled into the Bruins' ranks. "The problem tonight was that we didn't put it together," Sanderson said. "We knew they were going to be tough. New York has always been tough."

As in the previous contest, Rangers fans were out in full force, screaming obscenities at the Bruins in warm-ups and purposely thrusting their thumbs downward like an ancient Roman emperor issuing a death sentence. Their signs were colorful, too. "We Will Bury You," "Derek Is Dead," and "Don't Talk to the Animals—Kill Them" were among the most noteworthy. "Before the series," the *New York Times* observed, "The Bruins' fans were in a league by themselves for well-timed epithets, personal slurs, and a noise level that incited riots." That honor had now passed to their hockey cousins to the south along the Hudson River.

As both clubs headed back to Boston for a pivotal fifth game, Harry Sinden tried hard to rally his dispirited troops. "We don't have to panic," he told the *Globe*. "But we must get back to one thing. I said before this series started that the important thing for us was to play sound positional hockey against a team like New York, which has such good passing." Left unsaid was the porous quality of Boston's goaltending. The Rangers had been allowed to score eight times in the previous two games, and that simply was not good enough for a team with serious championship aspirations. The Bruins needed a stopper in net. They needed Gerry Cheevers. It was a challenge the balding, outspoken veteran was more than willing to accept. Cheevers—a lifelong thoroughbred racing enthusiast—relished situations where the stakes were at their highest. "If you aren't ready to perform well in a game that means elimination, then you shouldn't play professional hockey," he always said.

Gerald Michael Cheevers got his first taste of goaltending at the age of eight, when he was playing for a Catholic Youth Organization team coached by his father in his hometown, St. Catharines, Ontario. The club had suffered through an 18–0 loss, and the elder Cheevers—a local car salesman who held the distinction of being a member of the Canadian Lacrosse Hall of Fame—decided to move his son from wing to net for the next contest. "The [regular] goalie didn't show up," Cheevers told *Sporting News*. "My dad didn't have the nerve to ask anybody else to play goal, so he put me in there." Although his team got blown out again, Cheevers genuinely enjoyed his time between the pipes and the adrenaline rush that went along with it. As he recounted in his entertaining 2011 autobiography, *Unmasked*, "I played with no mask, no fear then, only the desire to win. I met each attacker head on."

Cheevers showed enough promise by his late teen years to start for the St. Michael's Majors of the Ontario Hockey Association, where he earned top honors for being the Junior A league's best goalie. "The [OHA] was a great league," Cheevers recalled. "Each team produced at least three to four hockey players yearly who would eventually go on to play in the NHL." It was here that Cheevers developed what would become his trademark style as a pro—roaming far beyond the crease while brandishing his goalie stick the "way a jungle fighter uses a knife," according to *Hockey Illustrated*. This aggressive approach—"chopping 'em down," Cheevers called it—sometimes frustrated his coach, a Catholic priest named David Bauer who had been equally displeased with his goalie's marked aversion to practice. To put him in his place, Bauer switched Cheevers to forward for 12 games. It was an eye-opening experience. "I almost got killed," Cheevers said. "All the guys on the other teams who were mad at me, maybe because I took a goal away from them, started to take runs at me. I'm telling you, I'm lucky I survived." To add insult to injury, Cheevers did not even score a goal. "You'd think if anyone knew how to beat a goalie it would be another goalie. But I drew a blank," he confessed. "Once I had a clear breakaway, but I forgot to think. I shot right into the goalie's pads. I only wish everyone played forward the way I did. I'd never be scored upon."

Since St. Mike's was an affiliate of the Toronto Maple Leafs, Cheevers was given a strong look by the parent club, which was impressed enough to assign him to their Pittsburgh farm team. The Leafs also brought him up to play in a pair of regular-season games in 1961–1962. But the team already had established goaltenders Johnny Bower and Terry Sawchuk on the roster, and Cheevers did not demonstrate enough skill in his brief NHL audition to displace either one of them. "I was just a young prospect," Cheevers said. "Maybe I was going to develop, maybe I wasn't." Thus, Cheevers thus was not surprised when the Bruins claimed him in the 1965 waiver draft after Toronto left him unprotected. "Sure, I was disappointed," he admitted. "It's tough to leave a team you've been with since you were 15." Compounding his misery was the fact that he had always dreamed of being a Maple Leaf growing up and was now going to a club that ranked among the dregs of the league. On the plus side, Boston had virtually no goaltending whatsoever, using five backstops the previous year to tie a club record. It appeared as if Cheevers would see plenty of ice time.

But the agile 30-year-old goalie—"I covered more ground than a stewardess," he once bragged—got into only seven games for the Bruins in 1965–1966, as a knee injury robbed him of his natural quickness and derailed any hopes he had of becoming a regular. Cheevers was subsequently sent down to the Oklahoma City Blazers of the Central Professional Hockey League, where player-coach Harry Sinden started him. "Cheesey" responded with a banner performance, allowing a career-best 2.49 goals per game. Fans, however, did not know what to make of him. "This Cheevers did not even *look* like a hockey player," noted future *Sports Illustrated* hockey writer Jack Falla.

> He was sort of round and dumpy. There was this round face with thinning blond hair pushed to one side and these bullet-hole eyes and a noticeable pot belly made more obvious by the bulge in the goalie's pants and chest pad. He projected neither strength nor quickness. He looked to me like race car driver Cale Yarborough, just an easygoing good ol' boy. I figured he'd be happy in Oke City.

As it turned out, Cheevers immensely enjoyed his time in the "Big Friendly," as he led his team to a league championship and got to play for the first time with future Bruins teammates Wayne Cashman and Derek Sanderson. "We hung out at a place called the Jungle Pitt down there," Cheevers recalled.

It was owned by a guy named Jacko. He had a pet monkey that tagged
along with him everywhere, including the bar. By the end of each day,
Jacko was covered with whatever came out of that monkey's [posteri-
or] from dusk till dawn. It was foul! But a haven for some of the local
fly colonies, no doubt.

Cheevers became the number-one Boston goalie in 1967–1968, after
beating out veteran Ed Johnston and top prospect Bernie Parent for the
job. Harry Sinden's elevation to Bruins head coach certainly helped his
chances. Sinden had witnessed firsthand in Oklahoma City how cool
Cheevers was under pressure. "Cheevers? He's a money player," he said.
Indeed, Cheevers would end up ranking among the top 100 NHL goalies
in career playoff save percentage (.902). "I guess I can psyche myself up
pretty good," he said. "It's a long season you know, 78 games, and the
important ones are after that. I like to think I can get myself up for a game
that really counts." Cheevers's secret had to do with possessing a devil-
may-care attitude. A loss was truly an unfortunate thing but nothing to
lose sleep over. "You never win them all—no one does," he said. As
future Bruins coach Don Cherry told author George Plimpton, "Cheevers's idea is that it's only a game. . . . He'll just do the best he can. If it's
not good enough, the next time he'll do better. The fact is you've got to
leave your bad games out on the ice."

It helped that Cheevers possessed an irreverent sense of humor. He
once told reporters that he was unafraid of squaring off against his celebrated All-Star teammates in practice. Their shots could never touch him,
he claimed, because "they scored all the time." On other occasions, he
and Phil Esposito would huddle together on long road trips and pick
imaginary NHL rosters for all-stupid or all-ugly teams. Regarding the
former, Cheevers posited that Ken Hodge would be an ideal candidate at
right wing. When Esposito protested, Cheevers reluctantly agreed to drop
his name. "Okay, okay, but he's a close second," he said. "Cheevers was
a beauty," referee Bruce Hood revealed in Stephen Cole's 2015 best
seller *Hockey Night Fever: Mullets, Mayhem, and the Game's Coming of
Age in the 1970s.* "Someone would shoot the puck over the glass. I'd
point past the blue line and say, 'Face-off outside.' Hearing this, Gerry
would go, 'But Bruce, we can't play outside—there's no ice!' He was
always joking."

Not everyone appreciated Cheevers's droll wit. Former Bruins general
manager Hap Emms, in particular, became upset after he confronted

Cheevers in the locker room following a lopsided defeat. "What the hell went on out there?" Emms demanded to know. Cheevers swatted away the question as easily as a rookie's backhander. "Roses are red, violets are blue, they got 10, we only got two," he said. Emms's front-office successor had a similar experience. When Milt Schmidt asked Cheevers whether he felt "like a complete asshole" for letting in a key goal during a loss against Montreal, the goaltender calmly disagreed. He suggested an adult gay man would be a more apt comparison. "What do you mean?" a puzzled Schmidt asked. "Let me put it this way, Miltie," Cheevers explained, while referencing the rampant homophobia that plagued the United States and Canada at the time. "If you had 15,000 people call you a cocksucker, what would you feel like?"

Cheevers further established his puck-stopping prowess in 1968–1969, when he won 28 games and made the All-Star Team with a .912 save percentage. "He was a Godsend for a team like we were, a team that played so wide open," Esposito later told writer Gerald Eskenazi. "He was special for putting up with us. We used to leave him all alone in his net quite a bit." But what really garnered Cheevers widespread notoriety that season had nothing to do with how he performed, but rather how he looked while performing. He started sporting what would become an iconic stitch-patterned goalie mask, as familiar to hockey fans as Joe Namath's white cleats were to football enthusiasts. "It began during a practice," Cheevers recounted. Fred Stanfield tagged a shot that deflected off the arm of Ted Green and hit him squarely in the mask. Cheevers then took the opportunity to retire to the Bruins dressing room, ostensibly to recover from the shock of the blow. In reality, Cheevers was not hurt at all. "If I wouldn't have had my mask on, [the puck] wouldn't have even cut me, but I was faking it and trying to get out of practice, like I tried to do every day," he said. It seemed like a foolproof plan, especially when Cheevers enlisted the aid of team trainer John "Frosty" Forrestal. Forrestal declared Cheevers unfit to return to action, but Harry Sinden knew better. "You're not hurt; get back out there!" he snarled. Cheevers, who had not bolstered his own credibility by being caught red-handed by Sinden smoking a cigar and reading the *Racing Form*, timidly complied with the order. But before he did, Forrestal came up with a mischievous idea. Using a black magic marker, he drew a jagged 12-inch stitch on Cheevers' mask. "I went out and said to Harry, 'I really got hurt bad like this,'" Cheevers said.

Everyone had a good laugh, but Forrestal continued to add stitches— 76 in total—by the time Cheevers retired from playing. "We kept an accurate count," Cheevers maintained. "I'd estimate how many stitches a shot was worth—I'd say, 'That's a tenner under the chin,' or 'Give me a niner over the eye'—and Frosty would draw them on." No longer the butt of jokes, the mask became the goaltending version of the *Red Badge of Courage*. "Drawing all those stitches on it showed people how dangerous the position was," Cheevers said. The "cuts" also made the previous all-white visor the most identifiable piece of hockey equipment in history. "I guess it was voted the best mask, and it hangs on my grandson's wall," Cheevers said in a 2018 interview. "I turned down a lot of money for it. It's just one of those things that, when I did it, I didn't know what was going to happen with it, but it turned out pretty great."

"Pretty great" describes how things went for the Bruins in Game 5. Sparked by a pair of third-period goals by Phil Esposito, the Bruins outlasted the Rangers, 3–2, in a satisfying come-from-behind victory at Boston Garden. "We can win it now," a relieved Esposito told reporters afterward. Bobby Orr fed Esposito with the game-winner on a picture-perfect lead pass near the Rangers' blue line at 7:59. "Espo went in and let it go from 15 feet, and it went through Giacomin's pads," Jack McCarthy of the *Boston Herald-Traveler* wrote. Orr had gained posses-sion of the puck on a prior steal at center ice. The Rangers were in the middle of a line change, and the opportunistic Orr swooped in to take advantage. He spied Esposito on a breakaway down the ice and con-nected. "Bobby's pass was beautiful," Esposito said. "All I decided was that I was going to shoot. I wasn't going to fool around." There was also an element of luck involved in the play. Esposito was able to be open because he had missed a check on Brad Park. "He wasn't even hustling," Park fumed. "He was coming back across our blue line slowly." Esposito had registered his other goal, which tied the contest at 2–2 minutes earli-er, on a Wayne Cashman pass from the backboards. "I had a pretty good opening," the center said. "Cash got the puck to me nice, and the opening was there."

Orr had kick-started the Boston offense in the first period when he split the Rangers defense and scored on a brilliant end-to-end rush. "That Orr, he is impossible," Rangers forward Rod Gilbert said. "Hockey is a team game, right? One man is not supposed to beat a whole team, right? But what else can you say. You saw it." The New Yorkers, however, did not go quietly. They picked up a pair of goals and held a 2–1 lead going into the third period. Things looked even brighter for the visitors when Esposito was assessed a five-minute major penalty for "accidentally" hitting Jean Ratelle in the head with his stick. "You can't believe how badly I felt," Esposito claimed. "All I could think of was [an earlier regular-season game] in New York when we took the same kind of penalty and they scored three or four times." Fortunately for the Bruins, history did not repeat itself. Orr was able to eat up most of the penalty on some brilliant keep-away moves, and the Bruins defense was able to hold the fort until Esposito bested Giacomin twice in the final period. Gerry Cheevers heroically did his part, too, turning away 28 New York shots. "The thing that woke us up was the realization that it [the third period] was the most critical part of the season," Harry Sinden said. "[The team] fully realized what could happen if we had lost this one."

The Bruins closed out the series the next day when Orr scored two goals in a 4–1 drubbing of the Rangers on their home ice. The defenseman's tallies gave him a total of seven for the six games, setting a new NHL playoff record. "He killed us," New York coach Emile Francis said.

Money in the bank: Gerry Cheevers in net. *Lewis Portnoy, HHOF Images*

Orr's first goal came early in the second period on a rebound off a Pie McKenzie bullet from the right point. "It looked accidental or lucky, but it wasn't," Orr revealed to *Sports Illustrated.* "I was in the right place, and the puck was in the right place." Orr was in the right spot again a period later. He took a Ken Hodge feed along the right boards and slammed home a 55-footer. "There was no wasted motion as the puck whirred over into the far side [of the Rangers net]," the *Boston Globe* reported. Wayne Cashman and Derek Sanderson registered the other Boston goals. Sanderson's keeper midway through the third period on an Ed Westfall pass was particularly sweet for the Bruins centerman. It represented the final goal for either team in the series as well, as his own personal Bronx salute to the Madison Square Garden faithful, who again made sure to heap abuse on Sanderson and his teammates. "Some fans threw eggs and ball bearings at the players on the ice," *New York Post* columnist and author Hugh Delano wrote. "They tried to attack the Bruins' players, and when the outcome no longer was in doubt, they set fires to the mezzanine." Things were considerably more civil when the Bruins and Rangers lined up for their traditional postgame handshakes. "Way to go, kid," Giacomin told Sanderson. For once, Sanderson appeared at a loss for words.

Having dispatched the Rangers in six hard-fought games, the Bruins looked upon their next opponent in the round with nervous trepidation, as the Chicago Black Hawks had bested them in the regular-season standings, albeit barely, with a talented lineup that boasted future Hall of Famers Bobby Hull and Stan Mikita. If that wasn't enough to give Boston pause, the Hawks had retained their top playoff seed in the East by effortlessly sweeping the Detroit Red Wings in their opening-round clash. "They were well rested and waiting for us," Bobby Orr remembered. "We knew the series wouldn't be easy." Indeed, the Hawks were a confident club after having fully recovered from a disappointing 1968–1969 season during which they missed the playoffs for the first time in a decade. Much of their turnaround was due to the emergence of prize 26-year-old goaltender Anthony James "Tony O" Esposito. "If I had to pick a key, it would be Esposito," Chicago coach Billy Reay said. "He has given us the big save, the save that gives you a lift. So many times you get that big save, and bang! You go right down to their end and put the puck in the net." Esposito, brother Phil's college-educated younger sibling, had been claimed on waivers from Montreal before the start of the season with only

13 games of NHL experience under his belt. But the former Michigan Tech All-American surprised everyone by playing in 63 games and establishing a new league rookie record of 15 shutouts, with a 2.17 goals-against average. "We thought Tony might be good someday," Reay revealed. "He fooled us all. It turned out he was already one of the best in the game."

Esposito easily secured Rookie of the Year honors and ended up an All-Star teammate of Phil's on the East squad. "Not bad for a goalie the Canadians discarded," Esposito said. As his sarcastic comment indicated, there was no love lost between Esposito and his old team. "Tony O" had been buried deep on the Montreal bench the previous season behind veteran backstops Rogie Vachon and Lorne John "Gump" Worsley. He did, however, manage to post a 5–4–4 record, with two shutouts, in limited action. Alas, it was not enough to satisfy a skeptical team management. "The coach, Claude Ruel, was always barking at me if I let in a bad goal," Esposito recalled. "I didn't need that. I needed support and encouragement. I didn't get it in Montreal. I was glad when they let me go."

The Hawks were too, especially when Esposito displayed an entertainingly unorthodox style that left teammates and Windy City fans in a near-constant state of suspended disbelief. "I've never seen a goalie do the things he can do," said Gerry Desjardins, Esposito's backup in 1969–1970. "He has a way of dropping to his knees and spreading his pads out to either side on certain kinds of shots, mostly from the point. That way he's in better shape to take care of rebounds than I am after I've done the splits on the same shots." Esposito's spread eagle stance proved unusual in another important way. He "give[s] the shooter a target between his pads, then drop[s] down at the last second to close it off," Desjardins added. "It requires great timing, and he has it down perfectly. His timing is terrific and he always seems to know exactly where the puck is with his back turned."

Opponents could be forgiven, however, if they first mistook the wide-faced, barrel-chested Ontarian for some yokel out of a beer league. "He looks like hell out there," Bobby Orr said. "The guy does everything wrong. He gives us shooters all kinds of openings, and he doesn't play the angles very well. Heck, he doesn't even keep his legs together, giving you big holes to shoot at." Yet, at the end of the day, even Orr conceded that Esposito got the job done. And that was all that mattered to Esposito. "I want the shutout," Esposito said. "I don't want to win 5–3, I want to win

5–0." Still, the mental stress incurred by taking such a driven approach exacted a heavy price. Esposito never had much fun in hockey. "It's a job," he said. "I have to do it. But it's tough. I don't like it. To be playing well as a goalkeeper, you have to be afraid. Not afraid that you'll get hurt, but afraid that they're going to score on you. Every time they come down the ice with the puck, I'm afraid the puck is going to go in."

That fear of failure was magnified whenever his high scoring older brother was near the net. "If I made a save on Phil, he'd crack afterwards that I was lucky, but we don't kibitz in a game," Esposito said. "That's all business. Off the ice it's a lot of fun needling each other, but on the ice there's no way Phil's going to score if I can prevent it." Such "healthy combativeness" had been a hallmark in their relationship since early childhood. The two brothers would stage epic hockey contests in the basement of their family home using a rolled-up woolen sock as a puck. Sometimes, however, their competitiveness got the better of them. "We had some groovy fights with each other," Phil later told Jack Olsen of *Sports Illustrated*. "Once I knocked a hole right through our basement wall when we were fighting. My father never found out. We covered the hole with a picture of Jesus." Phil also revealed how far their singular devotion to the sport went when they ventured beyond the comfortable confines of their Sault Sainte Marie home. "We used to get up at 4:30 or 5 in the morning," he said,

> load Tony's goal pads and everything on the toboggan, and pull it right through town to the rink so we could practice before school. Usually I did the shooting and Tony the goaltending. It's like baseball; every kid wants to get up and take his swings, and every Canadian kid wants to shoot the puck. I was a year older, so I did the shooting. Maybe Tony didn't like it, but he didn't have much choice.

Tony faced Phil professionally for the first time while playing for the Canadians on December 5, 1968. Although Tony allowed only two goals to the high-octane Bruins offense that day in Boston, both came courtesy of Phil in a 2–2 tie. "Hey Tony, I'll bet Mom's gonna be mad at Phil for spoiling your night," a teammate joked afterward. For his part, Tony dismissed each score as "lucky," but the first goal near the eight-minute mark of the opening period proved particularly bothersome. "I swept around [Montreal defenseman] Larry Hillman and tried to shoot the puck between Tony's right pad and the post," Phil recalled. "The puck bounced across, hit the other post, and went in." Tony raged at his misfortune. He retrieved the puck from the net with his stick and angrily launched it down the ice. "For a second I thought he was aiming at me," Phil said. "He was teed off, the same way he used to get when I'd beat him in our pick-up games as kids. But this time he was just shooting the puck . . . so he would have a little more time to recover from my goal." Tony's then wife Marylyn exhibited no such restraint in her response. She told Phil in a heated telephone conversation after the game that he was a "dirty dog."

While Tony Esposito had been a major factor in Chicago's success, Bobby Hull remained the team's central driving force. It was easy to understand why. Hull *was* Chicago hockey. Since breaking in with the club in 1957–1958, the brawny, high-scoring forward had led the league in goals seven times and overall points three times. If that wasn't impressive enough, Hull held the honor of becoming only the third player in history to score 50 or more goals in a season, a feat he would duplicate on four other occasions during his superlative 15-year NHL career. "He's definitely the toughest shot in the league," contended New York's Eddie Giacomin.

Hull was able to pile up the goals courtesy of a devastating left-handed slap shot that rival goaltenders like Giacomin struggled to draw a bead on. "I've fanned on shots of his when I reached for the darn thing, and, all of a sudden, it would take a drop of about a foot or something and go in," said Toronto's four-time Stanley Cup–winning goalie, Johnny Bower. "At first you think you can glove the puck without putting your body behind it, but the dip fools you." Bower candidly admitted to having panic attacks before games facing Hull. "Sure, I'm scared," he told an interviewer. And not just because of the Chicagoan's ability to peel off a game-winner. Bower was most fearful of how close Hull's shots came to his head, as these "sledgehammer blows" often travelled at velocities approaching 120 miles per hour. "If [one] ever hit I'd hate to say what would happen," Bower said. "I've never worn a mask in a game before, but I'd be tempted to wear one against him because I'm just liable to get one where I don't want to get it." Some of his peers threw in the towel altogether rather than face Hull head-on. "When the Canadians had a game with Chicago, Gump Worsley would always manage to pull a muscle in the warm-up, like a lot of guys," remembered Montreal sports columnist Red Fischler.

Adding to the explosive force of Hull's shots was his pioneering use of a curved blade on his hockey sticks. "It's helped him," teammate Dave Dryden said. "With the curved stick he can just lean forward and slap that thing on the net. With a straight blade the puck would slip off the end of the stick. With the curve the puck can be a little bit ahead of him and he can reach forward past a defenseman and still let a heckuva shot go." The "banana blade" also had the advantage of sowing confusion among opponents. "When you're looking at a guy with a straight stick you can see the angle; you can almost read it. With a curved stick you can't tell where the puck is coming off the stick, and with Bobby you just can't read the stick at all," Dryden said.

Hull adopted the curved blade based on a discovery made by teammate Stan Mikita at the end of a Black Hawks practice session in 1962. Mikita had badly cracked the blade on his stick but was too tired to go to the clubhouse for a replacement. "I took a couple of shots at the boards [with the broken stick] and noticed that the puck made an unusual sound when it hit," Mikita recalled. "That made me inquisitive. Why did the puck sound different? And why did the puck feel like it was moving faster off the blade?" Chicago's all-time scoring leader soon came to the conclusion that it was due to the curvature of the blade. That's all he and Hull needed to know.

"Soon [they] were warping the wooden blades on their sticks into scoop-like curves by soaking them in hot water and wedging them under door jambs overnight," noted one magazine account. Still, the notion that Hull's record-breaking success was due solely to the innovation is a bit of a stretch. "I think he'd be scoring just as many goals with the conventional stick," Minnesota's Cesare Maniago told Stan Fischler in 1969. "After all, he did score 50 goals one year using the conventional stick, and he was just on his way up then." Of course, it didn't hurt Hull's offense that he was one of the swiftest end-to-end skaters in the game, reaching speeds of as fast as 30 miles per hour. "Bobby is so fast, everybody in the league feels slower when he is on the ice," Gordy Howe once said. Bobby Orr—no slouch himself in the speed department—did not dispute the fact. "Let [Hull] get outside you, and he was . . . so fast that there was no way to keep him from cutting back in," he wrote. "Generally, you had to stand him up early."

Hull exhibited these extraordinary hockey gifts with the casual aplomb of a Hollywood matinee idol. Indeed, with a muscular, lean body, and dimpled cheeks and blond curls, he was often mistaken for Paul Newman, the leading man of such popular films as *The Hustler* (1961), *Cool Hand Luke* (1967), and *Butch Cassidy and the Sundance Kid* (1969). As Bill Furlong of *Sport* magazine wrote in 1966, "[Hull] is color personified—the hero as he should be: strong, dauntless, upright, unyielding under pressure, unflinching under attack. He is the wish dream in all of us, the personification of what might-have-been." Hull was billed as the "Babe Ruth of hockey," a larger than life figure for whom even nonsports enthusiasts could embrace. "Hull was a certified star," agrees biographer Gare Joyce. "The NHL was the second or third priority at best in New York, Boston, and Detroit, but in Chicago Hull had the highest profile of all the stars of the city's hard-luck sports teams." For sure, the "City of Broad Shoulders" could boast of having other dominant athletic talents like baseball infielder Ernie Banks and football linebacker Dick Butkus, who played for the Cubs and Bears respectively. But, as Joyce points out, their teams never won anything and rarely contended. Hull was different; his Black Hawks usually went deep in the Stanley Cup playoffs and captured several divisional flags. "Hull didn't own the city but of all the pro stars he owned the biggest piece of it," Joyce writes. "He made [Chicago] Stadium [the city's] most exciting venue." Nor was Hull's electric popularity confined to his home arena; he became a premier gate attraction throughout the league. "Even in Montreal, where they have the most partisan of fans," noted a Toronto sports editor, "Bobby Hull is saluted as no player for a rival team ever has been."

Hull's soaring fame was confirmed when a LeRoy Neiman portrait of him appeared on the March 1, 1968, cover of *Time* magazine, the first time a hockey player had been accorded such an honor by the immensely popular American news weekly. The accompanying article, written by magazine staffer Arthur Shay, proved equally flattering. "The sight of Robert Marvin Hull, 29, leaning into a hockey stick is one of the true spectacles of sport—like watching Mickey Mantle clear the roof, or Wilt Chamberlain flick in a basket, or Bart Starr throw that beautiful bomb," Shay wrote. "It is a thing hockey fans go to see. . . . And it is the thing that makes Bobby Hull the superstar of his blazing sport. A legion of partisans [who] call him 'the Golden Jet' and 'Mr. Hockey' regard him as the greatest player of this or any other day—and rare is the expert who says to them nay."

In spite of the accolades, Hull was no "golden boy." A heavy drinker and serial philanderer, the thrice-married Canadian liked to step out on the town after games to unwind. "Let's go get laid," he'd invariably tell teammates and opponents, sometimes within hearing distance of their mortified wives. Needless to say, this kind of loutish behavior did not make Hull an ideal husband. His second wife, Joanne McKay—a former ice show performer with whom Hull tied the knot in 1960—could attest to that. McKay frequently confronted her wayward spouse in public regarding his infidelities. "I was incredulous about what I saw between [them]," longtime hockey journalist Vic Grant said. "They were yelling at each other at airports. He'd tell her to go fuck herself, and she'd turn around and do the same. It wasn't just the team and reporters who were around. There would be dozens of people around." McKay would divorce Hull in 1980, after claiming she had suffered years of mental and physical abuse at his hands. In fact, she vividly described a 1966 incident at a Hawaiian hotel where Hull "threw" her into a room and proceeded to "knock the hell out of me." "He took my shoe—with a steel heel—and proceeded to hit me in the head," she revealed in a 2002 ESPN documentary. "I was covered with blood. And I can remember him holding me over the balcony, and I thought this is the end, I'm going." On a separate occasion, Hull reportedly aimed a loaded shotgun at her. In 1987, Hull pled guilty to an assault charge after allegedly assaulting a suburban Chicago police officer responding to a loud domestic disturbance in a condominium parking lot between himself and his third wife, Deborah. "I didn't have a lot of admiration for Bobby Hull because I saw what the public didn't see," Grant said. "Just like his teammates did. He was a hard man to admire, and I doubt many of his teammates did, even if they would never admit it."

The eldest son of a cement plant foreman and a homemaker, Robert Marvin Hull Jr. grew up in modest circumstances with his 10 brothers and sisters in the tiny community of Point Anne, Ontario, after World War II. A frustrated amateur athlete who had failed to see his hockey dreams come true, Bobby Hull Sr. had high hopes for his namesake. To this end he gave the boy a pair of hockey skates as a Christmas present when the latter was only three. Young Bobby wasted no time putting them to use. "I looked out the window [overlooking the frozen Bay of Quinte off Lake Ontario] a couple of hours later, and I could hardly believe it," his mother recalled. "Here was this little gaffer skating by himself. He fell down

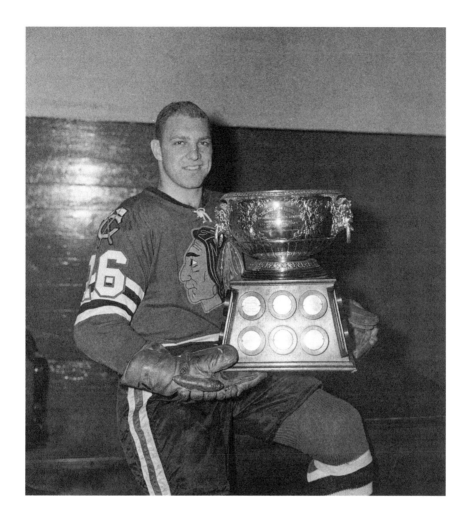

Bobby Hull won three Art Ross Trophies for being the NHL's top scorer during his celebrated Chicago career. *Le Studio du Hockey, HHOF Images*

often, but he would always get up, brush off the snow, and keep on skating."

Hull made a point of repeating the ritual on a daily basis until he became proficient enough to pick up a hockey stick and play in games. As he remembered, "I would get up in the morning to put on the porridge pot, then go out to skate until breakfast was ready. I used to skate all morning and afternoon, and I only came home for meals. After dinner, I always went out again, and Mum would have to send my sisters out to bring me home to bed." Bobby Sr. was duly impressed, especially after witnessing Hull compete against older boys at a local rink. "I couldn't believe what I saw," he said. "He was making plays as well as kids twice his age. I said to myself, 'If ever I've seen an NHLer this is it.'" The elder Hull was not content to just leave it at that, however. He constantly challenged his son to be a better player. "He was sometimes impatient," Bobby Jr. admitted, "but he liked to skate with me. 'Let's try it again, Robert,' he would say. 'Keep your head up. If the stick blade is angled properly, the puck will feel right on it.'"

Hull started playing organized hockey at the age of 10 and not long thereafter caught the attention of Chicago's chief scout, Bob Wilson. "It was strictly luck that I spotted him," Wilson said. "The kid was so outstanding any man in the business would have spotted him if he had been there first. I look at 10,000 kids a year, but you see a boy like Hull once in a lifetime." Wilson signed the promising teenager, and after only a few short years of seasoning at the junior level, Hull made his professional debut with the Black Hawks in 1957. "I felt the kid belonged in the NHL," remarked Hawks general manager Tommy Ivan, who fast-tracked the promotion. "Sure, he was young [only 17], but he had the moves of a big-leaguer."

Hull's first goal came in his seventh game against the Bruins, although it was hardly the stuff of legend. "Somebody rapped me a good one, and down I went right on top of the puck," Hull said. "All I did was slide into the net with the puck underneath me." He would tally 12 more goals that rookie campaign and go on to collect his first individual league scoring title two years later. In 1961, he led the Black Hawks to a Stanley Cup championship, their first since the Great Depression. But any rundown of Hull's early career accomplishments would be incomplete without mention of the cool methodical way he approached most pressure game situations. "You don't waste your energy," he said.

> You pick your spots, and you go when you know you have the edge. It's an instinct. You get so that you can anticipate when you should outrace or outbody or outmaneuver. You sense your opening, and you react. There's a lot in knowing what you yourself can do. If you see an opening, something tells you if you can make it or not make it.

Neither Hull nor his Black Hawks teammates encountered enough promising openings to pull off a victory in Game One of their semifinal

matchup with the Bruins on April 19. The favored Hawks fell victim to a
6–3 shellacking by Boston on their home ice, courtesy of a hat trick by
Phil Esposito and individual goals by Johnny Bucyk, Pie McKenzie, and
Ken Hodge. "No sir," Esposito responded to reporters' questions afterward about whether he felt bad about "running up the count" on his
brother Tony. Tony O had played the entire game despite being temporarily knocked unconscious in the opening moments on a blistering Hodge
shot that ricocheted off his goalie mask. "I don't think of him as my
brother out there," Phil said.

> I couldn't help it when he was hurt, but when I was shooting against
> him, he was just another guy on the other team. If my mother was
> tending goal for the other team, I'd try to beat her. I'm sorry he lost,
> but I'm glad I won. He's a good goaltender. He proved that all season.
> He beat me plenty this season. He may beat me next game. I beat him
> this game. It's a team game anyway. It's not a battle of brothers.

Still, Esposito grew worried when he saw his brother lying motionless
face down on the ice. "God," he whispered to himself, "I hope he's not
seriously hurt." His concern was only alleviated when Bobby Hull skated
up to him near center ice during the lull in action. "[Tony's] all right," his
former teammate informed him. "He was lucky he got it in the head. You
can't hurt an Esposito hitting him in the head."

The Bruins won again two days later when they demolished their
Chicago hosts, 4–1, to take a commanding two games to none lead in the
best-of-seven series. The margin of defeat was the worst suffered by the
Hawks in their own building that season. "When we came here, we
wanted to win one game," Bobby Orr said. "Winning two is super." Orr
started the Bruins off on the right foot with a breakaway goal off a nifty
feed by teammate Fred Stanfield at 5:08 in the first period. "Stanfield was
practically perfect on his timing with the pass," the *Boston Globe* said.
The goal gave the club a lead it would never relinquish and represented
Orr's first against the Black Hawks all season. "I came out the net to
charge him, and he got the puck over me," Tony Esposito said. "It was
my own fault. I should have stayed in the net and made him make the first
move." Pie McKenzie, Don Marcotte, and Phil Esposito added to Boston's advantage with solo tallies in the next two periods.

"The Hawks look lifeless," Derek Sanderson told reporters afterward.
For sure, Chicago played listlessly throughout, in part due to Boston

coach Harry Sinden's decision at the start of the series to have forward Eddie Westfall shadow Hull wherever he went on the ice. Westfall carried out his assignment brilliantly, frustrating Hull to the point that he was getting into the Chicago star's head. Hull, held scoreless in both games, later joked that when he got up to shave one morning, he was startled to discover Westfall staring back at him in the bathroom mirror. "It doesn't make sense," observed a rival scout. "A player of Bobby's ability should be allowed to go out there against anybody and play his game. He's as good, if not better, than any forward in the league. He shouldn't be hampered mentally, and that's exactly what's happening to him." The situation did not paint a pretty picture for Chicago fans.

"These are the darkest of days for the Black Hawks, and the dawn is not imminent," Ted Damata of the *Chicago Tribune* wrote. "Not even where they lost the first five games of this National Hockey League season was hope so faint." Having squandered their home-ice advantage, the Hawks faced a potential playoff sweep if they failed to win Games 3 and 4 on the road in Boston Garden, a veritable house of horrors for the club. Since 1966–1967, the Hawks had only claimed one regular-season victory there—a 1–0 squeaker on January 17. Any hope for a club turnaround now depended on getting increased production from Hull and the other half of Chicago's dynamic scoring duo—Stan Mikita.

The Slovak-born center led the league in overall goals and assists four times during the decade and earned MVP nods in 1967 and 1968. "If [the Hawks] lost Mikita, they might fall right out of sight," assessed Toronto Maple Leafs assistant general manager King Clancy. "He's a better defensive player than Hull, and he's the best checking center in the league. He scores well and he's the biggest part of their power play. He's the guy that makes them go. There's no two ways about that." Other opponents concurred. "Mikita, he'll always makes the big plays that'll kill you," said veteran goaltender Gump Worsley. "He won't pass the puck if a man isn't clear. He won't give the puck away to a guy that's half-covered just to get rid of it." For sure, "Stash" played a cerebral game that made his teammates around him better. He was the hockey equivalent of a point guard in basketball—setting the tempo of play and making sure everyone knew their respective roles. As Bobby Hull observed, "It's actually tough to go too far wrong when you play on a line with Mikita. All you have to do is follow his directions. If he says skate for the net, you do it. If it's go to the boards, you go. He'll get the puck to you, and there isn't a smarter player in the league."

Apart from brains, the wiry 5-foot-9, 169-pound Mikita also displayed an abundance of grit. He once recalled taking off his skates between periods and being surprised to discover they were filled with blood from two broken toes. "He can take the rough stuff a little longer than most centers," Worsley said. "The more you hit him, the harder he comes back." Still, the normal aches and pains acquired during a long hockey season were nothing compared to the kind of torment Mikita endured from chronic back injuries. This required a special kind of physical courage that few professional athletes in that era or any other possessed. "[The pain] gets so damn bad sometimes I think I can't stand it," Mikita confessed to Bill Libby of *Hockey News* in 1970. "It's like a dull toothache. It just never lets up. But in the games, unless I twist sharply or something like that, I just forget about it." Of course, Mikita did not improve matters by pointedly ignoring doctors' advice about wearing a back brace. "They said it would help, even though it was uncomfortable and restricted my movements" he lamented. "But I found it was too uncomfortable and too restricting while playing, so I've begun to take it off when I go on the ice. I'll wear it off the ice."

The dogged perseverance notwithstanding, Mikita was often judged a slacker. The misperception was largely due to a well-publicized aversion to practice. Mikita preferred to move at half-speed and "clown outrageously" on such occasions to conserve energy for contests that mattered. Unfortunately, others saw this behavior as a sign of personal laziness and lack of commitment. Adding fuel to the criticism was the fact the Black Hawks were chronic underachievers. Outside of a lone Stanley Cup championship in 1961, the talent-laden Hawks of this period always seemed to fall short of expectations. "Wherever we go around the league we are accused of choking," Mikita confirmed. "There is a loudmouth behind the bench in Boston, and he gives it to us all the time—accusing us of quitting when it counts. You can't hear him when you are out on the ice, but you hear him when you are on the bench, and that's enough." And more times than not, Mikita was blamed for the team's shortcomings—a verdict Billy Reay hotly disputed. "A lot of people misread him," the Chicago coach said.

The truth is, he's just about the proudest and most dedicated player I've seen in 30 years of being around hockey players. Sure, sometimes he clowns, but often that's because he's covering up for something that's been bothering him, about his own play or somebody else's. But just put him on the ice and there isn't a player who works harder for himself and for his team than Stan.

Comparisons to Bobby Hull didn't help. The tall, ruggedly handsome winger could do no wrong in the eyes of starstruck Hawks fans, whereas the diminutive Mikita came across as unattractive and wanting. "Bobby's got the image," Mikita once explained. "He's the fair-haired boy. The public thinks of me as number two, which is fine. Being number two isn't bad. Let's face it—I can't do anything about it, and I've never tried to." Mikita added that the only thing he could do was be himself and try not to compete with Hull's image. "Look, I haven't got the good looks that Bobby has. But then, he's got a few scars now, too. But the fact is, he looks a lot better in a Jantzen swimsuit than I do." Mikita always denied published reports that he begrudged Hull for his greater fame and status. "We laugh at this, Bobby and I," he claimed. "When I first came to Chicago and walked into the dressing room, he came over and put his arm around me. He took me in, and we lived together for a year and a half. We have been in business together."

Mikita did concede that they possessed different approaches when it came to dealing with the public. "Bobby has the type of personality that allows him to stand and sign autographs after losing a game, but I am not built that way. I will walk away, and I can hear what people are saying about me. Maybe it is wrong, but that's Stan Mikita." Indeed, Mikita's rabbit ears became exceptionally attuned to unreasonable fan expectations. A case in point was the 1968–1969 season, when Mikita's goal total dipped from a career-best 40 the previous year. Chicagoans mercilessly heckled him. "It's hard to figure them out," he said afterward.

I guess they expect me to score 90 goals and get 144 points like Esposito. A perfect game as far as they're concerned is one where we win 10–9, and Bobby Hull scores nine goals. It's their privilege to boo though. They pay my salary. But people seem to forget real fast. It's not what you've done in the past that counts.

The past haunted Stan Mikita. Growing up in Nazi-occupied Czecho-slovakia, present-day Slovakia, during World War II, Stanislas Gvoth and his family struggled to survive in the tiny village community of Sokolce.

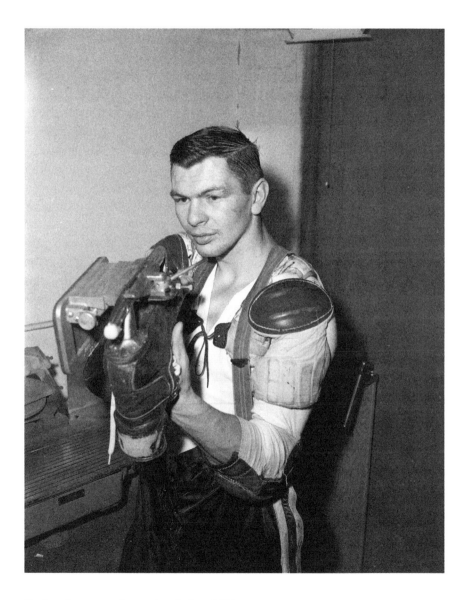

Paying close attention to detail: Stan Mikita sharpening his skates in 1963. *Le Studio du Hockey, HHOF Images*

"We lived in what I would call a bungalow consisting of two small rooms," he later revealed in his autobiography, *Forever a Blackhawk*.

> Behind the house was a barn where we kept a cow, a horse, chicken, geese, and a couple of pigs. Indoor plumbing was only a rumor; when it came to take a bath, Mom would have to get water from the pump outside, heat it up over a primitive wooden stove, then pour the water into the tub, along with me.

German soldiers became an everyday presence in his life; they frequently billeted at his home and forced his parents, older brother, sister to reside in the barn. "I recall them being nice to me, maybe because I was so young and cute," Mikita wrote. "They would assign me certain chores, like fetching food or soup from their mess hall nearby, and once in a while I would get some candy as a reward." Even more memorably, they took him to a rifle range, where he learned to shoot. "I would stand beside and behind a soldier when he fired," Mikita recalled. "I felt the vibration through my whole body. What a recoil."

The end of the war did not end the hardship for Mikita's family. Russian communists replaced the Nazis as the new totalitarian rulers of Czechoslovakia, and this harsh truth did not go down well with young Stanislas's parents. They yearned to give their children a freer and better life. Enter Aunt Anna and Uncle Joe Mikita of Canada. The childless couple had visited the Gvoth household during the 1948 Christmas holiday season with the intention of adopting Mikita and bringing him to live with them in their home in St. Catharines, Ontario. "I had no idea that years earlier my uncle and aunt . . . had asked my parents to let them have their second child," Mikita said. "I guess, to make them happy, my parents said okay. But I don't think they meant it." They were not serious, but the circumstances had now changed. "[My uncle] kept pressing [my parents], explaining what life was like in Canada and the opportunities that were available," Mikita said. The Gvoths finally relented and gave their reluctant approval. Not that any of this registered with Mikita.

The wide-eyed eight-year-old initially thought he was just going on a long trip. "I was lying in bed and got hungry, and asked my mother for some bread and jam," Mikita recalled.

> They had discussed going to America with me, and they were talking about it [with his aunt and uncle] when I hollered for the bread and

jam. I came down the stairs and my mother said, "No," because she thought I shouldn't have the bread and jam then. I thought she was saying "No" to my going to Canada. I began to cry, and everyone cried.

Mikita would replay the heart-wrenching scene several times over in his head. "Talk about a life-changing moment," he related. "What if I hadn't been hungry that night? What if I had just gone to sleep and never cried while my parents resisted saying good-bye to their youngest son?" The days ahead would not get any easier. Mikita broke down when his aunt and uncle brought him to the train station in Prague to begin his journey. Realizing his parents were going to be left behind, he wrapped his arms around a pole and wept. "Every inch of the train ride I plotted to jump off and go back to my mother and father," he said.

Life in St. Catharines was initially a jarring experience. Reared in extreme poverty, Mikita was not used to the relative opulence of his new home. "Joe and Anna's house was very nice, a mansion compared to our home in Czechoslovakia," he wrote. "They had electricity instead of kerosene lamps, and they had all those electrical appliances, like an actual refrigerator. Plus, there was a place to cook and a separate place to eat and another place to sleep. And we didn't have to sleep four to a room." Mikita still experienced strong bouts of homesickness magnified by his struggles to learn English. His new schoolmates were unsympathetic, constantly badgering him and calling him "foreigner." "Kids can be pretty cruel at that age," he said. To fit in, Mikita took up hockey—a sport he had a passing knowledge of from his days in Sokolce, where he used a cork as a puck. He now played with a real one in St. Catharines but he gave no hint of future greatness. In fact, the first time he was handed a hockey stick and asked to shoot by a friendly neighbor, he completely humiliated himself. "I didn't know how [to shoot], but I wanted to be good," Mikita said.

> So I took the big swing, like I was hitting a golf ball. I missed the puck and hit the guy right in the shins. He was a nice guy—he didn't hit me. He just took me by the hand and with sign language showed me the right way to shoot the puck. Then he taught me my first words of English, "stick," "puck," "shoot," and "goal."

As Mikita's shaky command of English improved, so did his hockey skills. He soon realized he had a deep and abiding passion for the game. "In the morning I used to get up at 5:30 and ride on my bike out to a rink and just stand around and wait to be asked to play," he said.

> It took half an hour to get to the rink, and sometimes I could practice for two and a half quarter hours before school began. There was an instructor there, and a hard one. We used to have to do things right or he would hit us hard in the shins with a broom. I remember that broom very well and appreciate now what it did for me.

Indeed, the tough love approach helped Mikita earn a coveted spot on the Black Hawks' junior-league team in St. Catharines at 16. He led the league in scoring, with 97 points, and showed a marked ability to mix it up with opponents. Mikita, who the *Toronto Star* once described as being "as abrasive as a barroom bouncer—and about as diplomatic," piled up the penalty minutes, although it did not seem to bother him. "I don't know where the aggression stemmed from," Mikita wrote, "but it might have had something to do with feeling like an outsider for so long." Whatever the source, Mikita's roughhouse style earned him the respect of opponents and Rudy Pilous, his St. Catharines coach. "He used to get into fights with guys who outweighed him by 40 pounds," Pilous said. "He'd get beat, but he'd never back off. Stan always had a burning desire to be the best, although that chip on the shoulder got in his way occasionally."

When Pilous became head coach of the Black Hawks in 1958, it surprised no one that Mikita, now recognized as the "best junior hockey player in Canada," followed him. Mikita scored only eight goals in his rookie season, however, an output he later characterized as embarrassing. "I was real tight," he said. "In the NHL I was afraid of making mistakes. On top of that, I was doing a lot of checking. You can't score that way. About the only good thing about that first year was playing with Ted Lindsey." Lindsey, a combative, high-scoring forward who compiled 1,808 minutes in penalties during his 17-season Hall of Fame career, went out of his way to mentor Mikita. "He was a little guy like me, and he taught me plenty," Mikita recalled. "For instance, he told me when I got into the corners, I should keep my stick chest high for protection. And when I throw a pass, don't look where you're going, watch for a guy tryin' to [hit] me."

The lessons took hold. In the seasons ahead, Mikita would become "Le Petit Diable," one of the toughest players in the league, a human wrecking ball, the *Toronto Star* said, who "left behind a trail of welts, bruises, and resentment as he warred his way around the NHL circuit." The pugnaciousness in turn helped Mikita reclaim his old scoring touch and emerge as an elite performer. "I knew that I couldn't become a player who ran away from trouble," he explained. "When you're a scorer, you've got to give back the punishment or you'll be a target for every elbow, knee, and stick in the league. I'd always retaliate instantaneously when the referee was watching and end up in the penalty box." Nevertheless, Mikita, who accumulated a career-high 154 penalty minutes in 1964–1965, experienced a major change of heart two seasons later. He abruptly abandoned his reckless approach and became a two-time recipient of the Lady Byng Trophy, the NHL's highest award for good sportsmanship. "It was like Atilla the Hun refusing to sack Rome," one bemused Chicago fan said.

Mikita attributed his pacifism to his infant daughter Meg. "I came home from a game one night, and Meg was still up, after watching it on television," he told Toronto columnist Jim Proudfoot. "She asked me why it was that I spent almost the whole game sitting down while all the other players were out on the ice, skating around." Mikita felt as if he had been doused with a bucket of cold water. "If a two-year-old kid could see there was something wrong, why couldn't a supposedly intelligent 26-year-old figure it out? What was I doing in the penalty box so much? Good question, eh? The game is played on the ice, after all." Mikita came to the conclusion that his own aggression had gotten the better of him and was hurting his team. He resolved to still play hard but smarter and without committing any unnecessary in-game infractions or misconducts. As a result, his penalty minutes dropped to 12 in 1966–1967. "I found I was scoring just as much, so I simply decided to keep it up," he said. The tactical shift represented Mikita at his finest—a shrewd and selfless competitor willing to make needed game adjustments when the situation warranted. That's why the thought of Mikita wearing another uniform was unimaginable to longtime Chicago general manager Tommy Ivan, an inductee into the Hockey Hall of Fame in 1974. "You simply don't trade players of his caliber," Ivan said. "What more could the man possibly do?"

Mikita could not rescue the Black Hawks from defeat in Game 3, as the struggling team dropped their third straight to the Bruins, 5–2, at Boston Garden. Johnny Bucyk paced the Bruins attack with a pair of goals, but the turning point in the game came off a spectacular glove save by Gerry Cheevers at 2:32 of the third period. With his team down, 4–2, Chicago defenseman Keith Magnuson, a gap-toothed rookie from Saskatoon, Saskatchewan, launched a missile directly at Cheevers on a breakaway pass from Mikita. "That was a big stop . . . a big stop," Harry Sinden said. "We weren't playing all that well. If Magnuson had got that goal, I don't know if we could have snapped out of it and held them." Indeed, Boston had played sluggishly throughout most of the contest, coming back from 1–0 and 2–1 deficits in the first period. "We read the papers the last couple of days," Eddie Westfall said. "There were complimentary things written about all of us. What saps we are. We let those things lull us into complacency. We could have lost this game, and we would have if we played the rest of the game the way we played the first period." Fortunately, the team woke up in the second period, with Bucyk netting both his scores and Wayne Cashman adding what turned out to be the go-ahead game-winner off Tony Esposito at 4:17. Chicago regrouped between periods and seemed to control the pace of play at the start of the third, that is until Cheevers made his clutch stop. "Unbelievable that [Magnuson's shot] wasn't in the net!" exclaimed Chicago coach Billy Reay. "One of the greatest saves I've ever seen. That's the kind of play when all you can do is throw your glove up." Phil Esposito added an insurance goal later in the frame to finish off the Hawks. "I never thought at any time—never—that we'd get up to 3–0 against Chicago," Harry Sinden told reporters afterward. "I don't want to take anything away from our guys who've played great hockey, but I think it's a cold fact that the puck has bounced our way most of the time. Very few breaks have gone against us."

The breaks continued to go the Bruins' way in Game 4, as the team completed their playoff sweep of the Hawks with a thrilling 5–4 victory in front of a boisterous Garden crowd of 14,835. "Don't ask me why, I just knew that we'd win if we played all night, if we had to have a dozen overtimes," Gerry Cheevers told reporters in the wild Boston locker room celebration that followed. "These guys have come too far to even lose one game—and this was a damned important game that we had to win." Pie McKenzie knocked in the game-winner with a 35-foot blast that whistled over Tony Esposito's left shoulder with 1:41 remaining. "I remember McKenzie cutting in from the right side and then [Johnny] Bucyk move in front of the net, blocking my view," Esposito said. "I didn't see the puck. I went low and prayed. But when I heard that roar from the Boston crowd I didn't have to look for the puck. I knew it was in the net." McKenzie, whom one writer described as "close to perpetual motion on skates," had initially received the puck off Stan Mikita's stick on a broken play. "I passed it over to Freddie Stanfield," McKenzie said. "The puck hit his pad and he passed it pack to me. It's a shot I've had a lot of luck with. I've scored with it a lot. I just lifted it over Esposito's shoulder." McKenzie had had high confidence it would go in. "You get that feeling," McKenzie said. "I had missed a couple early in the game and kept thinking the chance would come again." His teammates had also shared in the certainty. "That is John McKenzie's shot," Derek Sanderson said. "Ask any goaltender in the league."

Up to this point, the Hawks had been playing their best hockey of the series, overcoming first-period goals by Don Marcotte and Bucyk with a three-goal explosion in the second. "This is where the Hawks regained their first-place form by playing the man instead of the puck," the *Chicago Tribune* said. "They had the Bruins staggering from checks, and one of those gave them a 3 to 2 lead." Indeed, after Orr uncharacteristically coughed up the puck on a rush up the ice in the Chicago zone, Hawks left-winger Dennis Hull, Bobby's younger brother, took advantage by slipping one by Cheevers from 15 feet out. "I wondered if maybe we hadn't been a little overconfident," Phil Esposito later speculated. "They were outplaying us, and we were struggling." But his brother Tony, who faced 54 shots on net, was running out of steam going into the final frame. Ken Hodge tied the game on a tip-in from the crease at 13:19, and then came McKenzie's clincher. "I had no stamina left," the younger Esposito said. "Hell, I couldn't even raise my arm."

Despite the disappointing final outcome, Esposito's standout performance in goal did not go unnoticed or unappreciated. "He was terrific," Bobby Orr said. "They can't rap Tony. There was no knock on him during the series, anyway. They only gave him six goals up to today, and you can't win many games that way." But such high praise, coming as it did from arguably the greatest player in the game, did not deter Derek Sanderson from delivering his own snarky assessment. "Aw, your brother's a cocky bastard, and he's not really that great a goalie," he informed

Phil Esposito in the clubhouse afterward. Esposito understandably took exception. "Who's calling who cocky?" he testily responded.

All chippiness aside, the Bruins were one step closer to hoisting the Stanley Cup for the first time since 1942.

6

BEATING THE BLUES

The final obstacle standing in the way of the Bruins achieving hockey glory was in the form of the St. Louis Blues, a recent expansion team and winner of the West Division for the third straight year. They were Stanley Cup finalists in their first two seasons and gave the eventual champion Montreal Canadiens all they could handle before bowing out in a pair of closer-than-they-looked sweeps. Led by dynamic young coach Scotty Bowman—a former minor leaguer who would win a record nine league titles with Montreal, Pittsburgh, and Detroit in the coming decades—the Blues boasted a solid, if nondescript, offensive attack. Four players—Phil Coyette, Gordon "Red" Berenson, Ab McDonald, and Gary Sabourin—scored 25 goals or better, while four others finished in double figures. "The Blues aren't a superstar team," Berenson told *Hockey News*. "We're just honest hockey players, who, if we work hard, can be in the money."

The real strength of the squad, in truth, lay with the veteran goaltending tandem of Jacques Plante and Glenn Hall. The previous season both had shared Vezina Trophy honors for their outstanding play in net. While Plante and Hall's performances fell short of that level in 1969–1970, they were still quite formidable. "Having Plante and Hall together on the same team is like having Bob Gibson and Sandy Koufax on the same pitching staff," Bowman said. Of the two, Plante was the clear standout, posting a 2.19 goals-against average, with five shutouts in 32 regular-season games. The 41-year-old was even tougher in the playoffs, allowing only 1.25 goals per contest. "He's both hot on the ice, hot under the collar, and, after a week's layoff, somebody like this could be the Bruins' undoing," the *Boston Globe* said. For sure, "Jake the Snake" had plenty of experience winning high-stakes games. He was the backbone of six Stanley Cup–winning Montreal teams in the 1950s and early 1960s. "He never wanted to lose," remembered longtime Montreal teammate Bernie Geoffrion. "He had outstanding reflexes, and his hands were so fast you could just forget it. Even the great goal scorers like Gordie Howe and Ted Lindsay never did much against him."

Much of the success was attributable to Plante's innovativeness. He, for example, became the first goalie to roam far outside the crease to clear pucks. "I started wandering in self-defense when I first played junior hockey with the Quebec Citadels," he said. "The team had one defenseman who couldn't skate backwards, one who couldn't shoot the puck up to the blue line, and two who couldn't pivot on their skates without falling down. Somebody had to clear loose pucks, so I did it." Such boldness raised eyebrows when Plante broke in with Montreal in 1953. Many observers thought his wanderlust would create too many open-net opportunities for opponents. But the opposite ended up being the case, as Plante went on to win five consecutive Vezina Trophies from 1956 to 1960. "The shoot-and-chase approach had become big in hockey," Plante explained.

> Teams would come up to the blue line and shoot the puck around our boards deep in our zone, then swarm in after it forechecking, trying to regain possession. If I skated out of the crease behind the net, blocked the shoot-in, and left the puck there, the other team did not have as good a chance to get it again as when it slid into the corner.

In spite of the championships and personal honors, Plante was never popular with his coaches, teammates, or hockey contemporaries. He eschewed socializing and preferred his own company. On team bus rides, Plante would make it a point to sit several rows apart from everyone else. "We were all from a strange breed," noted fellow goaltender Johnny Bower of the Maple Leafs. "But Jacques was a very, very strange guy. Even Bernie Geoffrion would say, 'Oh, that Plante—he's a very good goalie, eh, but he don't go to no parties.'" Plante never apologized for his loner tendencies. "No, I never make friends," he said, "not in hockey, not elsewhere, not since I was a teenager. What for? If you are close to someone you must be scheduling yourself to please them. . . . I have always kept my own schedule."

Trendsetter: Jacques Plante revolutionized goaltending by adopting a protective face mask during his Montreal days. *Alain Brouillard, HHOF Images*

This individualist streak led Plante to make hockey history by intro-ducing the goalie mask. The momentous event occurred on the evening of November 1, 1959, in a game against the New York Rangers at Madison Square Garden. Plante was in the middle of leading Montreal to a 3–1 victory when popular Rangers forward and team captain Andy Bathgate aimed a slap shot at his face that almost took his nose off. Bathgate was upset that Plante had violently checked him into the boards earlier in the contest. "I thought," Bathgate recalled, "I'll give him a little boo-boo to let him know there are always ways of getting even." A profusely bleeding Plante was forced to temporarily leave the game and go into the dressing room to be stitched up.

When he returned, he was sporting a fiberglass mask that a sales and promotion manager at a Montreal manufacturing company had specially made for him. Plante had experimented with the model in practice, but Canadians coach Toe Blake—an authoritarian figure who Plante frequently clashed with—nixed his request to use it in games—that is, until Bathgate almost permanently maimed him. "We carried only one goalie at a time [then]," Plante said. "I told Toe I would only return if I could wear the mask, so there was no choice. But he never wanted me to wear the mask because he thought it would make me too complacent." Blake reluctantly gave his approval, and professional hockey would never be the same. No longer would goaltenders have to worry about flying pucks traveling at speeds exceeding 100 miles per hour rearranging their unprotected faces. The mask "gives me more confidence," Plante said. "It's like wearing a parachute when you have to jump out of an airplane . . . a real lifesaver."

Joseph Jacques Omer Plante had become a goalie by sheer accident while growing up in impoverished conditions in Shawinigan Falls, Quebec, during the Depression and war years. At age 12, he found himself watching his school's hockey team practice at a local outdoor rink one cold afternoon when he noticed a commotion on the ice. "The goalie was having trouble, and the coach accused him of not doing his best," Plante recalled. "The goalie was mad and took his skates off. I rushed toward the coach and volunteered to take his place. There was no other goalie around, so I went in the net and played with them the rest of the season." This would prove to be the launching pad to a storied career in professional hockey that would last 23 years. Not all of them were without their trials and tribulations, however.

Plante seriously injured his knee during the 1960–1961 season and was forced to undergo a painful surgical procedure to remove cartilage in the offseason. "I thought it might be the end of my career," he said. "But I was lucky. I did a lot of exercise during the summer and knew I could come back after the first week of training camp." Plante won his sixth Vezina Trophy in 1961–1962, and became only the fourth goalie to receive the Hart Trophy for the league's most valuable player. But his increasingly idiosyncratic ways, which included knitting his own underwear and loudly second-guessing coaching decisions, proved too much for Toe Blake to stomach. He was traded to New York for goalie Gump Worsley the following year. "Blake couldn't have taken much more without punching Plante in the mouth," longtime Montreal general manager Frank Selke claimed. "Jacques was probably the best goalie I'd ever seen, but that didn't mean he could run the hockey team."

The trade came as an unexpected shock to Plante, and while he played well for the Rangers, he was never happy in the Big Apple. Unlike the powerhouse Canadiens, the Rangers were perennially out of the playoff picture. If this wasn't bad enough, Plante had grown tired of the constant grind of performing in the National Hockey League and the accompanying strain it was putting on his family, specifically his wife Jacqueline. Her doctor informed Plante that she was on the brink of a mental collapse after losing 27 pounds and showing signs of acute depression. Deeply alarmed, Plante determined it was best to retire from the game at the age of 37. "I have been away from my wife and family an awful long time during my hockey career," he said. "My two boys, Michel, 14, and Richard, 10, are growing up, and I believe it's time to spend more time with them."

While Plante remained active in hockey during the next three years as a popular television and radio broadcaster, and president of the Quebec Junior Hockey League, he could not shake the feeling that he could still compete at a high level. And so, when Scotty Bowman approached him about the possibility of playing for the Blues before the start of the 1968–1969 season, he leapt at the chance. "My wife had regained her health completely, and she told me that if I'd like to go back to hockey, it was fine with her," Plante said. "I was relaxed and confident I could play again. I maintained good conditioning, and the St. Louis offer was a good one." Plante told reporters that life began at 40, and that he felt like a rookie again. He was not far off the mark. He compiled a sparkling 1.96 goals-allowed average to lead the league and was a major reason why St. Louis was able to make a second straight appearance in the Stanley Cup Finals. "I keep telling myself that all this can't be happening," Plante enthused to *Hockey News*. "It really is hard to believe, isn't it? I mean it when I say I never played this well before."

Glenn Hall missed the start of the 1969–1970 season, owing to a surprise announcement during the summer that he was walking away from the sport to take up farming in rural Alberta. Not everyone believed Hall would remain retired for long. "What's he going to do when the crop's in?" a skeptical Plante asked. "That farming all summer is fine. But when the snow comes, Glenn will be pacing the floor. He'll be back with us." Plante proved himself a seer. Hall returned to action in December and performed ably between the pipes. "I would have regretted [not reupping with St. Louis]," he later said. Indeed, Hall and Plante once again propelled the Blues to the top of the Western division standings. But that did not necessarily mean Hall enjoyed the ride.

A natural worrier, "Mr. Goalie" had trouble coping with the pressure cooker atmosphere of NHL competition. "I hated it so much," Hall once confessed, "that sometimes I wished I could stand out there in the middle of the 160 acres of farm I've got in Canada and scream at the top of my lungs, 'Bleep you, Bleep you' to everybody, and then hear the 'You . . . You . . . You' echo back across the fields. That's how much I hated it." Hall's anxiety was etched in his intensely drawn face before every contest—"an hour or so of hell," he called it—when the 11-time All-Star made a ritual of emptying his stomach. "I was just so uptight I didn't know what else to do," he said. "Although it may sound strange, each time I did it I felt better and knew I was ready to play." On some occasions, Hall would vomit between periods. "It was very surprising that he could endure all that and still be one of the very best goalies who ever played the position," Plante observed. "I think the challenge of the job kept him going. There was no way it was going to get the best of him."

Hall prided himself on being "up" for whatever challenges opposing clubs threw at him. "I was always completely ready," he said.

> Five minutes before a game or between periods, I didn't hear what a coach was saying because I was in total preparation. All I would be thinking about was what I had to do. During a game, when somebody got ready to shoot, I'd already looked at the shot in my mind. I tried to prepare myself for every option.

Much of this preemptive strategizing stemmed from self-preservation. Hall, like most goalies of the era, was slow to adopt a protective mask based on fear his line of vision would be impaired. "A mask might throw me off," he told Roger Angell of the *Saturday Evening Post*. Thus, a premium was placed on avoiding direct facial contact with the puck. "We tried to get our feet over in front of the puck and the head out of the way," Hall said. "When we got hit, it was a real accident because we weren't trying to stop the puck. We got hit in the face because we were doing something wrong, in a bad position, or one would get away from you." Only late in his career did Hall revise his thinking and begin wearing a mask. "I've had over 250 stitches in my head and face," he said. "I don't want my paycheck mailed to the Good Samaritan Hospital . . . or cemetery."

The son of an engineer for the Canadian National Railway, Glenn Henry Hall spent most of his youth hanging out at outdoor ice rinks in his hometown of Humboldt, Saskatchewan. Although his early ambition was to follow in his father's footsteps and work for the railroad, Hall's growing obsession with hockey caused him to alter his career trajectory. "I liked forward," he recalled. "But when I began playing in the local Bantam league, we had no coach. The other kids tagged me captain. Nobody wanted to play goal, so I took over. I became serious at it at 12. I wanted to become a pro, but I had my doubts about that." His doubts evaporated when the Detroit Red Wings signed him in 1951, and he made steady progress in their farm system. Along the way Hall developed a unique "butterfly" style of goaltending where he lowered his torso to the ice and spread his legs wide into an inverted Y position to block shots. "I liked the deep crouch that I saw [Red Wings regular] Terry Sawchuk use," he recalled.

> Most goalies would try to look over the players screening them, but Terry would often look underneath the screen. That worked well for me too, but in those days, goalies never talked about goaltending. I was called up a few times to fill in for Terry when he was injured, but he never told me a thing. No goalie ever did.

Hall got the opportunity to start in Detroit when team GM Jack Adams unexpectedly traded away Sawchuk before the start of the 1955–1956 season. "We had to make a decision between Sawchuk and Hall," Adams said. "We decided to go with Hall, and it was no snap decision. . . . [Hall] had shown us enough to prove he belongs in this league. He was more advanced at that time than Sawchuk was when he joined us." Sawchuk had been a popular mainstay on three Motor City title teams, and Hall was nervous about succeeding him in net. "I didn't want to let the other guys down," Hall said. "That's what worried me the most. Remember, this is a world championship team I'm playing for." Although he fell short of delivering Detroit another championship, Hall proved his worthiness by winning the Calder Trophy as the league's top freshman player and tying Sawchuk's single-season goaltending record of 12 shutouts.

The singular performance notwithstanding, Hall was deemed expendable by the Red Wings the following summer and sent off to the Chicago Black Hawks with fading All-Star defender Ted Lindsay. "I can suggest a couple of reasons why I was traded," Hall said afterward. "Number one is that [Jack Adams] didn't think I could play well enough to be good over the long haul. The other is that you should never tell your general manager to go fuck himself. The combination of the two made it easy to trade me." Hall added that while there were few people he actively disliked in the game, "Trader Jack" was one of the exceptions. "[Adams] was at the top of that list," Hall maintained. "It made it great for me in Chicago to try and prove him wrong."

Hall did not let his new team down. He continued to excel in goal and was crucial to the Hawks' victorious Stanley Cup playoff run in 1961, when they upended the Canadians in the finals, four games to two. Hall led all goalies that postseason with a superlative .927 save percentage. "I always knew Hall was a tough guy to beat, but I never realized just how great a goalie he is until I played on the same team," Chicago center Joseph Rudolph "Bronco" Horvath said.

> He makes fantastic saves. One night in Toronto, he had three or four Leafs talking to themselves. He made a stop on [All-Star forward] Bobby Nevin that was one of the greatest I've ever seen. Nevin had one-whole side of the net open and let go the shot. Hall flashed out his foot and deflected the shot with the toe of his boot.

Hall, who played Ping-Pong to strengthen his reflexes, also proved his stellar worth by performing in a record 502 consecutive games during a five-and-a-half-year stretch from 1959 to 1962. "I've been lucky, I guess," he told *Sporting News*. "A lot of goalies get broken bones when they're injured, things like fractured cheekbones, fingers, things like that. Most of my injuries have just been facial cuts, nothing that would keep me from playing." Hall's "iron man" streak came to an end on November

6, 1962, when he sustained a lower back injury in practice and reluctantly removed himself from a scheduled game against the Bruins. "I guess the fact that I had the string going made me want to play against Boston just that much more," he said. "However, I felt sure I would [not] be able to play well. They pay me to play, and I feel that I should whenever it's possible, but there's no point in harming your body or your team's chances." Still, the magnitude of what he had been able to accomplish was not lost on him. "Playing 500 straight games is something I'm proud of," he said. "But in this league, you don't make a living on your past reputation. My ambition is to stick in the NHL for the next few years, and I know I'm not going to do it because I played 500 games in a row, but only if I can do a goaltending job in the future that's up to NHL standards."

To keep Hall fresh and injury-free in the seasons ahead, the Hawks helped pioneer the two-goalie system—a development the 13-time All-Star wholeheartedly welcomed. "Playing in every game, especially those back-to-back games most weekends, wore a goalie down," Hall said. "With two goalies, I had some time to recover from the bruises of a tough game before I had to play again." The setup worked so well that Hall and talented backup Denis DeJordy were declared cowinners of the Vezina Trophy in 1967. But at season's end, the Hawks concluded that it was time to cut ties with the springy-legged veteran. Hall had turned 36—old by goalie standards—and had not performed particularly well in the playoffs. He was left unprotected in that year's NHL Expansion Draft, and the Blues snatched him up. While this might have appeared like an ideal time to retire after 14 superb seasons, Hall decided otherwise. He wanted to prove he could still play another year and was especially appreciative of the $47,500 salary the Blues had tendered him—the most ever commanded by a goalie in a single season. "He was our only big-name player," Scotty Bowman explained, "and he gave our franchise instant credibility."

Credibility is exactly what the Blues sought when they squared off against the heavily favored Bruins in Game 1 of the 1970 Stanley Cup Finals. But the Blues' hopes were rudely dashed when their sharpshooting visitors delivered a 6–1 trouncing in front of a near-capacity crowd of 16,715 at St. Louis Arena. Johnny Bucyk led the Boston scoring parade with the first playoff hat trick of his 15-year career, while teammates Wayne Carleton, Derek Sanderson, and Phil Esposito added single tallies.

Mr. Goalie: Glenn Hall with the Black Hawks. *Imperial Oil-Turofsky, HHOF Images*

"I feel strong now, and after this game I feel even stronger," said Bucyk, who scored the first, second, and fourth goals of the game. "I can't believe it. Me scoring three goals. Just being here is super." Making Bucyk's offensive onslaught possible was an unorthodox defensive maneuver devised by Scotty Bowman. The Blues coach tasked speedy forward Jimmy Roberts—who scored the lone St. Louis goal early in the second period—with shadowing Bobby Orr throughout the game. "Why?" Bowman responded to a reporter's question. "Because when Orr's on the ice, he controls the game. I'd rather play their four against our two if Orr wasn't around." Bowman's instructions to Roberts left no room for doubt about what he expected. "I want you to stick with that guy everywhere he goes," Bowman said. "I want you right next to him, in his face, so close you can tell me what kind of gum he's chewing." Roberts, however, might have taken Bowman a little too literally. When the physically spent Toronto native returned to the St. Louis bench near the close of the contest and caught Bowman's eye, he could barely spit out what he wanted to say. "Well?" Bowman thundered. "Juicy Fruit," Roberts replied.

Although a visibly frustrated Orr was held scoreless—"Naturally I'd like more room," he said—Harry Sinden voiced minimal concern about the Blues' strategy. "It hurt us a lot," he commented sarcastically. "All we got was six goals. But here's where something like that can hurt them more than it will help. Scotty makes the mistake of thinking that the Bruins are Bobby Orr, nothing else. The team is built around him. He's our best player, our leader, the guy we look to. But there are a lot of good players, very good players, on this team, and there's no way he can put a cover on Orr and leave a man unprotected for such stretches without hurting himself." Bucyk backed up his coach's analysis. "When they shadow Bobby," he said, "that's like giving us a 4–3 advantage."

Jacques Plante, receiving the starting nod in goal for the Blues, suffered a bad break early in the second period off the stick of Fred Stanfield. After intercepting an errant pass in the St. Louis zone, the Bruins center whistled a rising shot that hit Plante flush in the face mask. He "went down like he had been shot," the *Boston Globe* reported. The game was delayed several minutes as an unconscious Plante had to be carefully placed on a stretcher and taken to a nearby hospital, where he was diagnosed with a concussion. "My head hurts every time I try to move it from side to side," Plante said afterward. "All I remember is Stanfield winding up for the shot. After that, I don't remember a thing." Plante claimed the incident, which he likened to experiencing the "world's worst hangover," marked the first time he had ever been struck down in a game. "Without the mask, who knows what would have happened?" he added.

Plante did not play for the rest of the series and was sold to Toronto in the offseason. In a surprise move, Bowman replaced Plante in the game with Ernie Wakely, a green newcomer who had been Plante's primary backup during the regular schedule until Glenn Hall returned from retirement. "It amazed us because we thought Bowman would go with [Hall], who is more experienced," Derek Sanderson told biographer Stan Fischler. "It was a tough situation for the younger Wakely. Bowman deserves credit for his decision because he showed the kid he had faith in him." Alas, the faith went unrewarded, as Wakely gave up five goals in less than two periods and was officially charged with the loss.

In spite of the pasting, Wakely was back defending the crease two nights later for Game 2. Hall, boasting a goaltending record of 110 playoff appearances, had been the expected starter until the lingering aftereffects of an earlier injury to his catch hand convinced Bowman to sideline him and go with Wakely. It turned out to be an unwise move, as the Bruins lit up the rookie for six more goals in a 6–2 romp to take a commanding 2–0 lead in the best-of-seven series. They also picked up their eighth straight playoff victory. "From the moment we took the ice," Sinden said, "we dominated everything. [The Blues] weren't in the game for one second from start to finish, not one second of it." This was no exaggeration, as St. Louis came off as a cartoon version of Wile E. Coyote to the Bruins' Roadrunner. The only thing missing was the familiar splat sound the former made when he hit the canyon floor. "I had great respect for that club (Blues), and I still have," Ken Hodge said. "But I never thought for a second, even when I was dreaming about winning everything, that it would be this easy. Our guys just walked through them."

Sanderson and Eddie Westfall secured top Boston scoring honors with a pair of goals each, while Bucyk and Stanfield connected on solo efforts. "Frankly," Sanderson opined, "I thought St. Louis was going to be a lot tougher, but they never threw a check all night, and they're supposed to be the tough guys of the West. What a laugh!" Orr went scoreless again but had a major hand in setting up two of the goals, one of which came after a nifty pass to Westfall when the Bruins were shorthanded during the opening period. Orr "took [the puck] from in back of our net and [after drawing away the St. Louis defense on a breakaway] just fed it to me in front," the Bruins forward said. Orr made the contributions despite the continued best efforts of Jim Roberts to hound him all over the ice. "There is no way they could contain Bobby," Westfall maintained. "I don't care what they try. He's too good to be held down. He skates too fast and well for any one man or even two to check him. And he knew what to do to get one or two of us loose when they tried it." As for the likelihood of the series returning to St. Louis for a possible Game 5, at least one Bruin did not give the idea any serious thought. "I sure as hell hope not," Sanderson said. "This town is okay, except on Sunday. You can't get a drink. You've got to go back to your hotel and drink beer out of the bathtub."

The Bruins playoff express inexorably rolled on when the series resumed in Boston for Game 3. Although the final score was the closest yet of the three contests played, the Blues were no match for their supremely confident hosts, as the Bruins romped to an easy 4–1 win. "The way we are playing, no team in the NHL could handle us," Phil Esposito said.

"It's not just the Blues, it's the momentum we have as a team." Glenn Hall, answering the call in net for the first time in the series, learned this painful reality all too well when he made 42 saves on 46 Boston shots and still found himself on the losing end. "I've never seen him any better," Scotty Bowman said. He got no argument from the Bruins. "Hall was fantastic," Fred Stanfield said. "You have to score a good goal to get by him. No flukes, that's for sure." Added Harry Sinden, "I thought he was going to beat us. . . . I told our team to just go out and keep peppering, hopeful that something would get by." This sage advice proved useful to Wayne Cashman, who scored the second of his game-high two goals in the third period on a rebound after Hall repeatedly denied him during a steady Boston barrage on net. "I don't know how Hall did it," the left-winger said.

> There were passes between [Ken Hodge] and me. Then [Esposito] was in for a shot. The rebound came to me, and I swung wide to get it with my forehand. Somehow Hall saved on that and again with his glove on a close one. Finally I made it with a shot up on high on him. I don't know when I've had three shots on a guy like that.

Bucyk and Pie McKenzie accounted for the other Bruins scores, while a still-"shadowed" Orr remained active in the team's passing game. "Bobby did what you'd expect him to do in the situation," Sinden said. "He kept getting the puck up to our forwards, and you know he does that very well." For the third consecutive time in the series, Gerry Cheevers had a quiet night, giving up only one goal on a falsely credited first-period power play bid by Blues forward Frank Marselle. The puck had actually been directed into the Boston net on a botched clearing play by Dallas Smith. "I asked Dallas about that later," Sinden revealed, "and he told me he doesn't know what all the talk is about Cheevers being so tough to score on."

Now one victory away from their fourth Stanley Cup title in franchise history, the Bruins were confident they would complete their sweep of the overmatched Blues. No one expressed greater aplomb than Robert Gordon Orr. "We're not going to blow this game now," Orr told *Herald-Traveler* columnist Tim Horgan on the eve of Game 4. "When you're ahead 3–0 in the final round of the playoffs, you don't lose your concentration. In fact, that's when winning the Cup is all you can think about." Indeed, Orr, who became the only defenseman in history to lead the NHL in scoring during the regular season, had dreamed of becoming a champion from the moment he picked up a hockey stick as a bashful, blue-eyed, freckle-faced youngster growing up in Parry Sound, Ontario, in the 1950s.

Located 160 miles north of Toronto along the frigid eastern shore of Georgian Bay at the mouth of the Seguin River, Parry Sound was and still is a small, tight-knit community named in honor of nineteenth-century Artic explorer William Edward Parry. "People knew everybody else's children and kept an eye on them," Orr later recalled. "If someone got into trouble, the word spread quickly, and sooner or later a brother or sister, mother or father would know all the details of your problem." Such exposure was usually enough to deter individuals from getting into trouble. Orr, the third of five children to a Royal Canadian Navy veteran and a stay-at-home mom, did not buck this trend. He was by all accounts a "real good boy" and never got into any serious scrapes. Like so many of his postwar Canadian contemporaries, he was too busy playing hockey. "I remember watching him when he was three," his father, Doug Orr, said. "He'd take a stride, fall on his face, get up, and keep on skating."

The elder Orr, who scratched out a modest living packing dynamite into crates for an explosives factory, had been a fair hockey player in his day. "Doug was a terrific skater," remembered one local. "From a standing start or a face-off, there was no one faster." The Bruins had scouted him in high school in the early 1940s and thought enough of his talent to offer him a minor-league contract to play for the Atlantic City Seagulls. He flatly turned them down, however. World War II was raging, and Orr wanted to do his part, serving aboard a Canadian corvette ship tasked with escorting merchant vessels across the treacherous U-boat-infested waters of the North Atlantic. "Sure, I think I could have made it," he once told *Sports Illustrated* writer Frank Deford, "but I was young and wanted to travel."

A former Parry Sound teammate—left-winger Pete Horeck—did turn pro and enjoyed a lengthy NHL career with the Black Hawks, Red Wings, and Bruins. "He made a lot of money, [but] I'll tell you, I could skate better than Pete Horeck," Orr said wistfully. Frank was not the only standout athlete in the Orr family. His father, Bobby Sr., had reportedly been a professional soccer player from Ballymena, Ireland, before deciding to emigrate to Canada in the early twentieth century. Little could he have dreamed that one day his namesake grandson would surpass his own considerable accomplishments, as Bobby Orr had the look of greatness about him from the age of eight.

Although short in stature and scrawny in build, young Bobby skated with tremendous skill, élan, and purpose. "He could skate through a whole team," his father said. "The other boys wouldn't try to tackle him because of his size. I can remember his mother coming down to the river bank and watching him go." While Orr spent countless hours out on the ice with his friends burnishing his shooting and stickhandling skills, academics were a different matter. As Orr later wrote,

> During the long winter months, I would sit at my school desk, and that big clock on the classroom wall would take more of my attention as the afternoon started to wind down. I couldn't wait to be dismissed so I could get through the front door of that school once all my books had been put away.

He would then lace up a pair of skates and play pickup hockey games outdoors with his friends until the sun went down. Orr's study habits did not improve when the weather got warmer, as he preferred casting a fishing line to cracking open a textbook. "I don't recall much from my geography classes," he confessed, "but I clearly remember what it was like to be sitting on the shore of the Seguin River, waiting to see what I could pull from the water."

When he began playing organized hockey inside the spacious confines of the Parry Sound Memorial Community Center, Orr drew even more attention to his budding talent. "He was really something," recalled Orr's bantam coach, Wilfred Kennedy "Bucko" McDonald. "He could make that puck do tricks on the end of the stick." McDonald had been a rugged All-Star defenseman with the Toronto Maple Leafs in the 1940s and knew immediately that Orr was something special. "If I've ever seen an NHL prospect," he said, "this kid is one." Crucially, McDonald dissuaded his prized pupil from shifting to forward, which Orr's father had been advocating due to the latter's superior offensive abilities. McDonald believed such a move would prove a colossal mistake. "Bobby was born to play defense," he said. For sure, McDonald felt that Orr's explosive speed and ability to improvise with the puck made him a natural backliner. This fit nicely with the old Leaf's overall philosophy regarding the position. He wanted someone with a "creative streak" who was not afraid to take bold chances and use the entire length of the ice to his advantage.

"So," wrote biographer Stephen Brunt, "when Orr rushed the puck and left his position, when he led the team's offense, when he skated deep into the opponent's zone and then had to scamper back to cover his position, McDonald didn't tell him he made a mistake." McDonald instead encouraged him. Orr was forever grateful, claiming McDonald taught him "almost everything" he knew about hockey. "It was just a lot easier to make plays when you were in motion, and Bucko helped to reinforce that concept with me," Orr explained. "After all, the best play in hockey is still the give-and-go, and you can't run that play unless at least one player is in motion."

While Orr had acquired a reputation for being a local hockey prodigy, he still was not well known outside of Parry Sound. That situation would dramatically change on Good Friday 1961, when the top brass of the Bruins organization paid a visit to Gananoque, Ontario, to check out a pair of promising young players named Rick Eaton and Doug Higgins. The latter's team was playing host to Orr's Parry Sound squad in a provincial bantam playoff. "They were the boys," Orr later said. "The Bruins weren't there to see me. They didn't know me or anyone from Parry Sound." What transpired next was nothing short of magical. Although his team lost, Orr, age 12, was seemingly everywhere on the ice, controlling the flow of action and skating circles around his more physically imposing opponents. "This little bugger had the puck most of the time on us," Eaton remembered more than a half-century later. "So young, just a little guy, eh? You knew he was going to rise up the ladder, but no one could know he was going to get to where he did." Eaton's teammates paid the ultimate tribute to Orr after the game when they bumped into him at a local café while celebrating their victory with milkshakes and French fries. They jumped out of their seats in unison and applauded. "It had been a battle," Eaton said.

Bruins officials were impressed, too. Orr seemed like a revelation from the hockey gods; they couldn't keep their eyes off him. "I remember his baggy pants and his shock of blonde hair, and that he was playing defense, although he was one of the smallest boys on the ice," Bruins chief scout Wren Blair said. "What attracted me most aside from his uniform, the way it fit, was the fact that he was a defenseman. He was a small boy, but he was a general. He was directing the team, telling them what to do, doing it himself, and seeing to it that they did it too." Lynn Patrick had a similar reaction. "Jesus, isn't he something," the Bruins general manager said. He instructed Blair to give organizational top priority to Orr's signing. Blair did so with alacrity, frequently showing up at his games and dropping by the Orr family homestead on Great North Road for dinner. "He was always around talking to Mom and Dad and me," Orr recounted. So ubiquitous was Blair that a local neighbor joked he was beginning to think of the sweet-talking hockey lifer as an Orr family member. "I didn't have to try too hard to be nice to the Orrs," Blair said. "They're just nice people, and I sincerely liked them all. And I respected their solidarity. They are truly a one-for-all, all-for-one family." But Blair never pretended he was there merely to socialize. "From a professional standpoint, it was always a fact that if you wanted the boy, you had to get to know the parents. It's not who sees him first but who signs him that counts. Salesmanship is most important. You've got to go into those living rooms if you want a young player badly enough."

Blair's persistence paid off in 1962, when Orr turned 14 and became eligible to play Junior A League hockey. Blair persuaded Orr's reluctant parents to let their son skate for the Oshawa Generals, the Bruins' Ontario Hockey League affiliate, located 168 miles away, along the twisting banks of Lake Ontario. "I'll find a fine family for him to live with in Oshawa," Blair assured them. "He'll get the best of care. If he stays here [in Parry Sound] another year, he'll just deteriorate as a hockey player. He's too good for these boys. He'll just learn bad habits." The financial terms came to a little more than $10,000 and included a badly needed stucco job for the Orr's weather-beaten house and a used car for family use. Blair exhaled a heavy sigh of relief. Montreal, Detroit, and Toronto had also entered the sweepstakes to land the five-star prospect. "My dad and I talked it over," Orr later revealed. "The Bruins were down on the bottom of the league. I guess I thought they'd be the easiest team to make. They had to go up. Other teams had set lineups. But Boston . . . I thought I'd be able to get to the NHL faster with them."

Orr got off to an inauspicious start when he reported to Oshawa. "They had a roll call when we arrived for the first day of training camp," he remembered. "The players had to call out their names and the position they played. There were some big guys there, and when my turn came, I called my name." Then he revealed his position. "I said defense—and everybody laughed. I guess it was kinda funny at that. There I was with all those big guys and me in the middle of them—14 years old and weighing 125 pounds, and claiming I'm a defenseman." The laughter stopped when Orr got onto the ice. During his next four seasons with the Generals, he was almost unstoppable, compiling 116 goals and 205 assists for 321 points. "He amazes me every time I see him," Lynn Patrick said. "The way he can anticipate what's going to happen is sometimes uncanny; you know, sensing where the puck is going to be and moving there even before the puck does. I never saw a more promising player."

Orr became so dominant in games that his teammates got into the lazy habit of passing him the puck and then standing back to see what amazing things he would do with it. Oshawa coach Jim Cherry told the *Toronto Star* that his young charge reminded him of Red Kelly, the Hall of Fame defenseman who skated with eight Stanley Cup winners in Detroit and Toronto. "He plays 35 to 50 minutes a game, and he's the team leader," Cherry said. "He can't miss. He'd make the NHL at any position." Cherry did start Orr at center in some contests, although the future eight-time Norris Trophy winner made plain his position preference. "I feel more in the game on defense," he later said.

> You can see everything that goes on from there and can be better prepared to take the puck in whenever the chance comes. In fact, you can see chances develop. But when you're playing center you're always up the ice, where the only thing you know is what you and your wings are doing. And when the other team gets the puck, you have to check back all the time. Besides, I miss the challenge of stopping forwards when they come at me with the puck. You miss all that as a center.

Interestingly, Orr also showed he had the chops to be a top-flight goaltender. "We were down a goal to the Toronto Marlboros," Wren Blair recalled. "We pulled our goalie in the last minute of play, but Jim McKenny of the Marlboros broke free for a shot at the empty net." What followed next defied explanation. "Instinctively, Bobby raced back into the net," Blair said. "McKenny came in alone and tried to fake him, then shot. Bobby stood his ground like an experienced goalie and blocked the shot with his chest."

Orr's outstanding play made him a household name in Canada at age 16, when his boyishly handsome visage appeared on the February 20, 1965 cover of *Maclean's*, the country's top weekly news magazine. "Briefly," the lengthy accompanying article inside said, "Bobby Orr is the finest hockey player in Canada today, and Boston owns title to his services." The piece, written by the prolific sportswriter Trent Frayne, went on to declare that Orr had the potential to become the "finest offensive defenseman" in history. "Bobby Orr," Frayne wrote,

> is a swift, powerful skater with instant acceleration, instinctive antici- pation, a quick accurate shot, remarkable composure, an unrelenting ambition, a solemn dedication, humility, modesty, a fondness for his parents and his brothers and sisters that often turns eyes moist. Put simply, Bobby Orr is too good to be true. But there he is.

The big publicity buildup worried the Bruins, especially Wren Blair, who feared such "Hollywood adulation" would create unrealistic expectations for Orr moving forward, not to mention a "swelled head." To his credit, Orr tried to keep things in perspective; he made a concerted effort not to read stories about himself or exhibit diva-like behavior. By all accounts, he was remarkably successful. The only serious spat he had with Generals management was when he suffered a groin injury and was ordered to sit out the league championship playoff series in his final season with Oshawa. "I had spent four years of my junior career trying to get to this point," Orr wrote. "I was the captain of the team, and even if I had to head over the boards with only one good leg, I was determined to do it." Orr played, and while his team still lost, he never regretted the decision. "It was a great learning experience in high-level payoff hockey," he explained. "The experience would come in handy down the road during my hockey career." That was typical Bobby Orr—offering no excuses while taking a glass half-full attitude. People around him could not help but be impressed. "Those who know [Orr] best say he never was a boy," noted Red Fisher of *Sport* magazine.

Orr's mature behavior extended well beyond the rink. "You've never seen a boy so polite," recounted Eva Wild, whose Oshawa boarding house hosted Orr during this period. "I remember telling a friend about him once, and she insisted no boy could be as perfect as I described. Then she met Bob—and agreed." Nonetheless, the transition from the quiet, small town life of Parry Sound to the more fast-paced, gritty urban envi- ronment of Oshawa had been jarring. Orr suffered from bouts of acute homesickness that led to emotional scenes when he reconnected with family members. "Every time Bobby phones, I cry, and I can hear him start to blubber, too," his sister Pat told Trent Frayne. "I always cry when I see him. Dad thinks we're nuts, we'll all be watching a television program, and I look over to see if Mom's crying, and she is, and she looks at me and we both look at Penny and we're all sitting there blubbering. Dad looks at us, and he just shakes his head."

There would be more head shaking when Orr signed a lucrative deal to become a member of the Boston Bruins in the summer of 1966. After some tough back-and-forth wrangling, team management agreed to give Orr a two-year contract worth $50,000, along with a $25,000 signing bonus. No previous rookie in NHL history had achieved such a windfall. In fact, the highest salary for any player in the league at this time was in the vicinity of $40,000. Orr's signing was nothing less than revolutionary; it moved the financial goalposts for professional hockey. Henceforth, such outstanding performers as Gordie Howe and Bobby Hull would demand and receive paydays commensurate with their talents and overall status in the game. As hockey historian Stan Fischler wrote, "What matters is that [Orr], even while he was in his teens, was teaching hockey's supposedly sophisticated old pros what life was all about; and one of the first lessons is that you get the kind of bread you deserve."

Instrumental in Orr achieving this economic breakthrough was Alan Eagleson, a streetwise 33-year-old attorney from Toronto who Orr's father had met summers earlier when the two had competed against one another in a regional softball league. Doug Orr, weary of Bobby being taken advantage of by Bruins management, asked Eagleson to represent his son in the contract negotiations. Eagleson, who would go on to become the first executive director of the National Hockey League Players' Association, was more than happy to oblige. He was fully aware of the younger Orr's talent and sensed a great financial opportunity. "My mother wanted to know what he was going to charge," Bobby Orr recalled later. "I remember Al looking away as if he was adding up figures in his head; then he turned to my mother and said, 'I tell you what Mrs. Orr, if Bobby makes some money, then I will make some money.'" Bruins general manager Hap Emms was less than happy, however. He felt uncomfortable dealing with someone as sharp as Eagleson and tried to low ball Orr in the team's initial tender. "We have offered [Orr] a sum that is absolutely our best—a $5,000 bonus and an $8,000 salary," Emms told reporters. "After all, the boy has to prove himself. He hasn't played big-league hockey. He scored a lot of goals rushing up the ice from defense in junior hockey. A lot of people say he'll never be allowed to do that in the

NHL. We've got big men up here who may knock him down when he rushes."

Emms was forced to change his tune as the start of the 1966–1967 season approached. "He sure as hell didn't want to open camp with the greatest young hockey player in the world not there and all the Boston players giving him shit for being such a tightwad and maybe blowing the chance of a lifetime," Eagleson wrote in his 1991 autobiography, *Power Play: The Memoirs of a Hockey Czar.* "It would have been something like waiting for the Second Coming and then nothing happens." Eagleson also threatened that Orr would play for the amateur Canadian national team if the Bruins did not come up with a better offer. "The National Hockey League isn't the only place Bobby Orr can play hockey," he said. Outmaneuvered and losing the battle for public opinion—"If the Bruins don't sign Orr, the fans won't do anything except burn down Boston Garden," one sportswriter posited—Emms waved the white flag. Orr got the deal he was looking for and was now officially a Bruin. "I guess there'll be a lot of sleepless nights for me if I don't live up [to expectations]," he said.

Orr's apprehension was unnecessary. He had an impressive first season, scoring 11 goals, with 20 assists in 46 games, while receiving the Calder Memorial Trophy as the league's top rookie. "I always said he'd be a better pro than a junior," New York Rangers coach Emile Francis said.

> In the pros, I'd figured they'd throw the puck to him and then set themselves up for a return pass. That's what happened. I've looked at my scoring sheet after each Boston game, and there's Orr with six, seven, eight shots. One game, he's got 12 shots. Hell, he's a defenseman. He's not a supposed to get that many shots. . . . He's some meal ticket, isn't he?

Hap Emms offered no rebuttal. Setting aside his earlier reservations, Emms now counted himself among Orr's biggest boosters. "I don't think I've ever seen such a complete hockey player," he gushed. "Some players are great shooters, others fine passers and skaters, but Orr has everything. He also has something special—God-given ability. He makes the right move instinctively. All he needs is experience."

Orr made his official Bruins debut on October 19, in a 6–2 victory against the Detroit Red Wings at Boston Garden. "Bobby was a star from the moment they played the national anthem in that first game," Harry

Sinden said. While he didn't score any goals, Orr notched an assist, blocked several shots, and impressed teammates with his poise and smarts. "When he gets the puck, he knows right away what he's going to do with it," said veteran defenseman and former five-time All-Star Bill Quackenbush. "He sees a man open and doesn't hesitate. That enables that player to get going. And if he sees a man breaking, his pinpoint passing puts the puck right on his stick." Milt Schmidt was even more enthused. "When did you ever see an 18-year-old block shots the way he does," the Bruins executive said. "And did you notice when he couldn't find anybody clear to pass the puck to [and] clear it out of his zone, he nonchalantly flipped it into center ice instead of icing it."

As reporters swarmed his locker after the game, a humble Orr tried to downplay his contributions. He claimed that his credited assist to teammate Wayne Connelly on a second-period power play goal was a fluke. "That wasn't a pass," he said. "I fanned on my shot. It was too close to my feet. My shot just trickled along, and Wayne knocked it in." Still, the crew-cutted teenager had shown enough flashes of brilliance to grab the attention of Gordie Howe. "He'll do, for sure," the great 38-year-old Detroit winger said. "He anticipates well, he makes good passes, and he does just about what you'd expect of a good defenseman." Howe also taught Orr a valuable lesson on keeping his guard up. "I was watching a pretty pass that I had made, and Gordie wanted to let the young player know the old guy was still around," Orr said. "He stepped into me, and I went down hard. That was my welcome to the NHL. I had my head down, and the old fella nailed me."

Orr's first goal came two nights later in a losing 3–2 effort against the Montreal Canadiens at home. Manning the right point inside the Montreal zone, Orr launched a screaming missile that Habs goalie Gump Worsley had no chance of stopping late in the game. "The puck burst into the back of the net so powerfully that [Worsley] seemed practically chained to the spot," the *Boston Globe* reported. What happened next would stay with Orr for the rest of his days. The Garden faithful spontaneously rose to their feet to give the rookie a rousing standing ovation that lasted a full five minutes. "Those fans went out of their way to make me feel at home," Orr wrote. "I always found the cheers deeply humbling. When you hear that, you just want to give back. So that goal was the start of a very special relationship." In fact, the bond forged that evening was so strong that when Orr submitted a rare poor performance against Detroit during a blowout loss a week later, the Bruins fans in attendance were unusually restrained and sympathetic. "They would have forgiven him if he had been on the ice for 15 goals," Harry Sinden said. "He could have slipped five of them into his own net and they would have forgiven him. The kid is so good most of the time that everyone forgives his mistakes. He doesn't make enough to worry about anyhow."

Orr's budding superstardom drew parallels to another highly touted young athlete who had taken his sport by storm at about the same time— Joe Namath of the New York Jets. Like Orr, Namath was named Rookie of the Year (for the upstart American Football League) and breathed new life into a losing franchise with his electrifying play at quarterback. But there the comparisons ended. As a NHL insider confided to Jack Olsen of *Sports Illustrated*, "Bobby Orr is a whole 'nother ball game, a whole new breed of superstar. He brings a new image to the game. He's modest, he's restrained, he's understated. He's the exact opposite of a Joe Namath." Indeed, Namath was a vain exhibitionist who craved all manner of attention. "Being able to get up and go wherever you want to go, isn't that what life is all about?" he asked. Orr deliberately sought a lower profile, keeping the media at arm's length while maintaining some semblance of privacy. Fame was something to be tolerated, not embraced. "I'm almost afraid to go back to Parry Sound after the season," he confessed. "You know how it is . . . you're walking along the street and don't happen to notice someone. The next thing you know word gets around that 'Orr has gone snooty on us. He doesn't even say hello to his hometown people anymore.' Maybe I'll just disappear and go fishing."

When it came to charitable causes, however, Orr showed no such reticence. He gave tirelessly of himself and his time. *Lawrence Eagle Tribune* sportswriter Russ Conway once recalled complaining to Orr about a lousy day he was having when the Bruins were holding a morning skate at the Garden. Orr chuckled and told Conway to meet him afterward in the team dressing room. Conway complied and was asked by Orr to accompany him on a road trip after Orr filled up the trunk of his car with team souvenirs. "He drives away, and he doesn't say a word," Conway said. "I have no idea where he's headed. Then he pulls off the highway and into the parking lot of a big hospital." After securing Conway's word not to report anything he was about to see in his newspaper, Orr unloaded the trunk and led them to the hospital's children's ward. "He doesn't ask directions," Conway said. "It's obvious he's a regular at this place. He goes from bed to bed, talking to every kid and handing out his gifts—sticks and pucks and autographed photos." Conway found himself overcome with emotion, as many of the young patients were stricken with cancer and other serious maladies. "To see their excitement, the joy on their faces, I'll never forget it," Conway said. "He lit up that ward like he lit up the Boston Garden every time he put on his skates." And he wasn't even halfway done. "We've got two more floors to cover," Orr said. When they finally left the hospital and returned to the Garden, where Conway's car was parked, Orr gave him a big grin and an even bigger life lesson. "Well, Russ," he asked, "how's your day now?"

"He's a bleeding heart and do-gooder, that's all," Alan Eagleson told *Sports Illustrated* feature writer Jack Olsen.

> And most of it's private. He doesn't even tell me about it. He doesn't get receipts, and we lose all kinds of tax deductions because he doesn't make a record of it. Every once in a while, he cleans out his whole wardrobe and gives it to the priest at the Sacred Heart in Watertown. No, Bobby is no Catholic; he's barely even a Baptist. But he's the most Christian man I've ever known. He'll get $500 for an appearance somewhere, and he'll give it to the first charity worker he sees. I asked him what happened to his bonus check last year. He says, "Oh, I remember, I endorsed it over to Father Chase."

When Olsen asked Orr to explain the basis for his altruistic behavior, Orr initially demurred, as was his habit on the subject. But he eventually opened up after Olson persisted. "O.K., I'm lucky, right?" Orr said.

> I've been gifted, right? But the world is full of people who've not been gifted. Not only haven't been gifted, but have had things taken away from them. All I have to do is see one of them—some little girl that can't walk and yet she keeps on smiling at me, some lady . . . who goes home to an iron lung every night and still gives me a kiss and a hug after every hockey game. All I have to do is see someone like that, and then I don't think I'm such a big hero anymore. I think that to those people I'm a very small article! A very small, lucky article! It knocks me down pretty bloody fast. It cuts deep into me, and I'd rather not talk about it.

Orr continued to amaze the hockey world during the next two seasons, racking up impressive offensive totals and winning consecutive Norris

Trophies as the league's top defenseman. In 1968–1969 alone, he averaged almost a point per contest after amassing 21 goals and 43 assists in 67 games. No NHL defenseman had ever done that before. Orr might have posted even better numbers had he remained healthy, but "Brittle Bob," as some in the league began to call him, suffered through a bewildering series of injuries. They included a fractured collar bone, a dislocated shoulder, and a severely damaged left knee that eventually cut short his career. "It's just that he's always at the center of the action and is therefore exposed to danger more often," Harry Sinden told Jim Proudfoot of *Hockey World*. "It's just part of being such a dominant player that every game seems to revolve around him."

Orr had first injured the knee during his rookie season in a game against the Maple Leafs. Toronto defenseman Marcel Pronovost hip checked him into the boards as he tried to thread his way up the ice. "It was a clean check, but my knee was pinched and twisted under the force of the hit, and pinned there," Orr wrote. The ailments might have slowed him down, but they did not prevent Orr from regularly bringing fans to their feet with his dazzling end-to-end rushes, superb stickhandling, and brilliantly improvised sweeps around defenders. In short, he was a human highlight reel—a Michael Jordan on ice. As Boston sports columnist and author Ray Fitzgerald wrote,

> Orr played hockey for a living. That is like saying Picasso drew pictures for a living. His was a style of hockey never before seen in Boston, or anywhere else for that matter. Orr played the game with the grace of a Bolshoi balleteer. He was Nureyev on skates. When he was into his game, the Boston Garden was transformed into Swan Lake.

Orr was at a loss to explain his transcendent acts of athleticism. "Hockey is a game of instinct," he explained.

> After a game I sit in the dressing room and ask myself why I did certain things that night on the ice. Most of the time I have no answer. I had the puck on the other end of the ice and there were two players checking me pretty closely. The next thing I knew, I was all alone in front of the goaltender. I honestly do not know what I had done to get there.

The one and only Bobby Orr. *Graphic Artists, HHOF Images*

Neither did opponents; Orr was too quick, too smart, and too tough to be stopped. It was like trying to nail custard to a wall. "Bobby Orr simply shouldn't be allowed on the ice any time the opposing team is short-handed," former Toronto coach Punch Imlach once joked. "He's the best player in the league, and a team like Boston shouldn't have the added advantage of playing against a shorthanded opponent." Indeed, Orr could blow by any forechecker a rival club could throw against him in power play situations. "It's almost like being two men short," Emile Francis said. "I figure you're better off lining up your players across your own blue line." None of this surprised Gordie Howe. "Any time you play against [Orr] you're aware of his talent," the six-time league MVP said.

It's not only his puck control, he's also one of the most accurate passers in the league, and he can get away his shot as quick, if not quicker, than anyone I've ever seen. With that quickness, plus the ability to walk around anybody, and that heavy shot—I think he's got one of the better shots in hockey—he's got everything going for him. And he doesn't make mistakes—and how can you improve on that?

Orr was faulted for being too offense-oriented, but hockey old-timers like Milt Schmidt felt such criticism was unfair. "That's nonsense," he said. "What would they do, take away his best weapon, his ability to score and set up goals? If he doesn't get trapped in the other end, what difference does it make?" Eddie Johnson concurred. "They say Bobby doesn't play defense," the veteran Boston goaltender said. "Heck, he makes hockey a 40-minute game for us. He's got the puck 20 minutes by himself. What better defense is there? If Orr has the puck, we're going to score—not the other guys." Interestingly, Orr could be a far harsher critic of his own play. "I back in too far on our goalkeeper," he once confessed. "I keep trying to remind myself to stay up at the blue line, forcing the guy to commit himself sooner. I don't mind blocking shots, but if I back in too far I'm apt to screen our goalkeeper. And anyway, it's better if I can force the other guy to make his move when he's well out." Such unvarnished candor was perhaps Orr's most endearing quality, according to Sinden. "In those areas where he's weak, he knows it himself," the Bruins coach said admiringly.

Less appreciated was Orr's ability to fight. "There was so much to talk about with Bobby, I think people overlooked how tough he was, I mean really tough," Derek Sanderson said. For sure, Orr ranked among the best pugilists in the league, always getting in the first punch that left many an opponent sprawling helplessly on the ice. Brian Conacher of the Maple Leafs was one such victim. Orr once beat the "living daylights" out of him when the Toronto forward made the mistake of slamming his stick into Orr's face. "I felt he was too far away for it to have been an accident," Orr explained. "I was bleeding like a stuck pig, and I was hot. If a guy wants to beat the hell outta me with his fists, that's okay but not with his stick." While the *Boston Globe* and other publications criticized Orr afterward for lacking self-control and risking serious injury to himself, Orr was unapologetic. "Conacher got me in the nose," he said, "and frankly, I didn't want to fight. But if they see you backing up in this league, it's no good. So, if they want to fight, I'll fight." Orr won the majority of his bouts and earned the reputation of being someone who was not above unleashing a sneaky elbow or two at an unsuspecting opponent's head. "The kid's got a mean streak," said late Hall of Fame linesman Bill Chadwick. Brad Park agreed. "He'll throw a cheap shot at one of our guys," the Rangers defenseman wrote in his autobiography. "Naturally, it makes us a little wary of him, which is probably his intention. The trick is to hit Orr cleanly and get him good and angry. The problem, however, is to catch him."

Toronto's Pat Quinn accomplished the rare feat with a violent body check that left Orr unconscious during a rowdy 1969 home playoff contest. Orr was later taken to nearby Massachusetts General Hospital, where he was held overnight for observation and diagnosed with a mild concussion and whiplash. "At first, it was deathly quiet as Orr lay there," Quinn recalled. "I was just standing by myself. Then, as soon as they got him up and off the ice, it was bedlam." Beer and garbage rained down from the Garden rafters as outraged Boston fans focused their anger on the rugged 6-foot-3, 215-pound rookie defenseman. "Something hard hit me, and I looked down to see one of those metal change holders bus drivers carry," Quinn said. "Unfortunately, there wasn't any money in it." Things got so out of hand that Boston police officers on duty became concerned about Quinn's safety. "They should get him out of the building now," one of the officers said. "The fans here don't like anybody to touch Orr. He's like their Frank Merriwell and Jack Armstrong rolled into one."

The incident unfolded when Orr picked up a loose puck from behind the Boston net in the second period and rushed up the ice along the right side close to the boards. He lost control of the puck in his skates and momentarily gazed downward to retrieve it. That's when Quinn struck. "It was a monstrous hit," Sanderson said. "It was a bouncing puck. Bobby never has his head down, ever. His head just dipped to pick up a loose puck. . . . I don't doubt that Paddy felt a little shitty afterwards, hitting a superstar that hard. Wayne Gretsky *never* got hit that hard." In fact, Quinn did not feel any remorse. "I hit him with a clean check," Quinn said. "That's the way I've always played hockey. I don't retaliate. He had his head down when I hit him. That's not my fault." Angry Boston fans begged to differ. Several tried to assault Quinn in the penalty box after he was assessed a five-minute major for the hit. "Call it Animal Farm, if you like," *Toronto Telegram* sports editor Charles McGregor wrote. "If Lord Stanley had wanted to put up a trophy for this kind of competition, he would have issued all contestants with flails, halberds, broadaxes, and maces." While Orr suffered no lingering physical aftereffects from Quinn's check, he did receive a curious proposition. "Do you want me to take care of Pat Quinn?" a mysterious figure asked Orr after he was discharged from MGH. A shaken Orr declined, telling the man, who looked like he could have walked out of the pages of a Raymond Chandler novel, that he would take care of Quinn himself. Remembered Orr, "It was kind of a scary moment, because the look in his eyes and his general demeanor made me think that the guy meant to do some serious damage."

Orr and his teammates planned to do some serious damage of their own against the Blues in Game 4. Yet, performing before a sweltering Mother's Day crowd of 14,485 in Boston Garden, where the outside temperature hovered above 90 degrees, the Bruins fell flat out of the gate. They appeared to be already making plans for a postgame victory party while their visitors had a meaner and more determined look about them. "The Blues were different," Phil Esposito acknowledged. "They were really up for the game." Only 19 seconds into the contest, Blues defender Bob Plager unleashed a hellacious hit on Derek Sanderson at the St. Louis blue line that sent the center tumbling end over end. "That was a big check for us," Scotty Bowman said. "It showed the Bruins we weren't going to just let them have it. They were going to have to work." Sanderson, who arrived in the Bruins clubhouse before the game resplendent in a white tuxedo with matching white boots and tails, had a slightly different take. "Plager's check was a tonic," he posited. "I thrive on combat, and a hip in the face wakes me up as well as anything."

Sanderson proved his point five minutes later. Fighting for a loose puck in the St. Louis end as a hard-charging Plager closed in on him for another big hit, Sanderson opted to respond with an old-fashioned sweep check—something his father had taught him years earlier. He dropped to one knee and turned his stick flat on the ice in a blanketing counterclockwise motion that corralled the disk. "I continued the motion and swept it right through Plager's legs and out in front of the net," Sanderson told writer Stan Fischler. Teammate Rick Smith, who had watched the play unfold, skated in from his position on the blue line to take advantage. "[Smith] got hold of the puck about 25 feet in front of [Glenn] Hall and drove it home before the goalie could make a move," Sanderson said. The Blues, who outshot the Bruins, 14–10, in the period, for only the second time in the series, tied the game on a Red Berenson goal late in the frame. The St. Louis team captain converted on a stray rebound. The teams exchanged goals the next period, including a history maker by Esposito at 14:22, off a draw he won in the Blues' left face-off circle. "The puck bounced, and I took a stride to my left and snapped a shot," Esposito recounted. The goal was Esposito's 13th of the playoffs, which broke an all-time NHL postseason record shared by Maurice Richard and Jean Beliveau of Montreal. "We got these guys," Esposito told linemate Ken Hodge during the celebration that followed. "We are not going back to St. Louis."

Esposito's prediction seemed premature when Blues forward Larry Kennan pulled his team ahead, 3–2, on a power play goal only seconds into the third period. Gerry Cheevers unintentionally provided an assist here, as a Kennan backhander found net after wildly careening off the goalie's head. "I couldn't have picked a worse time to drop the armor," Cheevers later confessed. The Blues maintained the lead until Johnny Bucyk stepped in to deliver what he later called the "biggest goal I ever scored in my life" at 13:28. Only a day away from his 35th birthday, Bucyk got the celebration going early by redirecting a Pie McKenzie pass at the goalmouth into the St. Louis net. "I knew Pie was going to get the puck to me," the Chief said. "And there was someone all over me, but I weigh 217, and I think I stuck my fat butt into him and he never moved me. Then I put it up high." The score remained 3–3 until the end of regulation.

As the unusually quiet Garden crowd waited anxiously for the required sudden-death overtime period to begin, the Bruins betrayed no nervousness in the locker room. They had come too far to louse things up now. Harry Sinden saw to that. "I just told our guys not to get too smart," he said afterward. "We didn't want to start making beautiful plays all of a sudden." Indeed, Sinden wanted the team to use its superior talent and strength to bury the Blues. "Last year," he pointed out, "we got beat a couple of times in overtime by Montreal [in the semifinals] when we tried to get too cute on defense. I figured in this game we had the advantage in manpower and games." That was all players like Bucyk needed to hear. "Listen, you guys," the beloved veteran told his teammates before they headed back onto the ice, "I don't want to come back to play another game."

Since St. Louis started its high-scoring Red Berenson–led line, Sinden decided to counter with his best defensive unit, consisting of Sanderson, Wayne Carleton, and Ed Westfall up front, with Orr and Don Awrey manning the back line. "Harry just wanted everybody to settle down and have a good shift," Orr said. Sinden got his wish and more. Forty seconds into OT, Orr scored the game- and series-winner in what the NHL would later officially declare the greatest moment in hockey history. "At precisely 5:10 yesterday afternoon," the *Globe* giddily announced on its front page the next day, "Boston Garden started rocking with a delirious tumult that surely must have sent tremors down into the foundations of the old building. The shock waves from that initial celebration undoubtedly were carried far into the night, because the ear-shattering din was set off by the Bruins' first Stanley Cup triumph in 29 years."

Orr had set off the bedlam when he swooped in from center ice on a give-and-go with Derek Sanderson and rifled the puck by the outstretched right arm and leg of Glenn Hall. "I just let it go," a beaming Orr told reporters afterward. "I didn't aim it for a special spot, but I saw that goal. It went between Hall's legs." The clutch tally—Orr's only goal in the four games—came as no surprise to Sinden. "I knew we had a good chance to score with those two guys handling the play," he said. "It was well executed by the Turk. It couldn't have been more beautiful." Prior to the play, Orr had outhustled Larry Kennan in the St. Louis end for a loose puck, which he slid to Sanderson behind the net. "Orr took a glance at me and backhanded the puck along the boards, right onto my stick," Sanderson recounted. "It was a perfect pass." Sanderson then faked a move on the Blues defenseman covering him to buy Orr a few extra seconds to cut toward the net for the clinching score. "I knew it was over when the puck left his stick," Sanderson said. "You can't stop a laser beam." Missing from this analysis, however, was the fact that had Orr lost possession of the puck to Kennan, the outcome likely would have been very different. "Red Berenson was breaking down the middle as soon as he saw Orr pinch, so if I got it out, he would have had a breakaway and might have won the game for us," Kennan later told Andrew Podnieks, author of the 2003 book *The Goal: Bobby Orr and the Most Famous Goal in NHL Stanley Cup History*. Orr never disputed this point. "I got a little lucky there," he later told David Davis of Deadspin.com.

Adding further drama to the occasion was the sight of Orr soaring triumphantly through the air after the red goal light went on—"I thought I was going right out of the arena," he said—courtesy of a trip by Blues defender Noel Picard. He "got his stick on me to slow me down," Orr wrote. "But he tripped me an instant too late. He brought me down, but not before I'd spent that moment airborne." Picard, who had won a Stanley Cup as a member of the Montreal Canadiens in 1965, prior to joining the Blues, was accused by some of exhibiting poor sportsmanship. But the future hockey broadcaster denied there being any malicious intent. He was just trying to catch Orr and stave off defeat. "Those things happen so quickly," Picard said. "My God, [Orr] went six feet in the air! At the time, you think only that he's scored a goal. He scored on the short side, right in front of the goal. Then you see the pictures and you admire the play."

One photograph in particular stood out. Taken by veteran *Boston Record-American* staff photographer Ray Lussier with his Nikon F camera with a 35 mm lens, the iconic black-and-white photo captures a victorious Orr frozen in mid-flight parallel to the ice with his arms raised in unfettered joy after Picard had tripped him. "Oh, that's a different picture," Orr thought when he first saw the image in a centerpiece newspaper spread a couple of days later. He had no idea. In the decades to follow, "Flying Bobby" would become the hockey equivalent of the Mona Lisa—a ubiquitous presence in the annals of the sport. "The photo is everywhere," Randy Lussier said of his late father's masterpiece in a 2016 interview. "In Boston, there's not a sports bar you can walk in and it's not up on the wall. I think one of the surprising places I saw it was in a geometry textbook." Future Bruins coach and Bobby Orr fan Bruce Cassidy kept a reprint of the picture in his Ottawa home growing up. "I used to deliver the paper when I was a kid," Cassidy said. "I cut it out, and it was on my [bedroom] wall. By the time I took it down, it was, what, yellow? Isn't that the color newspaper goes?"

Interestingly, Ray Lussier—a lifelong hockey fan since his early childhood days playing the game in neighboring Lawrence, Massachusetts—got the shot by sheer accident. Assigned to the opposite end of the arena, Lussier spied an empty photographer's stool behind the Blues net during the intermission before the start of overtime. The spot had been reserved for a thirsty *Globe* photographer who had decided to duck into the stands for a cold beverage. Lussier grabbed the seat and, by the time his tardy rival returned, had snapped the most famous photo of his career. "I never would have got the picture if that other photographer didn't go running off to get a beer," he said.

Orr was piled on high by his exuberant teammates the instant he hit the ice as the scorching hot Garden exploded in cheers. "The noise was deafening," confirmed one news account. "Everyone hugged everyone, women shrieked, and hot champagne flowed and flowed. Mascara ran like water, and shirts were ringing wet. Nobody cared about anything, except the Bruins, the Cup and, Number Four." Phil Esposito, who had witnessed the dramatic goal from the Boston bench, almost got injured in the process. "No kidding," he later related. "As the other guys jumped over the boards, the bench went flying, and I fell flat on my face. By the time I reached Bobby, he was at the bottom of a pile of players." Minutes later, Johnny Bucyk—the longest-tenured member of the team—formally received the Stanley Cup from NHL president Clarence Campbell and skated slowly around the rink with the gleaming silver trophy thrust proudly above his head to more thunderous applause. "I've waited 15 years for this," Bucyk said. "And I wanted it for these fans. They've been waiting even longer. They deserve it."

Ted Green had more mixed feelings. The sidelined defenseman had been invited to sit on the Bruins bench during the finals, and while he was genuinely happy for his teammates' success, Green felt strangely de-tached from the proceedings. Only when Bucyk and Esposito insisted he join them for the Cup presentation at center ice did he feel a measure of belonging. Indeed, the thoughtful gesture reduced Green to tears. Re-membered Green, "All the emotions came together—my injury, my miss-ing out on such a beautiful year, the memories of all those bad years I had lived through with the team, and the knowledge that when this finally happened, everyone wanted me to enjoy it, too." Still, Green could not shake the feeling he was undeserving. "How can you feel a part of some-thing that you haven't given anything to?" he asked himself.

The tumultuous celebration carried over into the Bruins dressing room. Players, coaches, and team executives sprayed one another with champagne when not drinking the bubbly straight from the Stanley Cup. "There was also the traditional shower baths for a number of fully clothed individuals and other characters," the *Globe* noted. Harry Sinden, Milt Schmidt, and Weston Adams Jr. were among those so specially honored. "It was perfect, just perfect," exclaimed a dripping Sinden leaning against a wall afterward.

A great game for our fans, an excellent hockey game for television, and Bobby Orr scored the winner. I couldn't have written a better script. The kid has been tremendous all season. Heck, he's been tremendous from the first game he played for the Boston Bruins. He shows me a new trick every game, never ceases to amaze me.

When a reporter asked whether future hockey championships could be expected in Boston's future, Sinden was equally upbeat. "Why not? We have talent, size, depth, spirit, harmony, fine goaltending, an excellent power play, good penalty-killing, and an unquenchable thirst for victory. What more could a coach ask?"

Bobby Orr initially had difficulty locating his father to share the great moment. That's because Doug Orr, who had made the long trek from Parry Pound to be with his son, found himself too emotionally spent. He needed time to collect his thoughts. "I cried like a baby," the elder Orr said. "I called home and spoke to my wife. She was crying, too. I'm the proudest man alive." When the two finally united at Orr's locker for an interview with local broadcaster Don Earle, there were warm embraces all around. "It's so great I don't know what to say," Orr said. "This team. Unbelievable. The guys that were hurt are out yelling for us between periods. They're in the stands. They're fighting for us. The guys that are playing. The goaltending. Put everything together, it's a great bunch of guys." Orr had an additional reason to smile. Teammate Ace Bailey had "promised a dollar to the guy to get the winner," he revealed. The only problem, Orr joked, was that Bailey had paid him in Canadian money. On a more serious note, the 22-year-old showered praise on the vanquished losers. "We had to work our butts off to beat those St. Louis Blues," he said. "We were fortunate to survive regulation time. They really carried it to us. . . . We took them four straight because we have a fine team. People forget we took the Chicago team four straight, and they were no pushovers."

Derek Sanderson spent most of his time revisiting the magic of Orr's clinching goal. "Bobby's got more anticipation and instinct than anyone," he said. "He was 40 feet away when he saw the play develop. It was give and take, baby, and it went right in." Gerry Cheevers, who concluded his brilliant goaltending playoff run with 28 saves and a personal-record 10th straight victory, shrugged off questions about whether the warm game-time conditions affected play. "The heat?" he asked. "It was so hot the water was dripping out of my mask, but the main problem with goaltend-

Making history: Orr scores the Stanley Cup–clinching goal on May 10, 1970. *Le Studio du Hockey, HHOF Images*

ing is waiting [for] your team to score, and I never had that problem." Instead, Cheevers chose to needle critics who believed he would be the weak link in the Bruins' championship run. "I was that good all along," he said. "No one noticed." Phil Esposito took the opportunity to remind everyone about a bold prediction he had made when he first donned the Black and Gold. "Three years ago, I said we would win this Stanley Cup," he beamed. "Know why? Because we have the team that stays together."

Unsurprisingly, the mood was funereal in the visitors' clubhouse. The Blues, who would not win a Finals until 2019, had put forth their finest effort in the series but still came up short. Glenn Hall, who had turned away 28 of 32 Boston shots in net, could barely hide his disappointment. "I suppose you could have stopped that shot," he snapped at a journalist when the latter raised the touchy subject of Orr's goal. "It dribbled between my pads. . . . I made a stupid play." Bob Plager visibly winced in agony as he dressed, revealing that he had played the game with a dislocated shoulder. But the real pain, the stoic defender emphasized, was being swept in the Finals. "Give us Orr and we could win it all," he said. Scotty Bowman did his best to sound gracious in defeat. "I can't complain," the coach said.

> It was a case of the better team winning. But three years ago, we started even with five other West clubs, and we've been to the Stanley Cup Finals three times. Am I frustrated at never winning? We've won $23,000 a man [in postseason player earnings] in those three years. That wipes away a lot of the frustration.

Bowman went on to praise his players' dogged determination "to go down fighting." "We had good chances to score when we had the goal lead," he said, "but that's been the story for us against this club. The only thing we did differently today was to play more offensively. We tried to play a little stronger, to attack more."

The Bruins Cup celebration resumed the next day. A raucous crowd of more than 140,000 greeted them with a shower of confetti during a downtown motorcade parade and reception at City Hall Plaza hosted by Boston mayor Kevin White. "The parade, almost a half-hour late in starting, was slowed as the crowds surged toward the cars carrying the Bruins," the *Herald-Traveler* reported. "There were no ropes, possibly because the police did not expect such a crowd, but this let the parade watchers get touching-close to their heroes." Too close, according to many of the players. Derek Sanderson had his stylishly mod red shirt torn in three places and his buckskin vest taken from his back. Orr, who had been named MVP of the playoffs by the NHL Board of Directors, unsuccessfully fended off the hugs and kisses of several young female admirers mobbing his car. Even the Stanley Cup didn't go unaffected. "I was holding it all day, and people kept grabbing at it," Johnny Bucyk said. "That made it very heavy." Phil Esposito was taken aback by the mob scene. "I got up this morning and said we're going to have a parade today, so what," he said. "I thought it would be a nice little thing, a band, a few handshakes, and that would be it. I never thought about anything like this."

By the time the motorcade reached City Hall, most of the Bruins had the unsettled look of trauma victims. To their credit, however, they were able to recover their bearings in time to have some fun at Mayor White's expense. While Hizzoner was congratulating them for the magnificent season they had provided their fans, a grinning Pie McKenzie dumped a pitcher of beer on his head.

It was the perfect coda for a team of "kooks and degenerates."

7

DYNASTY'S END

Just three days after registering the greatest triumph of his coaching career, Harry Sinden shocked Boston fans and most of the hockey world by abruptly announcing his retirement from the sport. "I never wanted coaching as a lifetime career," Sinden explained. "And for years, I knew that the day would come when I would get out of it completely." But even Sinden admitted he had not expected to step down so soon. For sure, the young coach had planned to stick around several more seasons with the Bruins. What forced his hand?

Sinden was unhappy with the relatively paltry sum of money the Bruins were willing to offer him to remain behind the bench. The previous December he had sat down with team general manager Milt Schmidt and asked for an $8,000 raise above his annual salary of $22,500. "The Bruins have become a real power in the NHL," Sinden told Schmdt. "Before I came along, they missed the playoffs for seven straight years. I think I deserve a raise for next season." But Schmidt appeared unconvinced. "Wow! That's a lot of money," he said. "Too much for me to approve." Schmidt went to Weston W. Adams Jr. for input and the penurious Bruins president voiced disapproval. He authorized Schmidt to tender Sinden a more modest $3,000 salary increase instead. Sinden became incensed. "For a long time I had entertained doubts about [my] future with the Bruins organization, and this incident was the clincher," Sinden recounted. "To me, a coach is a member of the club staff, not a hired hand. The Bruins thought otherwise—and that was that."

Sinden concluded that regardless of how well the Bruins performed on the ice in 1969–1970, the season would be his last professionally. "Living with that decision these past five months has been painful," he confessed to Will McDonough of the *Boston Globe* afterward. "There were times when it popped into my mind, and I had to shut it out. There were times

Gerry Cheevers with the World Hockey Association. *O-Pee-Chee, HHOF Images*

in the happiness of the days following our Stanley Cup win that it hit me hard that I wouldn't be associated with these kids—or be their coach any longer." Nor did it make the 37-year-old's decision any easier that the team he was leaving had the potential to be an annual championship contender. "Their future is all in front of them," Sinden said. "This Stanley Cup victory should be the first of many. As I've said before, they've got the ingredients and the courage to keep that Cup a long time."

Bruins players had equally kind things to say about Sinden. "He was the best coach I ever had in pro hockey," Phil Esposito said. "I have met a lot of great guys on the management end, and most of them have been with the Bruins, but Harry has been the best. He knows players better than anyone I have ever known." Fred Stanfield did not disagree. "It's a tough job keeping everyone on a hockey club happy," the center said. "I thought Harry did a great job. You can ask any of the guys. I'll bet 90 percent of them thought he did a good job." Derek Sanderson counted himself among the latter, claiming Sinden was irreplaceable. "I hope he reconsiders," Sanderson said. "This is a blow to us. A new coach won't be able to handle the club like Harry did. I hate to see him go." The disappointment about Sinden's departure did not end in the Bruins locker room. Fans were also upset, roundly condemning the move as "terrible" and the "worst thing in the world." "He deserves more money," Braintree resident Stephen Zoll told a local reporter. "A lot more. They should raise the price of tickets a dollar, and that would take care of the salaries."

Sinden's close friend and attorney Bob Woolf tried to persuade him to reconsider his decision in lieu of Sinden having never made any serious money in coaching. "Now he seemed on the verge," Woolf later wrote, "and he had decided to walk away from it." But Sinden refused to change his mind, claiming Bruins management had personally insulted him with their low-ball salary offer. "All my life," Sinden told Woolf, "I promised myself I would never work for someone who didn't appreciate me. I've seen so many guys lose their pride just because they needed a job. I don't need one that bad."

Sinden, in fact, had already lined up a job outside of hockey with an old high school friend who owned a modular home construction business in Avon, New York. His pay would be significantly higher than what the Bruins were willing to offer him. In addition, he would be afforded the opportunity to reclaim a normal family life. "I have three daughters approaching college age, and I haven't been around them as much as I should have been," he said. Still, regardless of how emotionally or financially secure he became, Sinden admitted he would miss hockey. "I know that," he maintained. "It was my life for more than 20 years. But I'm leaving as a winner—the coach of the Stanley Cup champions—and that is the way to go."

The Bruins did not let Sinden's hasty exit stand in the way of accomplishing a record-breaking performance during the 1970–1971 regular season. Phil Esposito, Bobby Orr, Johnny Bucyk, and Ken Hodge finished in order as the top four scorers in the National Hockey League, with more than 100 points each. Esposito's 76 goals and 152 points set new individual league marks that would not be broken until Wayne Gretzky of the Edmonton Oilers accomplished the feat in 1982. "How do you stop a guy like Phil?" asked Chicago goaltender Tony Esposito, who suffered the indignity of having his older brother score a hat trick against him in an early December game. "He's got everything going for him. He's got size and strength. He can shoot, he can stickhandle, he can check. He's the best around . . . just talk to some of the other players about Phil. They'll tell you he's almost impossible to stop once he gets the puck and lets it go."

Orr's performance was noteworthy as well. He was runner-up to Esposito in scoring, with 37 goals, and collected 103 assists, to shatter the old standard for defensemen. He also took home league MVP honors for the second year in a row. "Orr," wrote Larry Merchant of the *New York Post*, "is at least hockey's sixth dimension. He is one of those rare athletes who revolutionizes his game as Babe Ruth did, as Bill Russell did. Bobby Jones once said of Jack Nicklaus, 'He plays a game of which I am not familiar.' Orr plays hockey in a way that makes old-timers feel like dinosaurs, too." Indeed, the NHL might well have been Jurassic Park when the explosive Bruins lineup took the ice. The team compiled 399 goals, with an unprecedented 10 players netting 20 goals or better. Observed Esposito, "We didn't set records because of weak opponents. We did it because of our overall offensive philosophy. We hit, we get position in front of the net, we shoot, we help each other. . . . I think there's never been a hockey club that could tie our skates."

The Bruins coasted to a first-place finish in the Eastern Division with a league-best 57–14–7 record. But the playoffs proved a different matter. The team fell in seven games in the opening round to the Montreal Canadiens, who had finished 24 points behind the Bruins on the season. Les

Canadians possessed an aging roster that featured several past-their-prime stars, for instance, Henri Richard, Jacques Lemaire, Frank Mahovlich, and Jean Beliveau. "They say we are too old to win," Richard said. "We are not. Not all of us. We have that desire to win. We want the Cup back, want it bad. Last year we were not in the playoffs, and it was embarrassing. Now we are in, and we want to win."

Leading the Habs to their improbable triumph was rookie goaltender Ken Dryden. A brooding 24-year-old from Toronto who had been drafted and traded away by Boston, Dryden was a late-season call-up from the American Hockey League and an imposing physical presence in net. He stood 6-foot-4, with a lightning-quick left glove hand that allowed him to snatch an opponent's shot in midair. "That hand of his is something else," marveled Pie McKenzie. Yet, these superior physical skills were only part of the story. Dryden, who replaced veteran goalie Rogie Vachon as starter, remained cool in pressure situations and liked to intellectualize the game, as befit someone who had earned a bachelor of arts degree in history from Cornell University. As he later wrote in his 1983 best seller *The Game*,

> Behind a mask, there are no smiling faces, no timely sweaty grins of satisfaction. It is a grim, humorless position, largely uncreative, requiring little physical movement, giving little physical pleasure in return. A goalie is simply there, tied to a net and to a game; the game acts, the goalie reacts. How he reacts, how often, a hundred shots or no shots, is not up to him. Unable to initiate a game's action, unable to focus its direction, he can only do what he's given to do, what the game demands of him, and that he must do.

Dryden managed to stymie the high-powered Bruins offense throughout the series, stopping a total of 258 shots on goal, including 57 by Esposito. "My God, he's got arms like a giraffe," the impressed center said afterward. Other Bruins were inclined to agree. "Dryden?" pondered Milt Schmidt. "We saw too much of him. He has some kind of radar. Even the shots he couldn't see, the screens, were hitting him." Ken Hodge thought Dryden performed with a poise and savvy well beyond his years. "What a goaler," he exclaimed. "Words can't describe him. He baffled us right from the start." Dryden, possessing only six regular-season games of NHL experience going into the playoff, gracefully accepted the praise but admitted he had to pinch himself. "I couldn't let myself believe we had won," he said.

> I looked at the clock with 10 seconds to play [during Montreal's 4–2 Game 7 victory in Boston], and I said to myself, "Tick, you so-and-so tick." Then it was nine seconds and eight and seven. And I kept looking at the clock and at the Bruins' faces. They looked discouraged, disappointed. Even with five seconds I didn't dare tell myself we had won. I guess I finally believed it with three seconds to play. "We've won, we've won," I told myself.

There was considerable soul-searching among the Bruins in the aftermath of the Montreal loss. A consensus emerged both inside and outside the locker room that Sinden's laidback replacement as coach—the bowtie-wearing former All-Star Montreal defenseman Tom Johnson—had been too lax in the discipline department. Players had been allowed to come and go as they pleased while demonstrating a notable indifference to training rules. "Look guys, I'm going to give you free rein here," Johnson told the team at the beginning of training camp. That was something Sinden never would have said—or permitted. As a result, the club was softer than it appeared, which fact hurt them when they ran into a determined opponent like Montreal in the postseason. "Tom had his own style," Derek Sanderson later wrote diplomatically. "He was a fabulous guy and Harry's best friend, but when a team is used to one guy's style and all of a sudden they change, it changes the room and the atmosphere." He added the change probably cost Boston another championship.

Intent on avenging the previous year's playoff disappointment, the Bruins played like a team possessed in 1971–1972. For the second straight year, the club led the NHL in regular-season victories, with 54, and dominated most offensive categories. But when it came to the playoffs, there were no missteps this time around. They tore through Toronto and St. Louis in the opening rounds. "You have to look at them and size them up, and you have to admit it's one of the greatest teams in hockey," said St. Louis coach Al Arbour. "One of the all-time best. They've got so much depth, so much power. They go to the bench and they come up with players who could start for anybody else." Against the New York Rangers in the finals, the Bruins continued their relentless onslaught, taking four of six to win their second Stanley Cup in three years. No one was happier than Orr, who earned his third straight league

MVP Award. "I spent an aggravating summer," he told Mark Mulvoy of *Sports Illustrated.* "People kept asking me what happened against Montreal. This summer should be a lot better."

When their plane reached Boston's Logan Airport after their Cup-clinching victory at Madison Square Garden, the Bruins were greeted by thousands of boisterous fans who treated their hockey heroes as if they were the Beatles at the height of their musical fame. Orr had his clothes ripped from his back. "You fear for your life when people lose it like that," Sanderson wrote. Esposito initially reveled in the adulation but then contracted a bad case of claustrophobia. "In a second my watch was torn off my wrist," he said. "My suede coat was shredded. Women were trampled." Esposito spotted a side terminal door and attempted to make a hasty exit. "I found myself in a parking lot," he remembered. "I didn't know where my car was, so I wandered around." Esposito then heard a fan shout his name and panicked. "I leaped a fence, and within seconds I was gone," he said. Sanderson was more creative. He traded clothes with a ramp attendant on duty and successfully avoided the crush. "I rode into the employees' entrance on the back of a baggage truck," Sanderson wrote. "Nobody noticed me, and I sat in the hangar wearing the Eastern Airlines overalls and baseball cap until the crowds cleared." When they did, Sanderson hopped into his car and drove away. The Turk was far more relaxed when the newly crowned champions were honored at Boston City Hall. Mayor Kevin White finally got even with Pie McKenzie for dumping a pitcher of beer over his head in 1970. Hizzoner unexpectedly returned the favor this time around. "Revenge is a bitch," Sanderson observed.

Sadly, there would be no further Stanley Cups for this fun-loving, supremely talented bunch to celebrate. The World Hockey Association chiefly saw to that. The brainchild of a former political fund-raiser from California named Dennis Murphy, the WHA was an attempt to break the monopolistic stranglehold the NHL had on professional hockey. Murphy, along with business partner and attorney Gary Danielson, already had considerable experience as sport disrupters. A few years earlier, the duo had launched the upstart American Basketball Association to challenge the supremacy of the National Basketball Association. While both had grown tired of that particular venture due to myriad legal and financial issues, they thought they could make a better go at things with hockey. "We felt [the NHL's] weakness was their arrogance and selfishness,"

Murphy told Ed Willes, author of *The Rebel League: The Short and Unruly History of the World Hockey Association.* "The NHL thought they had it made and, if they ignored us, we'd go away. They could have knocked us out of the box before we even started if they wanted to. But they didn't, and we didn't go away."

The WHA formally debuted in the fall of 1972, with teams in 12 North American cities, notably New York, Philadelphia, Chicago, Los Angeles, Quebec, Winnipeg, Ottawa, and Alberta. Owing to the strong interest the Bruins had generated for the sport in New England, there was a team placed in Boston called the Whalers. But the really big news associated with the WHA's launching was the prying away of veteran superstar Bobby Hull from the Chicago Black Hawks. "I wasn't going anywhere," Hull later recalled. "I thought I had a Black Hawks emblem tattooed on my chest." That was before Winnipeg Jets owner Ben Hatskin floored him with a 10-year contract offer worth $1.75 million that called for a then-unheard-of $1 million signing bonus. "In those days, a million dollars might as well have been a billion dollars. Nobody had ever heard of a million for a hockey player," said Hull, who went on to play 411 games in nine seasons with the WHA.

The record signing of the Golden Jet gave instant credibility to the new league and encouraged other established NHL stars to follow suit, notably those wearing the Black and Gold. Gerry Cheevers was the first to cash in. After receiving what he described as a low-ball contract offer from the Bruins, Cheevers signed a seven-year, $1.4 million deal with the Cleveland Crusaders. "I added up 999 reasons to stay in Boston," the veteran goaltender later told writer Jack Falla. "Then I added up 999 reasons to go to Cleveland. The 1,000th reason was the turning point—money." Ted Green and Pie McKenzie soon followed, the latter jumping to the Philadelphia Blazers as a player-coach. This caught the attention of Derek Sanderson, who had been McKenzie's longtime roommate on the road. So, when McKenzie asked him to join him in the "City of Brotherly Love" at the behest of the Blazers ownership, he was intrigued, especially when the Bruins appeared to be giving no priority to his resigning. "Philadelphia figured I was *the* guy to get," Sanderson later wrote in his autobiography. "I was coming off a Stanley Cup championship, I was a pretty big name, and I was available." But not even Sanderson was prepared for the lucrative offer he received from Philadelphia: $2.6 million over 10 years. The team even agreed to give him the right of first refusal if they ever decided to sell or move the franchise. "I was stunned," Sanderson wrote. "That just did not happen in hockey."

While the lure of becoming filthy rich was undeniably tempting, Sanderson was reluctant to cut ties with Boston. He considered his teammates as extended family members and felt a deep sense of personal loyalty to the Bruins, particularly team owner Weston Adams Sr., who had first brought him into the organization. He decided to visit Adams at his luxurious home north of Boston to discuss his future. "Mr. Adams, I owe you this," Sanderson told the Hockey Hall of Fame executive upon his arrival. "You are responsible for me playing in the National Hockey League, but this is where the rubber meets the road." Sanderson handed Adams a copy of the Philadelphia contract to review. "Vandals, rogues, charlatans, and thieves!" Adams exclaimed as he angrily flipped through the pages. Pointing to the expensive furniture in his private library where they were conferring, Adams said the document made him feel that Philadelphia was hand-selecting his finest pieces and claiming them as their own. "There's something wrong in America when this can happen," Adams said. Nevertheless, Adams advised Sanderson to sign the contract. "Derek, if the money's there, you have to take it," he said. "You'd be a fool not to. You'll never have another chance like it in your life." Still, Sanderson hesitated. "The Bruins are the only friends I've got," he declared.

Only when Philadelphia sweetened their offer by agreeing to hire Sanderson's father as a scout and throw in an additional $50,000 cash bonus to make him the highest-paid professional athlete in the world did Sanderson finally relent. "Like the Godfather, they made me an offer I couldn't refuse," Sanderson said. Yet, like the title character from the 1972 Academy Award–winning movie, Sanderson would bitterly come to learn that material wealth does not come without a significant personal price. Indeed, Weston Adams had tried to tell him as much in their final encounter. "Money corrupts, you know," Adams warned. "You're only 26 years old. This is so much money, and you can't comprehend its power. Do yourself a favor and don't ever consider yourself a millionaire—keep living at the $25,000-a-year level until you can grasp the magnitude of this contract."

Despite the WHA defections, the Bruins remained a strong, contending club. Bobby Orr and Phil Esposito were still near the peak of their respective hockey powers, and the team responded with back-to-back 50-

Derek Sanderson in the Big Apple. *Peter S. Mecca, HHOF Images*

win regular seasons. Yet, something was missing. "The ingredients you need to win it all, the good luck and the hard work, and the sense of destiny, just weren't all there," Orr later wrote. The Bruins did return to the Stanley Cup Finals in 1974, but they lost to the Philadelphia Flyers of "Broad Street Bullies" fame in six games. Led by Hall of Fame center Bobby Clarke and bruising enforcer Dave "The Hammer" Schultz, the Flyers beat Boston at its own physical game to become the first expansion team to win the Cup. "The Flyers were bigger and badder, in a sense, than the Bruins were," noted writer Stan Fischler. A disappointed but gracious Orr visited the Flyers locker room afterward to congratulate the new champions. He was offered some victory champagne by his old rookie teammate, Joe Watson, now a Flyer. But Orr politely declined to take a swig, claiming he was undeserving. "Can you believe it?" Watson mused. "If anybody deserved anything, it was him. My goodness gracious, he's their leader. He was carrying the puck into our end all afternoon. He doesn't have to be dejected the way he played. My goodness gracious, whatta player!"

The Bruins were upended by the Chicago Black Hawks in the opening round of the playoffs the next season, and team general manager Harry Sinden, who had returned to the Boston fold two years earlier to replace the outgoing Milt Schmidt, decided a major club shakeup was in order. On November 7, 1975, Sinden traded Esposito and defenseman Carol Vadnais to New York for All-Star defenseman Brad Park, center Jean Ratelle, and a minor leaguer. Getting Park was the key to the deal. "Park is a defenseman of Bobby Orr's type," Sinden said. "He carries the puck a lot, but he is good defensively. That is something this team needs."

Esposito was devastated. Three weeks earlier, he had turned down a 10-year contract with a $1 million signing bonus with the WHA's Blazers to take a lesser deal with the Bruins. "I thought I had a home in Boston," Esposito said. "It has been a great town for me." Making the news even harder to digest was the fact that he had balked at the suggestion of a no-trade clause during his Boston contract negotiations. "Harry," he told Sinden at the time, "you and I have been through so much together, I don't need a no-trade clause. If you tell me you're not going to trade me, that's good enough for me." Sinden assured him he would remain a Bruin as long as he was general manager. That was good enough for Esposito, who finalized the deal with Sinden with a handshake. "I signed, and I

became the *guy*," Esposito remembered. "I became the Boston Bruins—
Bobby and I." That turned out to be wishful thinking.

Esposito learned of the trade at 7 a.m. in a Vancouver hotel room. The
Bruins had been in town for a road game against the Canucks, and Esposito was nursing a hangover from the previous evening. An ominous
knock on the door sounded, and in walked Don "Grapes" Cherry, a former career minor leaguer who had become the team's coach the previous
season. "I remember the whole thing, verbatim," Esposito later told Kevin Paul DuPont of the *Boston Globe*.

> Grapes is there in the worst pair of blue pajamas you've ever seen, and
> Bobby [Orr] came with him, wearing just a T-shirt and pants. I just sat
> there, with my head in my hands, and I was saying, "I know what it is.
> I got traded. Just don't tell me it's New York. Not New York. If it's
> New York, I'm telling you, I'll jump out the window."

Cherry, who later gained fame and fortune as the popular television
host of *Hockey Night in Canada*, then instructed Orr to open the window.

Esposito's thoughts immediately turned to the WHA's earlier lucrative
offer he had unwisely left on the table. "Me, I was more loyal than
anyone, including Bobby Orr, only to have the fuckers fuck me like that,"
Esposito later revealed. He was especially angry at Sinden, whom he had
numbered among his close personal friends. "It's 28 years later," Esposito wrote in his 2003 autobiography, "and I'm still not over it. I still
haven't forgiven Harry Sinden. We've talked and I've tried to be friends
and I've laughed with him and had a few drinks, but I treat him like
anybody else. There isn't that special feeling anymore."

Local reaction to the trade was universally negative. "You do not
improve a team by that's already short of talent by trading away its
quality players, even if you get equal talent in return," wrote *Boston
Herald-American* columnist Tim Horgan. "You improve a team only by
adding quality to quality. The trouble with the Bruins was not Esposito
and Vadnais. The problem with the Bruins is that they have too few
players of their caliber." The *Globe*'s Tom Mulvoy painted Esposito's
departure in equally stark terms. "He scored 453 goals while skating
under the Bruins' banner," Mulvoy noted. "That is a singular contribu-
tion. It's also irreplaceable, and that's bad." Fans were even more down
on the move. "It would have been better to give them Faneuil Hall," John
Limoli of Tewksbury complained to the *Globe*. "I'm moving to New

York." Reading resident John Fallon believed the Bruins were giving away too much scoring. "The trade will tighten up the defense, but Esposito has always been a hustler, and they should have gotten more for him." Outside of Boston, the move was seen as largely favoring the Rangers. "How do you replace the league's best scorer?" asked Buffalo Sabres general manager Punch Imlach. "What do you do about making up all those goals? In my memory, I can't think of the league's best scorer ever being traded by anyone."

While Esposito's departure hurt, it was nothing compared to the public uproar caused by Bobby Orr's decision to leave the team via free agency at the end of the 1975–1976 season. Orr had played in only 10 games that year due to yet another knee injury. But he still remained the face of the franchise, and new Bruins owner Jeremy Jacobs—a Buffalo, New York, concessions magnate who purchased the team for $10 million in 1975—was intent on signing him to a long-term contract. But Alan Eagleson had other ideas. Orr's longtime agent and business advisor was a close friend of Chicago Black Hawks owner Bill Wirtz, whose team had taken a nosedive in attendance since Bobby Hull's defection to the WHA. Wirtz needed a major box-office draw to bring back the fans, so he leaned on Eagleson to get him Orr. Orr was reluctant to leave the Bruins, however. "I thought of myself as a Boston Bruin," he later wrote. "I had done so for years. I had been part of the organization since I was in grade school. I loved the city and the fans. I had been surrounded with great people on and off the ice. I can't begin to explain what that city meant to me. . . . I wanted to stay in Boston." The city had become his adopted second home, and he was viewed as a hockey demigod in most fans' eyes. "He was to us like Paul Revere," Mayor Kevin White said.

None of this mattered to Eagleson, of course, who was determined to deliver Orr to Wirtz and the Black Hawks. He manipulated Orr into signing a five-year, $3 million contract with Chicago, in spite of the fact that the Bruins had offered their franchise defenseman a far superior deal. Indeed, the team was willing to hand Orr an 18.6 percent ownership stake in the club, which translates into a hefty sum of more than $50 million in 2019. "Such an offer was unheard-of in any professional sport," Orr biographer Stephen Brunt wrote. "With franchise values [in the late 1970s] about to skyrocket, it would have set Orr up financially for life." Alas, Eagleson made sure his famous client knew nothing about it. He falsely suggested to Orr and the public at large that Jeremy Jacobs was

Phil Esposito's trade to the Rangers shocked Bruins fans and marked the end of a hockey era. *Lewis Portnoy, HHOF Images*

planning to kick him to the curb. "I suppose Jacobs feels it would be crazy to give this kid a couple of million dollars when he has a questionable knee," Eagleson said.

But this kid is not hamburger or a hot dog or a stale keg of beer. He's done everything they've ever asked him to do for the Bruins, and some people are forgetting that. He didn't get all those knee injuries playing for the Celtics. Bobby knows how he got them, and he never believed anyone could treat him this way.

Orr felt let down and abandoned. He would not even listen to new Bruins president Paul Mooney when the latter reached out to him to clear the air and explain the full scope of the club's good-faith offer. Instead, Orr grew testy and openly questioned Mooney's motives, suggesting the team executive was trying to sow division between Eagleson and himself. "Alan Eagleson's my friend!" he exclaimed. "Don't you ever try to divide him and me again, understand that?" Orr's mind was made up. The greatest backliner of his generation was taking his Hall of Fame resume and heading to Chicago. "My years in Boston have been the greatest years of my life," he told a gathering of friends, teammates, and journalists at a tearful farewell party he hosted at a restaurant in downtown Boston. "I've never had a complaint, not a single complaint with the press, with the fans, not with anybody," he said. "It was a very, very difficult decision I had to make." Only later would Orr come to bitterly rue his decision and Eagleson's Svengali-like role in maneuvering him into it. "I believed what he told me," Orr claimed. "There was no reason to even consider that he wasn't hammering out the best deal he could make for me. After all, he wasn't just my representative. He was a valued friend."

Bostonians were aghast. Respected Bruins beat writer and author Russ Conway, who did pioneer investigative reporting on Eagleson's controversial business dealings, likened the collective pall cast by Orr's departure to the loss of a loved one. "It was a sad day for New England," he asserted. *Globe* sports columnist Ray Fitzgerald admitted to having difficulty even accepting the news. "Funny," he wrote, "but right up until yesterday I thought someone would wave a magic wand, sprinkle some miracle dust, and Orr would remain in Boston." Fitzgerald's colleague and fellow columnist Mike Barnicle exhibited more bile in his response. He claimed the Bruins ownership was simply clueless about how much

Orr's name meant to Boston and hockey in particular. "It means nothing to economic royalists named Jacobs," Barnicle wrote.

> It isn't even Number Four. To them, it's just another number on a ledger sheet; something to be talked over with their accountants the same way they talk over how many peanuts have been sold and how much of a crowd they can attract with some all-male rock band . . . at $12.50 a head. And, in treating Orr like a vending machine, they show us the high regard they hold for the town of Boston. To the Jacobs bunch, this town looks must look like so much popcorn and beer to be packaged and sold; loyalty means mustard on the hot dogs.

Most fans agreed, claiming Jacobs and team management had made a mistake of historic proportions. As one diehard Bruins supporter vented to a local reporter, "It's like trading Ted Williams to the old Philadelphia Athletics [in baseball]. It's a boon to Chicago hockey."

Orr's exit did not spell the end of the Boston Bruins as a competitive hockey club. Thanks to the arrival of a talented new crop of stars like Rick Middleton, Ray Bourque, and Cam Neely, the team continued to qualify for the playoffs, setting a NHL-record 29 straight postseason appearances from 1968 to 1996. But the team came up short when it mattered in the Stanley Cup Finals, losing in 1977, 1978, 1988, and 1990. The Bruins had a consistently solid and entertaining team to watch, just not one capable of winning it all. Always there were comparisons to their 1970 champion forebears, especially that group's peerless leader—Bobby Orr.

Prolific author and amateur sportsman George Plimpton once recounted a conversation Orr's former teammates had about him during a Bruins training camp he attended in the late 1970s. It was after practice, and several of the players had retired to a local bar to unwind and swap boisterous tales of seasons past. The room grew noticeably more subdued when the subject of Orr arose. Wrote Plimpton,

> They told stories about him with a kind of reverence, with no interruptions or horseplay around the table, and if a waitress came around to take orders for another round of beers, she waited until the story was done, and very likely, being a Massachusetts girl, she would lean in to hear the rest of it because there is no one, ever, who matched Orr for the adulation he received in New England for his brand of play.

The Bruins fell on hard times as the millennium dawned, losing more games than they won and failing to make the playoffs. Players and coaches came and went with bewildering regularity. Local buzz about the club flatlined, as fans seemed more interested in discussing the phenomenal success of All-Pro quarterback Tom Brady and the newly crowned Super Bowl champion New England Patriots. The Bruins became an afterthought. Indeed, things got so bad around Causeway Street that the team's best player—39-year-old team captain and 17-time All-Star defenseman Ray Bourque—asked to be traded to a serious NHL contender. Team management obliged, sending Bourque to the Colorado Avalanche, where he promptly won a Stanley Cup championship in 2001. "The atmosphere wasn't good," Bourque confided to Michael Farber of *Sports Illustrated*. "To get the best out of myself, I needed a different environment. If I had stayed in Boston . . . I would've called it quits."

The Bruins returned to championship form in 2011, raising their sixth Stanley Cup in franchise history. The team was centered around the outstanding goaltending of two-time Vezina Trophy winner Tim Thomas, a former low draft pick who kicked around the minors for several years before finally finding his niche in Boston. The 37-year-old set an all-time Stanley Cup Finals record with 238 saves in seven games. "My whole career has been about proving to people that I can play in the NHL and that I can be very successful in the NHL," Thomas said. Even though the notoriously peevish netminder became a pariah around the Bruins for his refusal to attend the traditional White House victory celebration with President Barak Obama, Thomas helped make the club and hockey relevant again in Boston. But no one mistook Thomas or any of his champagne-drenched teammates for the Big Bad Bruins. That singular honor still belonged to a now-aging group of former champions who had weathered the turbulent waters of fame and glory with varying degrees of success.

8

BOYS OF WINTER

Ted Green miraculously returned to the Bruins lineup in 1970–1971, after a grueling offseason physical rehabilitation regimen supervised by an elderly, blue-eyed personal trainer named Gene Berde. Berde—a former Hungarian Olympic boxing coach who had whipped Carl Yastrzemski into peak shape for his 1967 MVP season with the Boston Red Sox— initially had his doubts. "I've had lots of players come here for help," Berde told a *Boston Globe* reporter at his suburban Boston gym that summer. "Almost all of these players have to be pushed. After 10 minutes they're huffing and puffing. You have to keep after them to do the work." Green was different. "He wants it," Berde said. "He has great determination. He wants to be better than he ever was, and I think he will be. You'll see. Teddy Green will be a great hockey player again." Green had already been working out extensively before he hooked up with Berde, running several miles a day, rain or shine. But Berde was a tough taskmaster.

He worked Green relentlessly, beginning with breathing exercises, calisthenics, and jumping rope every morning. Then came the really challenging part. Said Green,

> He had me running on a treadmill, operating wall pulleys, riding a stationary bicycle, doing deep knee bends, push-ups, high kicks, chin-ups, arm stretching, tossing the medicine ball, forward and backward somersaults, 60-yard sprints, and working on a devilish contraption called the Swedish wall ladder.

Green elaborated, "It's a heavy, multiple-rope ladder forming a vertical and horizontal grid. You scramble up like a monkey—or at least Berde does—and every muscle of your body is exercised." When he wasn't in the gym, Green spent much of his free time on a local golf course perfecting his swing. "I am normally a five-handicapper," he revealed. "I can hardly tell you how I felt when I was 110 my first time out. I kept at it until I shot in the 70s twice. Then, I knew if I had the coordination for golf I would surely have it for hockey."

Green reported to Bruins training camp that fall in great shape, 15 pounds below his regular playing weight of 210. But he was filled with self-doubt. He had not been on skates for more than a year, and the rust showed. "Maybe it's like swimming—you never forget—yet a year is a long time to be off the ice," he told Toronto sports columnist Bob Pennington. "I will need a few days to get the feel again." Green was also unsure how his teammates would respond to him. "He was on the spot in training," Phil Esposito admitted. "We all wondered if he'd be able to skate, let alone play hockey." For sure, it made for some awkward moments, especially with Green now wearing an ungainly black plastic helmet as protection against further injury. "All I know is that every single one of us was watching [Green] while trying not to," Esposito said. "We didn't want to embarrass him or make him feel like we were putting him through some kind of test. We all felt the same way—if he could come back we'd be a stronger team, and we were already the best team in the league. And once I saw him skate, I knew he'd make it back."

Yet, it was a slower, more tentative Green who returned to the ice. He displayed moments here and there of his past All-Star form, but overall, he was inconsistent and error-prone. He scored five goals in limited playing time. "His reflexes aren't the same," commented Detroit defenseman Gary Bergman. "He doesn't get a piece of every guy who comes down his side. That used to be like skating into a mine field. I notice when he takes a pass now he takes a long look before he passes. He used to zing those passes across. And he doesn't barrel up the ice like he did." Green never claimed he was the same player. "My timing was terrible," he confessed. "I couldn't adjust to guys coming down on me with the puck. Before, I'd instinctively know whether to skate up and meet them or hang back and wait. Now I had to debate with myself, and by the time I'd made up my mind, the guy was past me and heading for the cage."

The reality dawned on him that he had returned too early and was unprepared for the kind of intense popular attention his comeback drew. "I tried to do too much, too soon," he explained. "I expected too much of myself right away. I hadn't kidded myself and said, 'Oh, I'll step right back out there and, by the end of camp, I'll be ready to go again.' I knew better than that, but maybe because I had gotten myself in such great shape, I thought I could do more than I did."

Panic attacks were frequent and debilitating. "I felt that every eye in every rink was focused on me when I skated out to my defense spot," he said. "I felt they were waiting for me to make a mistake, that they were checking my reflexes. It was like I carried a mirror with me because I was conscious of my every move." It was only natural that he lost his confidence. "I'd make glaring blunders, mistakes I hadn't made since my rookie year," Green said. "The guys tried to help and were great at covering my mistakes. I never knew a man who could deteriorate so much in 17 months off skates." He received no shortage of sympathy from his teammates. "He made terrible demands on himself," Ed Westfall said. "Too many, in fact. This caused him to get down on himself, blame himself for lost games, for goals scored against us when he was on the ice. Nobody should chew himself out for these things. We're a team." Pie McKenzie agreed. "Few thought he'd ever be back, and here he is, and he's playing amazingly well under the circumstances," the Bruins forward said. "He has a lot of guts. And he's a great hockey player. He was before, and he will be again. I don't think he should be rushed, pushed into doing things before he's ready."

Green did his best to grind things out, but his efforts were complicated by the medical side effects caused by his head injury. To prevent any recurrence of a cerebral hemorrhage, doctors put Green on strong anticonvulsive drugs. But they only served to drive down his stamina and make him tired. In addition, Green experienced blinding headaches that would remain a constant source of pain and discomfort throughout his life. "Some nights," he once confided to a reporter, "it's like there's a guy banging to get out from under the plate in my head." His new helmet took some getting used to as well. "The damn thing worked loose and hung down over my eyes in one game," Green complained. He did entertain thoughts of ditching it altogether but realized that would have been "asinine" given his vulnerability to head injury. "I'm always going to have to wear it, but I still don't like it," he said. Bruins management did its best to dampen expectations and explain away the obvious decline in his skills. "Just give him time," said new coach Tom Johnson. "Don't draw conclusions too fast. It's unbelievable how fast he's come back, and I think he'll get all the way back eventually if people don't ask too much of him too soon. He's not hurting us right now, the way he is."

Despite the generous appraisal, Johnson used Green sporadically in the playoffs. He was no longer Terrible Teddy, a feared enforcer who could change the course of a game with sheer, brute force, but a potential liability on a contending team that could ill afford to play him in crunch time. If this wasn't bad enough, Bruins fans began to boo him at home. So much for the blood and toil he had expended on behalf of the team in seasons past. "You watched him and you wondered if your eyes lied," wrote *Montreal Star* columnist John Robertson.

> Sure, he'd still drop his gloves and take anyone on—but there was that flicker of hesitation, both by him and whoever he tangled with. With that plate in his head, could he really stand a good solid jolt—despite what doctors said? You watched him fight . . . and you cringed and your stomach flipped a little. You were afraid for him, and you had never been afraid for him before.

Robertson concluded that it was perhaps time for Green to hang up his skates. "In the cold, unyielding war of attrition in the NHL, there is no room for anyone who can't hack it right now—today. And this is why what Teddy has been and has meant to the Bruins in past seasons doesn't count once the puck drops."

Green had one final season with Boston in 1971–1972. Although he fulfilled a lifelong dream of playing on a Stanley Cup winner, he was benched down the stretch and had only one goal, with 16 assists. Likewise, he was a nonfactor in the playoffs, playing a grand total of 91 seconds in the Cup-clinching contest in New York. For a former two-time National Hockey League All-Star, the entire experience was a bit mortifying. "Am I sore?" he commented afterward. "Of course, I'm sore. But at a time like this, I've got to think beyond myself. It's not me anymore. It's the team. I don't like the way I've been used—or not used. I've told people right to their face exactly how I feel." He moved on to the upstart World Hockey Association the following season and was a major contributor on a New England Whalers team that won the league's first championship. As a sign of the deep respect his new teammates held for him,

Green was named squad captain. "He's mellowed a lot," Whalers coach Ron Ryan observed. "But I think Teddy is a more complete hockey player. We didn't sign him to be a bully." For his part, Green was just happy to be employed. "The idea of the game is to play, and I'm playing with the Whalers," he said.

In spite of a new team and league, Green was constantly reminded of his fateful run-in with Wayne Maki, who he had played against several times without incident in his final go-round with the Bruins. "People won't let me forget," complained Green of the fans and sportswriters pining for a return to form of the old Terrible Teddy. "They think there's something wrong with me, that I'm sick or scared or something because I don't play like I used to," he said. "I admit I used to go looking for trouble. But I like to think I'm more mature now. I'm a man, not a kid." In point of fact, Green now went out of his way to denounce the same roughhouse play he had employed against opponents in his younger days. "There's no place in hockey for high-sticking and slashing," he declared. "None at all." Green was especially irked by the lack of strong penalties meted out by game officials for such offenses. To him there could be only one explanation for this curious lack of accountability. "Why? Because the big shots who run the NHL and WHA haven't got the guts to do what should be done," he declared. "They're gutless. They think high-sticking and slashing is a part of hockey. Draws the fans. Adds color. Yeah, it adds color all right—the color of blood running."

Green went on to play six more seasons in the WHA, his final four with the Winnipeg Jets, where he skated for two more league champions. After retiring as a player at the end of the 1978–1979 season, Green became head coach of the Edmonton Oilers in the early 1990s. He compiled a lackluster 65–101–21 record before Oilers GM and former Bruins teammate Glen Sather finally saw fit to replace him. "I guess in the scope of world events, this is probably very small, but in my little world it's very devastating," Green commented. "Nobody forced me into this ring. I climbed in. I didn't go the distance."

Ironically, Green enjoyed a much longer professional career than Maki, who was diagnosed with a cancerous brain tumor in 1972. Maki had received the dire news after experiencing a series of pounding headaches playing for the Vancouver Canucks. "[The headaches] were real bad, like a knife stabbing into the head," Maki said. "They'd last a minute, go away, be gone five minutes, and then come back. They kept getting worse and worse." Maki died two years later, at the age of 29. By this time, Green had long since made peace with his old rival and the shared tragedy that forever linked them. "It was as much a trauma for Wayne Maki as for me," Green later told the *Toronto Sun*.

Harry Sinden returned to hockey glory as coach and manager of Team Canada during the 1972 Summit Series against the Soviet Union. Two years after leaving the Bruins surrounded by a cloud of controversy, Sinden led a Canadian team of top NHL All-Stars that featured Ken Dryden, Bobby Clarke, Vic Hadfield, and old friend Phil Esposito to a historic come-from-behind victory against the Soviets in what has been called a "Cold War on ice." Down 1–3–1 in the first five games, the Canadians rallied to win the best-of-seven series by sweeping its remaining contests, notably a thrilling 6–5 victory in the clincher that was played in front of a packed Luzhniki Ice Palace audience in Moscow. "What won it for us . . . was resiliency," Sinden told the *Globe and Mail* years later. "We never quit or got out of the game emotionally, never let the bad breaks or tough times beat us." Nor did they permit the petty intimidations of the dreaded Soviet secret police stand in their way. "The KGB is all over the place," Sinden revealed in *Hockey Showdown,* his firsthand daily diary account of the series.

> During the games you can see one positioned in almost every aisle of the arena. We know we are being followed constantly. I don't mind that, but I do mind the way they operate. They get physical with people, and they don't ask any questions first. And they don't care if you're Canadian or Russian. If you're doing something they don't like, they just come up and grab you, and shove you around until you get the message.

Sinden was hailed as a conquering hero when he returned to Canada, and his hockey coaching stock was never higher. He was approached by 10 clubs about potential job openings, including several from the WHA, but going back to the bench held no interest for him. He wanted to call the shots for an entire organization. The Bruins knew of this desire and came a knocking. "We always thought a great deal of Harry and still do," team president Weston W. Adams Jr. said. "When we learned that he wanted to get back into hockey and he preferred to rejoin the Bruins, we weren't averse to talking with him." A lucrative new multiyear deal was swiftly worked out. Sinden agreed to replace Milt Schmidt as club general manager, as the former Bruins playing great was bumped upstairs to the team executive suite. "Part of my job is to keep [the] Boston Bruins as the number-one team in competition," Sinden said. "We have to look to the future as a team."

Under Sinden's direction for the next 38 years, the Bruins continued to be a top championship contender, winning six conference championships and 10 division titles. The Stanley Cup proved more elusive. Sinden never got the opportunity to hoist another one. "It's something that we look at as a weakness in the organization and in me," he candidly told *Sports Illustrated*. Indeed, Sinden was criticized for being too accommodating to the penny-pinching ways of Bruins owner Jeremy Jacobs when it came to signing and retaining the kind of four-star talent believed necessary to lift the team to the next level. Recounted Phil Esposito, "The old story was Jacobs would say: 'Get me to the seventh game of the Stanley Cup Final—and lose. So I don't have to pay [the players].' That was the joke." Sinden had no better luck dealing with head coaches, cycling through them with bewildering regularity. He had a particularly nasty falling out with Don Cherry, the future Canadian television commentator who skippered the Bruins from 1974 to 1979. In his irreverent 1982 autobiography *Grapes*, Cherry devoted an entire chapter—"I'm Not Wild about Harry"—to what he considered Sinden's overmeddling in team affairs. The 1976 NHL Coach of the Year later reversed himself, however, and said he was mostly to blame for how badly things turned out between the two former friends. "I got awful cocky," Cherry confessed. "[Sinden] just got sick of it. And you know what? I would have, too."

Sinden did earn a reputation for being one of the shrewdest traders in the business, fearlessly pulling off a number of high-profile player acquisitions. "I lived by the principle," he said, "that when you come to the decision that you can do something to help your team, and you refuse to do it because you're worried about what the media and fans will think, then you need to get out. Sometimes it doesn't work, and sometimes it does." His biggest and most hotly debated trade involved moving Phil Esposito for Brad Park near the start of his tenure. "The deal was fraught with danger," he confessed. "The fans hated it, the team hated it, the press hated it. But I had a gut feeling that it would work because of Park, who was a dominant defenseman, and because we knew that Orr's knee was in peril." Sinden also played a crucial role in bringing Hall of Fame defenseman Ray Bourque into the Bruins fold, drafting him in the first round of the 1979 NHL Draft. "Our scouts were conflicted between Raymond and [fellow backliner] Keith Brown, who was ultimately chosen by the Chicago Black Hawks the pick before we selected," he said. "But I had seen Raymond play, and he caught my eye."

That he was able to last so long in one of the most demanding and high pressured executive positions in all of professional hockey always surprised Sinden. "I suppose few in pro sports ever feel they have real security," he once reflected. "Being the GM of an NHL team is a job where you tell your wife not to buy wall-to-wall carpets, which you have to leave if you sell the house, but to use area rugs instead because you can roll them up and take them with you to the next job. Funny, but when I took the job, I didn't think in terms of length of time I might have it. But the time just moved on, my duties expanded [he became club president] which kept the job varied and interesting, though the hockey part of it always is the big thing."

Spoken like a true survivor.

Gerry Cheevers thrived with the WHA's Cleveland Crusaders, becoming a highly respected veteran leader on the team and surprisingly earning the only two All-Star nominations of his hockey career. Yet, there were times, for instance, when an experimental blue puck was used in preseason contests, when playing for the gimmicky new league made him shake his increasingly balding head in dismay. "We had the blue puck our first game, and every time it hit the boards it would lose its shape because of the rubber [not freezing correctly with the special blue dye used]," Cheevers said. "It was like playing with a tennis ball after a while. It just bounced all over the place." Cheevers also had difficulty adjusting to the run-down, crime-infested area where the Crusaders played their home games. Several teammates were physically assaulted, while others had their cars stolen directly from the arena's parking lot. "If you didn't get mugged that first year, they didn't think that much of you," Cheevers joked.

Cheevers's tenure in Cleveland came to an unceremonious end during the 1974–1975 season. "We weren't faring well in the standings, and personally, I was having one of my worst years as a pro in net," Cheevers said. Fans were not bothering to show up to Crusaders games either, and this put a financial strain on the team it would not recover from. The team officially shuttered its offices in 1976, but not before Cheevers requested and received his release. "I had finally had enough," he said. Despite the sour way things turned out, Cheevers claimed to have no regrets. He had made substantially more money in Cleveland than he ever had with the Bruins and came away with some fond memories. "I took particular enjoyment in watching all the young guys work their butts off," he said, "each one hoping to maintain his status as a professional hockey player."

Cheevers rejoined the Bruins the following season and had an emotional first game back in the Black and Gold against the Detroit Red Wings in Boston Garden. In front of an enthusiastic crowd that included U.S. secretary of state Henry Kissinger, who was in town to be at his wife's side while she underwent a medical procedure at nearby Massachusetts General Hospital, Cheevers blanked Detroit with 22 saves in a 7–0 Boston victory. Said Harry Sinden, "It wasn't so much the shutout or the couple of tough saves—although I think he had more than he admits—it was the way he handled himself out there. He got one with the stick, and on others he used the glove or the skate. He really impressed me, considering he was supposed to be out of shape."

Cheevers never helped the Bruins to another championship, but he did play a vital role in getting them to the Stanley Cup Finals in 1977 and 1978. The injuries to his legs were mounting, however, and he decided to retire his stitched-up mask and skates in 1980, even though statistically he had one of his finest seasons. "I can't play anymore," he told the *Toronto Star*. "Believe me, I tried. I kept hoping over the summer my knees would get better. But when I would go downstairs in the morning, the noise in the knees was horrible. I'd wake up in the night and it would take five minutes to straighten them." Still, Cheevers was not quite done with hockey or the Bruins. He became the team's head coach in the early 1980s and compiled an enviable 204–126–46 record in 376 games. "I had to get used to coaching guys who were my teammates just a few months before," Cheevers recounted. "It was surreal, and I had a feeling I would have a tough time dealing with it in the years to come." Cheevers was not mistaken. By the middle of the 1984–1985 season, the Bruins front office determined that he had lost control of the club and fired him. "I don't think I was stabbed in the back," Cheevers declared afterward. "I don't think there were any punctures, but I feel a lot of the players really were second-guessing my coaching."

Whatever bitterness Cheevers may have harbored about the dismissal, he put it aside once he received word he had been selected for the 1985 induction class of the Hockey Hall of Fame. "I was stunned when it was confirmed, and I'm still in a state of shock," he said. "I honestly didn't think I was the caliber of player who gets into the Hall of Fame, but when you're in goal behind outstanding guys like Bobby Orr, Phil Esposito, Wayne Cashman, and all the rest, anyone has a shot at the big prize at the end of a career." Cheevers need not have been so modest. As one impressed hockey contemporary put it, "Cheevers plays goal two ways. When he isn't good, he's great. Mostly, he's great."

Johnny Bucyk became the Bruins version of the Energizer Bunny. He continued to perform at a high level for several more seasons, despite playing in constant physical pain. "I had muscle spasms and a partial disc problem in my back," Bucyk told Tom Heinshaw of *Hockey News*. "When I went into traction I was on my back for six weeks all told, and I lost two inches of muscle in one leg. When I went to skate, I just didn't have any strength or power in my right leg." Bucyk coped as best he could and lost 14 pounds of unneeded weight. "When I first came here a couple years ago, he looked like a sumo wrestler," Bruins coach Don Cherry said. "But you seem him now, he's right down."

The sands of time, however, were working against him. Bucyk officially retired at the end of the 1977–1978 season—his 23st in the NHL and 21st for the Bruins. That last season had been a frustrating one for the Edmonton product. Aside from his rookie year with the Detroit Red Wings in 1956, he had the fewest goals (8) and assists (13) of his career. His plus–minus average was a negative one, and he was benched throughout the entire playoffs. It was not exactly the capstone to a glorious career he had expected. "I know I can still play," he said unconvincingly. It was a delicate situation, and Harry Sinden did his best to finesse it. "With the service John has given this club, we don't want to take the initiative in deciding his future," the Bruins GM said. "If he wants to stay in hockey, whether coaching or scouting, or a post with [the] Bruins, such as Jean Beliveau has in management activities with the Montreal Canadians, we will find it."

Although Bucyk went reluctantly into that hockey night, he took tremendous satisfaction from the raft load of Bruins team records he set, including most points (1,339), most assists (794), and most games played (1,436). But the honor he was most proud of was the Lady Byng Trophy, which he won twice, in 1971 and 1974. "It's a trophy given to a player who shows sportsmanship play, without earning penalty minutes, and combines it with great ability," Bobby Orr explained. "[Bucyk] deserved it. In fact, Chief should have won it long before he did." It was an argument few, if any, of his NHL peers would contest.

Derek Sanderson floundered with the Philadelphia Blazers. Billed as a poster boy for the upstart WHA, Sanderson failed to live up to the advance hype or the huge contract. Owing to a painful lower back injury and an indifferent attitude, Sanderson played just eight games, scoring three goals, with three assists. "That's why it's all so tragic," his agent, Bob Woolf, later said. "He had everything there, and it's almost like he was destined for self-destruction. I don't know why. We took him to psychiatrists, doctors, the whole bit." Things went south from the get-go. "I was a day late for [training] camp," Sanderson remembered.

> It was wrong. I knew it. And [the season] started as a disaster. It was just that I was in a bad frame of mind. The money was new, and I was spending it pretty good. But I hadn't worked for it yet. And I'm not sure I came prepared to work for it. I was catered to, primped, and pampered. And hell, I liked it.

What he didn't like was his new surroundings. Philadelphia lacked the sophisticated cosmopolitan charms of Boston, and Sanderson missed the celebrity status he had enjoyed while wearing a Bruins uniform. "Nobody knew him," explained old Boston teammate Pie McKenzie, who had made the jump to Philadelphia along with Sanderson. "In Boston, he couldn't walk down the street. He was a big star." Deprived of his old support network, a lonely Sanderson spent most of his time tooling around the streets of Philadelphia in a shiny, new, silver Rolls-Royce convertible he had purchased for a then-astronomical sum of $31,000. "It was a rainy day, and I had nothing else to do," Sanderson explained. "I was wearing blue jeans and a sweat shirt, and I walked [into the local auto dealership] and saw something I liked." He lavished the same kind of attention on the car as a parent would a newborn child. The two were inseparable. "That Rolls is the only thing he ever took care of," McKenzie joked.

Sanderson's main social contact was with a group of young street thugs who he began calling the "Under the Hill Gang." They had tried to sell him some stolen hockey equipment when he found them suspiciously loitering around his Rolls one day. "I figured that they were about to break into it or something," he recalled. Sanderson frequently drove them around the city and treated them to lunch. "I knew they were skipping school, but I figured this was more important than any school could ever be," he said. Their wastrel ways reminded Sanderson of his own misspent youth in Niagara Falls, and he did what he could to brighten their days. Not all were appreciative. One scamp managed to sneak into the Blazers locker room and walk away with a teammate's game tickets. "They were tough little bastards—good kids at heart but rough around the edges," Sanderson said. "They were all smart, but they put their energy into the wrong places."

Blazers management felt the same about Sanderson. Looking to free themselves of his expensive contract and difficult personality, they negotiated a $1 million buyout after finding no trade takers from other WHA teams. That suited Sanderson just fine. "Getting out of Philadelphia is like getting out of Vietnam," he told the media. Sanderson regarded the WHA as a poorly run, low-rent operation that could barely draw fans, especially in Philadelphia. The NHL Flyers of Bobby Clarke, Dave Schultz, and Reggie Leach were already the toast of the town and in the process of winning back-to-back Stanley Cup championships. In contrast, the Blazers barely registered as a blip on the local sports radar screen, despite making the playoffs in their first season. Only four thousand fans per game even bothered to attend the run-down Philadelphia Civic Center, where the Blazers played their home contests.

Those few hardy souls who did found more to laugh at than to cheer. When the Zamboni ice-resurfacing machine plunged through the ice on opening night, team officials were forced to cancel the game due to player safety concerns. Fans vented their disappointment to Sanderson, who as team captain and designated face of the new franchise was tasked with making the public announcement. The crowd responded by pummeling him with souvenir orange pucks the team had unwisely handed out earlier. Sanderson did his best imitation of Gerry Cheevers and tried to block as many of the foreign projectiles as he could before making a hasty retreat down a hallway. "Hell, I didn't blame them for being angry," Sanderson confessed afterward. "I apologized on behalf of the club and told them not to run over each other in the parking lot."

Despite the depressing Philly denouement, there was no shortage of interest from other NHL teams willing to bring Sanderson on for their 1973 Stanley Cup runs. The Rangers, in particular, showed a keen interest. But Sanderson knew there was only one place he truly wanted to play—Boston. After some protracted negotiations with new Bruins general manager Harry Sinden, Sanderson got his wish. He signed a two-year deal worth $200,000. "I think you're an asshole for leaving us in the first place, but it's good to have you back," Bobby Orr informed him. Unfortunately, the return to Beantown proved disappointing. Never a stickler for conditioning, Sanderson appeared several pounds heavier and noticeably slower on the ice. "He has the body of a 50-year-old man at 27 years of age," Sinden cracked. It didn't help that Sanderson appeared more interested in resuming his active Boston social life than improving his game. "Hell, he didn't even try to get into playing shape," complained one teammate. "We have a gang of guys who work bloody hard and all get along well, and he was destroying this." Indeed, Bruins team chemistry had changed since Sanderson had left, and there was less tolerance for his lack of discipline and unconventional ways. "Things weren't the same," Sanderson said. Tensions boiled over when up-and-coming forward Terry O'Reilly got into a locker room fistfight with Sanderson, and Sanderson was suspended by club management. He also missed a team flight, blew off several workouts, and displayed a haughty indifference to taking instruction.

Sanderson's act was wearing thin, no more so than with new Bruins head coach Armand "Bep" Guidolin. A product of the "old school," the stocky, sharp-featured Ontario native resented Sanderson's lackadaisical attitude and overall disruptive behavior. "I did everything possible to help Derek," Guidolin claimed. "At one point, I broke up our best line (Phil Esposito, Wayne Cashman, and Hodge) to try to build a line around Turk, with Cashman on the wing. . . . Turk just wasn't in shape to help us much of the time." Sanderson felt Guidolin resented his lifestyle and was trying to break his spirit as a player. "Bep didn't understand me at all," he said. Sanderson theorized to reporters that the basis for this animosity stemmed from Sanderson's making more money than Guidolin, a charge the coach flatly denied. "Gentlemen don't discuss their salaries in public," Guidolin said. "When our players read what Derek said, they decided that they'd each donate $1,000 to bring me up to a decent wage. Phil Esposito said he was writing Turk a letter asking for the donation from him and then Turk could claim me as a dependent on his income tax." Harry Sinden had seen enough. The Bruins GM shipped his troublesome center off to the Rangers at the conclusion of the 1973–1974 season. "What happened to Derek was that he lost track of what he was," Sinden said afterward. "If a carpenter thinks he's an electrician, he gets a shock. Derek wasn't a sex symbol or a talk-show host or a philosopher. He was a hockey player. He made sense on the ice, the kind of sense he doesn't make off it."

Sanderson played well for the Rangers, amassing 50 points on 25 goals and 25 assists in 1974–1975. But his partying and drinking intensified in the glare of Broadway's bright lights. "I was too single," he said. "A professional athlete really only has to work one and a half hours a day. If you don't have a family, what do you do with the other time? How do you fill it? I filled my time going to the bars." If this wasn't bad enough, Sanderson developed a nasty cocaine habit that quickly spiraled out of control. He discovered the effects of the drug allowed him to stay awake longer and drown out his sorrows with a never-ending flow of booze. "I'm crazy, I admit it, but I'm also insecure," Sanderson told Canadian journalist Earl McRae at the time.

> I have to do crazy things to get attention. There are two Turk Sandersons. Did you know that? Well, there are. There's a private me and a public me that does things to get attention, to keep people off balance. . . . I'm 28 now and most of time I feel 35. I feel old. I don't want to be old, but it's happening. I don't like it.

The Rangers traded Sanderson to St. Louis the following season, and although he collected a career-high 67 points in 1975–1976, his days as the "Peck's Bad Boy of ice hockey" were coming to an end. His production numbers tailed off the next year, and the Blues front office grew weary of his extracurricular activities, which now included an addiction to painkillers. Nothing surprised Bob Woolf anymore. The longtime sports agent had just about seen it all when it came to Sanderson. "He'd call me in Hawaii and ask me to call the manager of the hotel there to tell them there wasn't enough hot water in his room," Woolf remembered. "Imagine that. Derek called me in Boston to tell the manager in Hawaii that, three floors up, he's not getting enough hot water. What a man." Sanderson was demoted to the minors and out of hockey altogether by 1979.

His departure from the game did nothing to straighten out his life. If anything, Sanderson fell deeper into a pit of addiction and personal despair. His money gone from a string of bad investments, Sanderson became homeless and gave serious thought to ending his life. His lowest point came in New York City's Central Park, where he tried to steal a bottle of booze from another unfortunate sleeping on a bench. "I reached for his bottle, and he woke up," Sanderson recalled. "He grabbed the bottle back and said, 'Get your own!'" Taken by surprise, Sanderson informed his antagonist that he obviously wasn't aware of the famous celebrity he was dealing with. "Yeah, I know," the man said. "You're a drunk, just like me."

With the help of a concerned Bobby Orr, who expended great effort in tracking down his old friend and teammate, Sanderson was able to receive the kind of medical treatment and counseling he needed to beat back his old demons. It wasn't easy. "I had to bottom out before I realized what happened," he told Dave Anderson of the *New York Times*. "I had to go on a diet of humility." Sanderson slowly began to rebuild his life. He went back to school and became a successful financial advisor, specializing in wealth management for professional athletes. "The money has to last a lifetime," he said. "With players making a lot of money all at once, it's easy to think it will last forever. I certainly did. Most players are not conscious of the fact that it will end someday." When he wasn't dispensing financial wisdom, Sanderson could be heard on local Bruins television broadcasts providing color commentary alongside longtime team voice Fred Cusick. His wild days were over, and that was okay by him. "I bought the world a drink," he once said. Now he preferred the quiet life.

Phil Esposito had difficulty adjusting to playing in the Big Apple. "My life is different than in Boston," he told *Hockey News*. "I have a longer, harder drive to games. The games aren't as much fun. My legs aren't as strong. I get tired faster. I try to get by on my wits more. I'm tired of the travel." Nor did Esposito appreciate the indifferent attitude many of his new Rangers teammates expressed toward winning. When the team dropped a 7–5 decision to the pathetic California Seals in his first year with the club, Esposito was appalled at what he witnessed in the locker room afterward. Players were laughing and clowning around without any hint of remorse or urgency about the loss. "What the fuck is this?" Esposito thought. "In Boston, if we lost a game, everybody was pissed. Especially if we lost to a team we never should have lost to, like California. Our philosophy was to always beat the teams you're supposed to beat. Especially the teams that are worse than you—you *have* to beat them."

To make matters worse, Esposito injured his ankle out of the gate, missing several games. Spurred on by a hypercritical New York media, which concluded Esposito was washed up as a player, fans got on his case when he returned to the Rangers lineup. Loud boos rained down from the Madison Square Garden cheap seats, putting Esposito in an unfamiliar and uncomfortable position. "I was devastated," Esposito recalled. "I had never been booed like that in my entire career, not by the hometown fans. I had been booed on the road, but I loved that. The more they booed and yelled, the better I played. But booed by the hometown fans? The Rangers fans were relentless." Esposito came back from the ankle injury and remained among the league's top scoring threats in the seasons ahead. But his old enthusiasm for playing the game had clearly diminished. He now fretted about the size of his paycheck and whether he would be able to earn enough money to retire comfortably. "I'm a businessman before anything else," he said. "After all the years I played for next to nothing I think I deserve it. If I have to go to Africa to finish out my contract, I will. If the fans throw rotten tomatoes at me for the next three years, I don't care."

Esposito still found time for controversy. While captaining the 1977 Team Canada squad, he threw a sucker punch at Czechoslovakian team coach Jan Starsi while streaking down the ice during a world championship tournament game in Vienna, Austria. "Any player who'd skate past the opposing coach who's following the play and slug him in the mouth must be sick," Starsi said. "I was spitting up blood for nearly an hour." Claiming innocence, Esposito shrugged off the episode as an unfortunate misunderstanding. "I didn't know who it was," he said. "I saw a guy reaching over the boards and grabbing one of our guys. So I let him have it to teach him to keep his hands off our players. That's all."

Esposito's Rangers, meanwhile, continued to underperform. And the reason was not hard to fathom. There was rampant alcohol and drug abuse on the team, as too many promising young players, for example, forward Donnie Murdoch, chose to frequent such trendy Manhattan nightspots as Studio 54 rather than put in the necessary hard work to improve their hockey skills. "You could smell the booze on [Murdoch] every morning," Esposito claimed. "He'd go out on the ice half in the bag, and even in games." Murdoch, who later served a 40-game league suspension for illegal drug possession, gained everlasting infamy by skating into a goalpost during a contest. "They had to get him out of there," Esposito wrote.

Despite the perpetual chaos surrounding the team, the Rangers did manage to put together a stellar playoff run in 1978–1979, reaching the

Stanley Cup Finals against the defending champion Montreal Canadiens. They dropped the series in five games to the Habs, but for Esposito it was like old times. He led the Blue Shirts in goals and overall points during the regular season and throughout the playoffs. "Yeah, I'm happy again," Esposito told John Iaboni of the *Toronto Sun*. "I feel good now after two and a half unhappy years here. I enjoyed every minute in Boston, and it was rough here for a while. But you know what? We've got something on this team now that I felt in Boston. The feeling you want to win; the feeling of togetherness. Yeah, I'm really happy." What made Esposito unhappy was talk he was staging a miraculous comeback at 37. "Last year I get 38 goals and 82 points, and this year it's 42 goals and 79 points, and they're saying what a fantastic year," he griped. "Look, I never thought I was away."

Father Time did catch up to Esposito in the middle of the 1980–1981 season. With the Rangers reverting back to their losing ways and his minutes on ice declining under a new coach, Esposito decided the moment was right to retire from the game he had first taken up as a precocious 12-year-old in Sault Saint Marie, Ontario. "His deadly shot strays more often than it finds the target, and the quick release that left goalies flatfooted has slowed," noted one writer. But Esposito, who had tallied only seven goals and 12 assists in 40 games, refused to concede that his offensive skills had eroded. "Physically," Esposito said,

> I believe I'm as fit as any guy on the team. The difference for me is mentally. I found myself getting down easily. I didn't score as I should have, and that added to the mental pressure. . . . When I was down—and I was down a lot more than I was up this season—the energy wasn't there like it always used to be.

He insisted that he had no regrets about quitting. In fact, he was eagerly looking forward to what the future might bring. "You're life isn't over," Esposito said. "It's like reading a book. You are enjoying that book, but you know sooner or later that book is going to end. And now you have to search for another book. You have to search for something that is going to give you as much pleasure and enjoyment as the last book."

Esposito found his niche in the front office, becoming general manager of the Rangers in 1986. Known as "Trader Phil," Esposito engineered a flurry of deals that added a number of high-quality players, for instance, future Hall of Famer Marcel Dionne, to the New York roster. But it was the trade that Esposito was not allowed to make that stuck with him throughout the years. "I worked out a deal to get Wayne Gretzky from Edmonton," he said. "Ownership said to me, 'Why do we want this guy?' I told them, 'I could win the Stanley Cup with Wayne on my team.' They said, 'We're already selling out the Garden every night, so why do we need the Stanley Cup?'" A disappointed Esposito severed ties with the Rangers shortly thereafter. "For Chrissake, I wanted to win," Esposito said. Elected to the Hockey Hall of Fame in 1984, Esposito moved on to run the Tampa Bay Lightning in the early 1990s, laying the foundation for the expansion team's 2004 Stanley Cup championship. Yet, he always felt unappreciated, especially in Boston, where his record-shattering performances had been overshadowed by Bobby Orr in his playing days.

The Bruins attempted to make amends by retiring Esposito's jersey in an unforgettable banner-raising ceremony at Boston Garden in 1987. But Esposito had his reservations going into the event. "I would have liked to have seen it done before, to be honest," he told a reporter. Esposito also voiced displeasure that other Bruins had been allowed to wear his beloved number 7 since leaving the Hub. "I hated Harry Sinden for that. I hated the man!" he later wrote. Such bitterness evaporated, however, when future Hall of Fame defenseman Raymond Bourque, now proudly sporting the number for the Bruins, performed one of the most chivalrous acts in hockey history. Skating up to Esposito during the ceremony, Bourque stunned everyone in attendance by taking off his number 7 jersey and handing it to Esposito. "It's all yours," Bourque said. "Number 7 has been retired for good," declared Bruins radio announcer and master of ceremonies Bob Wilson. Sinden had arranged for the classy gesture following several days of deliberation in the Bruins front office. The often-cantankerous GM concluded the move was necessary given Esposito's undeniable contributions to the team. "Phil Esposito is one of the Boston Bruins' greatest heroes," Sinden said. "He was our greatest scorer and one of our greatest players." Bourque voiced no opposition. In fact, he was genuinely delighted to be part of the surprise. "People weren't expecting anything like this," Bourque said, "and to see [Esposito's] reaction was really an emotional thing for me, too. . . . I'm sure he was shocked. It may have been the first time Phil was lost for words." Indeed, Esposito was rendered speechless. "I'm looking at [Bourque], like, is someone trying to play a joke on me here or what?" Esposito remembered. "We had talked about [both sharing the number], yeah, we'd put the number up, with my name on it, and when Raymond retired, they'd put his name on it. I had no problem with that, and Bourqee had no problem with that, but when he did that, man, that really . . . I'll never forget that as long as I live."

Neither would Boston.

Things did not pan out for Bobby Orr with the Black Hawks. Orr was limited to only 20 games his first season, as knee injuries again took their painful toll. Indeed, it was obvious in training camp that something was seriously wrong. "Bobby doesn't have that great acceleration anymore," said new Chicago teammate Stan Mikita, "and he doesn't make the sharp, quick cuts he used to." Orr tried to strengthen his damaged knees by riding a stationary bike and wearing a weighted boot when he wasn't out on the ice. But nothing seemed to work. "I could hardly walk, let alone skate," Orr confessed. "I wanted to play but just couldn't." Orr was forced to retreat to the sidelines, and the enforced inactivity gnawed at his confidence and now-fragile psyche. "You want to get back to doing what you should be doing," Orr explained. "But it is one thing going through your rehab when you believe you are on the way back to being as healthy as you ever were and something totally different when you are forced to confront the realization that things have changed forever." His depressed mental state only worsened when it was mutually decided with the Hawks front office that he should sit out the entire 1977–1978 season for medical reasons. "That was a particularly tough time in my life," Orr later wrote. "I worried that I couldn't live up to the expectations of the Chicago fans. I worried that my teammates would be let down. I worried that the management group who had brought me in would decide that they had made a mistake."

Orr had been able to recapture some of his old hockey magic prior to joining the Black Hawks in the fall of 1976. He played for the Canadian national team in the inaugural Canada Cup Tournament, which saw the roster of NHL All-Stars triumph in seven games against top international competition. Orr was the catalyst, scoring two goals, with seven assists. He received Most Valuable Player honors. "Not bad for a cripple," joked teammate and veteran Philadelphia Flyers forward Reggie Leach. "Even if he's only at three-quarters of what he used to be, he's still great." Don Cherry seconded that sentiment. The Bruins and Team Canada coach believed Orr had compensated for his diminished physical skills by carefully picking his spots offensively and defensively. "I can't put a number on it," Cherry said. "I just know that he's as effective now as ever. He's using his head more, taking the body more. . . . He's playing now the way I always wanted to see him play. He's moving the puck quickly—and you know he always could pinpoint his passes." For Orr, the Canada Cup victory was personally more rewarding than being a Stanley Cup champion. "There is nothing like winning for your country," he wrote.

> Sport brings people together, and the bigger the game, the bigger the community. It didn't matter to the guys on the bench what team they played for, or even what league they played in. And on a day like that, for fans and players alike, it didn't matter what province you were from, or what political party you voted for. We were all Canadians, and it was an honor to have been part of something that brought people together like that.

Orr made one final stab at playing for the Black Hawks in 1978–1979, following yet another operation on his ravaged left knee. "I know I've got a way to go," he told Jerry Kirshenbaum of *Sports Illustrated.* "But as long as there's a chance I can play, I've got to try. I feel it's too soon to retire. I want to be a hockey player." Although he harbored strong doubts, new Chicago coach Bob Pulford did his best to sound publicly supportive of the comeback attempt. "It's unrealistic to think Bobby Orr can be the same player he once was," he said. "But if the knee holds up, he's not going to be just another hockey player, either. . . . There's no way Bobby Orr will be ordinary." Alas, Orr *was* less than ordinary. Once the most gifted of skaters, with blinding end-to-end speed, he now discovered he could barely make it down the ice. And after playing in only six games, he decided to call it quits. "Bone spurs and arthritis left the [knee] joint swollen and immobile," he recalled. "I couldn't cut. I couldn't accelerate. I couldn't play at the level that I expected of myself anymore. I had always said I would play until I couldn't skate anymore. Finally, I knew that day had come." It was a bitter realization. "I had grown up believing I could do whatever I wanted on the ice," Orr later wrote, "and had convinced myself I could somehow conjure up the will to play through the injuries in order to continue as a pro hockey player as long as I wanted." In those heady days, Orr thought he could be as durable as his boyhood idol, Gordie Howe, who played for parts of six decades despite numerous injuries. "But there is only one Gordie," he reluctantly conceded, "and no amount of willpower or wishful thinking could prevent the inevitable."

Orr made his retirement official in a conference room full of television and newspaper reporters at Chicago Stadium on November 8, 1978. With tears flowing unashamedly down his cheeks, Orr told the sad gathering he had few regrets, despite the fact he was leaving the game at 30—an age when most players were entering their prime. "Hockey has given my family and me everything we have, and I hope now I can just give something back to it, even though I'll never play again," he said. Orr wasn't sure what lay ahead for him, but he was appreciative of those who had stuck by him to the bitter end. "There were my parents, who had supported me from the beginning," he recounted. "There was Peggy, who was there when I needed her most. My teammates and other people around the game. The journalists. The fans. I received hundreds and hundreds of letters in the weeks that followed, and I'll never forget those acts of kindness."

Boston provided Orr with another memorable act of kindness on January 9, 1979. Officially proclaimed "Bobby Orr Day," Orr was feted by city and state officials for being a civic asset, albeit a highly perishable one. "He epitomized all the best of Bruins hockey for a decade," Massachusetts House of Representatives speaker Thomas W. McGee said. "Back in 1967–68, we thought it would go on forever. Yet, we knew in our hearts that it couldn't. But did it have to end so soon?" Kevin White was less maudlin in his remarks. The upbeat Boston mayor told a packed City Hall reception in Orr's honor that he had recently read an article by famed British social critic Henry Fairlie lamenting there were too few heroes left in public life. "In it," White said, "[Fairlie] described a hero as someone you wouldn't mind being caught staring at. I can't think of a better description to fit Bobby. You'd never be embarrassed to be caught staring at Bobby because we saw in him something the rest of us could never be."

The day's festivities climaxed a few hours later at Boston Garden, where Orr's famed number 4 was formally retired to the rafters prior to a Bruins exhibition game with the Soviet Wings of Russia. Given the acrimonious way Orr departed from the Bruins, team management had at first been reluctant to stage such an event. But public pressure from fans to honor the hockey legend largely responsible for bringing two Stanley Cups to Boston proved too overwhelming to ignore. Orr would receive his proper due and then some. Standing mid-ice that evening in front of an ecstatic sold-out Garden audience chanting "Bobby, Bobby," Orr felt the unconditional love Bostonians had always held in their hearts for him. They gave him a thunderous six-minute standing ovation. "He was every middle-aged fan's ticket back to youth and every kid's fantasy," columnist Ray Fitzgerald wrote in the next day's edition of the *Boston Globe*. Never a comfortable public speaker, a visibly moved Orr was taken aback on how to respond. "I was going to say something formal tonight," he told the crowd. "But I'm finding it very difficult." After awkwardly trying a stab at humor, Orr revealed his true emotions. "I love you all so much," he said. "I spent 10 years here, and they were the best 10 years of my life. If you talk to athletes who have been around, they say Boston is the place to play."

Orr's subsequent retirement was as stormy and controversial as his playing days had been glorious and inspirational. He initially tried coaching and working in the Chicago front office, but the results were mutually disappointing. "The original contract with the Black Hawks was renegotiated, stretched out," Orr explained. "They thought I breached it and launched a lawsuit." The two parties eventually reached a settlement in 1983, with Orr receiving $450,000, but this modest financial windfall failed to lift his spirits. Orr felt increasingly isolated, ignored, and abandoned. "I had lost something I didn't think those around me would understand," he recalled. "My health, my career, my place in the game—it had all slipped through my fingers." Driving his depression was the shocking discovery that Alan Eagleson had betrayed him. Neither were Orr's spirits lifted when he learned the extent to which Alan Eagleson had betrayed him in his final contract talks with the Bruins. "The fact is I wouldn't have been in Chicago if I hadn't trusted Eagleson completely," Orr maintained. Orr also claimed the controversial agent and business advisor had left him almost penniless through a series of poor investments. "Where all the money went, I will never know," Orr wrote years later. "A huge part of what remained was eaten up by unpaid taxes. Whether this was due to incompetence, greed, or malice on his part is impossible to guess. At this point, it doesn't matter. What mattered to me then was that I was watching what remained all but disappear." He severed financial and personal ties with Eagleson. Eagleson, who later pled guilty to mail fraud and embezzlement charges in separate U.S. and Canadian court actions, was coldly unsympathetic to the plight of his former client and friend. "Bobby

An emotional Bobby Orr sees his number retired to the Garden rafters on January 9, 1979. *Le Studio du Hockey, HHOF Images*

decided he was through with hockey and me," he said. "It is like a divorce. It would have been nicer if it hadn't happened." Eagleson denied any wrongdoing and claimed Orr owed him an apology. "When Hell freezes over," Orr responded.

Down but not out financially, Orr painstakingly rebuilt his fortune in the years ahead. He entered the printing business and performed promotional work for Nabisco, a major American cookie and snack manufacturer. "This guy gets up 5:30, 6 o'clock every morning," said an impressed business partner.

> By the time I talk to him—and we talk every day between 7 and 7:30—I can tell by the sound of his voice whether our clients had a good or bad night the night before. He knows how everybody did; if someone's minutes are down, we know he's either injured or hasn't done what he should have been doing. And by the end of the conversation we have a list of seven or eight items for that day that we're going to address. Involved? He still lives and breathes it.

Orr eventually gravitated toward the sports agency business, launching the Orr Hockey Group in 2002, which represents such current young NHL stars as John Carlson, Kevin Labanc, and Cam Ward. "I suppose

The 1970 Stanley Cup champions. *MacDonald-Stewart/HHOF Images*

these is some irony that someone who lost so much to an agent would become one himself," Orr admitted. "But on the other hand, I think parents [of young clients] recognize that my experience has shown me a side of the game that not a lot of people have seen." Indeed, according to the company's official website, the group pledges to empower its clients and "offer a full continuum of advice and support—helping players reach their peak potential—on and off the ice." Orr refuses to provide investment advice or handle personal finances. "Any player," he argues, "whether he is a client or not, should learn from my experience and realize that he is ultimately responsible for himself and should not give complete control to anyone for any reason. The money a player earns during his career is his, and it is his duty to learn to protect that income." Financial self-education is the key. "After all," Orr maintains, "if a player's hard work is squandered because of bad advice, it will the player who pays the price. Professional athletes who accumulate wealth need to take the time to do their homework."

His hard-earned success in the business world notwithstanding, Orr never stopped missing the game he loved. He became acutely aware that had the advantages of modern sports medicine existed during his salad days with the Bruins, his hockey career most likely would have been extended by several years. "There's no question," he told writer Ryan Kennedy of *Hockey News*. "When I was playing, you'd ice [the knee], you'd heat it—there was a hot gel—and that was it." Still, Orr professed to hold no bitterness. "I can't stand here and say I would have done anything differently," he said. "In a game like hockey, there's a lot of contact, and I played a style where I got hit a lot. I handled the puck a lot, and I got hit a lot. That's the game. It was the way I enjoyed playing, and I'd probably do it all over the same way."

Perhaps the highest praise Orr ever received came from Larry Bird of the Boston Celtics. Although Bird had never seen Orr play, the three-time NBA MVP admitted at a local sports banquet late in his career that he had long drawn inspiration from the hockey legend. When the national anthem was played before Celtics home games at the Boston Garden, Bird made it a point to fix his eyes on Orr's retired jersey number hanging in the rafters. "It gives me a tingling feeling for some reason," Bird said. "I don't why it does. And I started [the ritual] back when I was rookie. You get there and all of a sudden you see this number, and you get fired up. I could never understand it but it's true." Bird added that he hoped he would be as beloved and respected by Boston fans when he finally retired. Orr, who was in attendance at the event, could scarcely believe his ears. "My god," he stammered. "My god."

This was the same kind of awed reaction most people had when watching Bobby Orr and the Big Bad Bruins perform during their epic 1970 Stanley Cup run.

SELECTED BIBLIOGRAPHY

BOOKS

Adrahtas, Tom. *The '60s: Goaltending's Greatest Generation*. Toronto: CreateSpace Independent Publishing Platform, 2018.
———. *The Man They Call Mr. Goalie: Glenn Hall*. Tampa, FL: Albion, 2003.
Ali, Muhammad, with Richard Durham. *The Greatest: My Own Story*. New York: Random House, 1975.
Ambrose, Stephen A. *Nixon: The Triumph of a Politician, 1962–1972*. New York: Simon & Schuster, 1989.
Arnold, Dale, with Matt Kalman. *If These Walls Could Talk: Boston Bruins*. Chicago: Triumph, 2018.
Beatles. *The Beatles Anthology*. San Francisco, CA: Chronicle Books, 2000.
Belth, Alex. *Stepping Up: The Story of Curt Flood and His Fight for Baseball Players' Rights*. New York: Persea, 2006.
Bock, Hal. *Dynamite on Ice: The Bobby Orr Story*. New York: Scholastic Book Services, 1972.
Bouton, Jim. *Ball Four: My Life and Hard Times Throwing the Knuckleball in the Big Leagues*. New York: Dell, 1970.
———. *Ball Four: Twentieth Anniversary Edition*. New York: Macmillan, 1990.
———. *I'm Glad You Didn't Take It Personally*. New York: William Morrow, 1971.
Brophy, Mike. *My First Goal: 50 Players and the Goals That Marked the Beginning of Their NHL Careers*. Toronto: McClelland & Stewart, 2011.
Brunt, Stephen. *Searching for Bobby Orr*. Chicago: Triumph, 2006.
Bucyk, Johnny. *Hockey in My Blood*. New York: Charles Scribner's Sons, 1972.
Cameron, Steve. *Hockey Hall of Fame Book of Goalies*. Buffalo, NY: Firefly Books, 2014.
Canellos, Peter, ed. *Last Lion: The Fall and Rise of Ted Kennedy*. New York: Simon & Schuster, 2009.
Caputo, Phillip. *13 Seconds: A New Look at the Kent State Shootings*. New York: Penguin, 2005.
Castle, George. *When the Game Changed: An Oral History of Baseball's True Golden Age, 1969–1979*. Guilford, CT: Lyons Press, 2012.
Cheevers, Gerry, as told to Marc Zappulla. *Unmasked: Autobiography of Gerry Cheevers*. New York: Sports Improper Publications, 2011.
———, with Trent Frayne. *Goaltender*. New York: Dodd, Mead and Company, 1971.
Cherry, Don, with Stan Fischler. *Grapes: A Vintage View of Hockey*. New York: Avon Books, 1982.

Cole, Stephen. *Hockey Night Fever: Mullets, Mayhem, and the Game's Coming of Age in the 1970s.* Toronto: Doubleday Canada, 2015.

Connelly, Michael. *Rebound: Basketball, Busing, Larry Bird, and the Rebirth of Boston.* Minneapolis, MN: MVP Books, 2008.

Conway, Russ. *Game Misconduct: Alan Eagleson and the Corruption of Hockey.* Toronto: Macfarlane Walter & Ross, 1997.

Cusick, Fred. *Fred Cusick: Voice of the Bruins.* Champaign, IL: Sports Publishing, 2006.

Damore, Leo. *Chappaquiddick: Power, Privilege, and the Ted Kennedy Cover-Up.* Washington, DC: Regency, 2018.

David, Lester. *Good Ted, Bad Ted: The Two Faces of Ted Kennedy.* New York: Carol Publishing Group, 1993.

Delano, Hugh. *Eddie : A Goalie's Story.* New York: Atheneum, 1976.

Denault, Todd. *Jacques Plante: The Man Who Changed the Face of Hockey.* Toronto: McClelland & Stewart, 2009.

Devaney, John. *The Bobby Orr Story.* New York: Random House, 1973.

———. *We Love You Bruins: Boston's Gashouse Gang from Eddie Shore to Bobby Orr.* New York: Sport Magazine Press, 1972.

Doyle, Tom. *Man on the Run: Paul McCartney in the 1970s.* New York: Random House, 2013.

Druzin, Randi. *Between the Pipes: A Revealing Look at Hockey's Legendary Goalies.* Vancouver, BC: Greystone Books, 2013.

Dryden, Ken. *The Game.* Toronto: Macmillan Canada, 1993.

Eagleson, Alan, with Scott Young. *Power Play: The Memoirs of a Hockey Czar.* Toronto: McClelland & Stewart, 1991.

Eskenazi, Gerald. *The Derek Sanderson Nobody Knows.* Chicago: Follet,1973.

Esposito, Phil, and Peter Golenbock. *Thunder and Lightning: A No-B.S. Hockey Memoir.* Chicago: Triumph, 2003.

———, and Tony Esposito, with Tim Moriarty. *The Brothers Esposito.* New York: Hawthorn Books, 1971.

———, with Gerald Eskenazi. *Hockey Is My Life.* New York: Dodd, Mead and Company, 1972.

Etter, Les. *Hockey's Masked Men: Three Great Goalies.* Champaign, IL: Garrard, 1976.

Fischler, Stan. *Bobby Orr and the Big, Bad Bruins.* New York: Dodd, Mead and Company, 1969.

———. *Boston Bruins: Greatest Moments and Players.* Oak Brook, IL: 1999.

———. *Heroes of Hockey.* New York: Random House, 1971.

———. *Hockey Stars of 1969.* New York: Pyramid Books, 1968.

———. *Hockey Stars of 1970.* New York: Pyramid Books, 1969.

———. *Hockey Stars of 1971.* New York: Pyramid Books, 1970.

———. *Hockey Stars of 1972.* New York: Pyramid Books, 1971.

———. *Hockey Stars of 1974.* New York: Pyramid books, 1973.

———. *Hockey's Great Rivalries.* New York: Random House, 1974.

———. *Stan Mikita: The Turbulent Career of a Hockey Superstar.* New York: Cowles Book Company, 1969.

———. *Those Were the Days: The Lore of Hockey by the Legends of the Game.* New York: Dodd, Mead and Company, 1976.

Fitzgerald, Ray. *Champions Remembered: Choice Picks from a Boston Sports Desk.* Brattleboro, VT: Stephen Greene Press, 1982.

Freedman, Lew. *The Original Six: How the Canadiens, Bruins, Rangers, Blackhawks, Maple Leafs, and Red Wings Laid the Groundwork for Today's NHL.* New York: Sports Publishing, 2016.

Gordon, William A. *Four Dead in Ohio.* Laguna Hills, CA: North Ridge Books, 1995.

Gould, Jonathan. *Can't Buy Me Love: The Beatles, Britain, and America.* New York: Random House, 2007.

Green, Ted, with Al Hirshberg. *High Stick.* New York: Dodd, Mead and Company, 1971.

Gretzky, Wayne, with Kirstie McLellan Day. *99 Stories of the Game.* New York: G. P. Putnam's Sons, 2016.

Grimm, George. *We Did Everything but Win : Former New York Rangers Remember the Emile Francis Era (1964–1976)*. New York: Sports Publishing, 2017.

Haldeman, Bob. *The Haldeman Diaries: Inside the Nixon White House*. New York: G. P. Putnam's Sons, 1994.

Hiam, Michael C. *Eddie Shore and That Old-Time Hockey*. Toronto: McClelland & Stewart, 2010.

Hirshberg, Al. *Bobby Orr: Fire on Ice*. New York: G. P. Putnam's Sons, 1975.

Houston, William, and David Shoalts. *Greed and Glory: The Fall of Hockey Czar Alan Eagleson*. Toronto: Warwick Publishing, 1993.

Hughes, Ken. *Fatal Politics: The Nixon Tapes, the Vietnam War, and the Casualties of Reelection*. Charlottesville: University of Virginia Press, 2015.

Hunt, Jim. *Bobby Hull*. Toronto: Ryerson Press, 1967.

Jenish, D'Arcy. *The Montreal Canadiens: 100 Years of Glory*. Toronto: Anchor Canada, 2008.

———. *The NHL: A Centennial History*. Toronto: Anchor Canada, 2013.

Johnson, Richard A. *A Century of Boston Sports*. Boston: Northeastern University Press, 2000.

Joyce, Gare. *The Devil and Bobby Hull: How Hockey's Original Million-Dollar Man Became the Game's Lost Legend*. Mississauga, ON: John Wiley & Sons Canada, 2011.

Kalman, Matt. *100 Things Bruins Fans Should Know and Do Before They Die*. Chicago: Triumph, 2010.

Keene, Kerry. *Tales from the Boston Bruins Locker Room: A Collection of the Greatest Bruins Stories Ever Told*. New York: Sports Publishing, 2011.

Kennedy, Edward M. *True Compass: A Memoir*. New York: Hachette, 2009.

Leonard, Candy. *Beatleness: How the Beatles and Their Fans Remade the World*. New York: Arcade Publishing, 2014.

Libby, Bill. *Phil Esposito: Hockey's Greatest Scorer*. Toronto: Longman Canada Limited, 1975.

Liebman. *Hockey Shorts*. Chicago: Contemporary Books, 1996.

Liss, Howard. *Bobby Orr: Lightning on Ice*. Champaign, IL: Garrard, 1975.

Lovell, Jim, and Jeffrey Kluger. *Lost Moon: The Perilous Voyage of* Apollo 13. Boston and New York: Houghton Mifflin, 1994.

Lukas, J. Anthony. *Common Ground: A Turbulent Decade in the Lives of Three American Families*. New York: Vintage, 1985.

MacInnis, Craig, ed. *Remembering Bobby Orr*. Toronto: Stoddard, 1999.

———, ed. *Remembering the Golden Jet: A Celebration of Bobby Hull*. Toronto: Stoddart, 2011.

McDonell, Chris. *Hockey's Greatest Stars: Legends and Young Lions*. Buffalo, NY: Firefly Books, 2014.

McFarlane, Brian. *The Blackhawks: Brian McFarlane's Original Six*. Toronto: Stoddart, 2000.

———. *The Bruins: Brian McFarlane's Original Six*. Toronto: Stoddart, 2000.

———. *The Rangers: Brian McFarlane's Original Six*. Toronto: Stoddart, 1997.

McIndoe, Sean. *The Down Goes Brown History of the NHL: The World's Most Beautiful Sport, the World's Most Ridiculous League*. Toronto: Random House Canada, 2018.

McKinley, Michael. *Hockey: A People's History*. Toronto: McClelland & Stewart, 2006.

McMillan, John. *Beatles vs. Stones*. New York: Simon & Schuster, 2013.

Michener, James A. *Kent State: What Happened and Why*. New York: Random House, 1971.

Mikita, Stan. *I Play to Win: My Own Story*. New York: Pocket Books, 1970.

———, with Bob Verdi. *Forever a Blackhawk*. Chicago: Triumph, 2011.

Milton, Steve, and Mike Ryan. *Hockey Hall of Fame: Unstoppable*. Buffalo, NY: Firefly Books, 2016.

Moran, Jay. *The Rangers, the Bruins, and the End of an Era*. Bloomington, IN: AuthorHouse, 2009.

Morrison, Scott. *100 Years, 100 Moments: A Centennial of NHL Hockey*. Toronto: McClelland & Stewart, 2017.

Nixon, Richard. *RN: The Memoirs of Richard Nixon*. New York: Grosset & Dunlap, 1978.

Norman, Philip. *Shout: The Beatles in Their Generation*. New York: Warner Books, 1981.

O'Brien, Andy. *Superstars: Hockey's Greatest Players*. New York: McGraw-Hill Ryerson Limited, 1973.

Olson, Jack. *The Bridge at Chappaquiddick*. Boston: Little, Brown and Company, 1970.

O'Neill, Gerard. *Rogues and Redeemers: When Politics Was King in Irish Boston*. New York: Crown, 2012.

O'Ree, Willie, with Michael McKinley. *The Autobiography of Willie O'Ree: Hockey's Black Pioneer*. New York: Somerville House, 2000.

Orr, Bobby. *Bobby: My Story in Pictures*. Toronto: Penguin Random House Canada, 2018.

———. *Orr: My Story*. New York: G. P. Putnam's Sons, 2013.

———, and Mark Mulvoy. *Bobby Orr: My Game*. Boston: Little, Brown and Company, 1974.

Orr, Frank. *Great Goalies of Pro Hockey*. New York: Random House, 1973.

———. *Hockey's Greatest Stars*. New York: G. P. Putnam's Sons, 1970.

———. *Tough Guys of Pro Hockey*. New York: Random House, 1974.

Page, N. H. *Bobby Orr: Number Four*. New York: Dell, 1982.

Park, Brad, with Stan Fischler. *Play the Man*. New York: Warner Paperback Library, 1972.

Pepe, Phil. *Talkin' Baseball*. New York: Random House Value Publishing, 1998.

Plimpton, George. *Open Net: The Professional Amateur in the World of Big-Time Hockey*. New York: W. W. Norton, 1985.

Podnieks, Andrew. *The Goal: Bobby Orr and the Most Famous Goal in Stanley Cup History*. Chicago: Triumph, 2003.

Pritchard, David, and Alan Lysaght. *The Beatles: An Oral History*. New York: Hyperion, 1998.

Richardson, Stewart, and Richard LeBlanc. *Dit: Dit Clapper and the Rise of the Boston Bruins*. Columbia, SC: PACTS Management, 2012.

Robenalt, James. *January 1973: Watergate, Roe v. Wade, Vietnam, and the Month That Changed America Forever*. Chicago: Chicago Review Press, 2015.

Roberts, Randy, ed. *The Rock, the Curse, and the Hub: A Random History of Boston Sports*. Cambridge, MA: Harvard University Press, 2005.

Robson, Dan. *Quinn: A Life of a Hockey Legend*. Toronto: Penguin Random House, 2015.

Russell, Bill. *Go Up for Glory*. New York: Coward-McCann, 1966.

Ryan, Bob. *The Four Seasons*. Indianapolis, IN: Master's Press, 1997.

Sanderson, Derek, with Kevin Shea. *Crossing the Line: The Outrageous Story of a Hockey Original*. Chicago: Triumph, 2012.

———, with Stan Fischler. *I've Got to Be Me*. New York: Dodd, Mead and Company, 1970.

Sears, Thom, and Brad Park. *Straight Shooter: The Brad Park Story*. Mississauga, ON: John Wiley & Sons Canada, 2012.

Sheffield, Rob. *Dreaming the Beatles: The Love Story of One Band and the Whole World*. HarperCollins, 2017.

Shinzawa, Fluto. *The Big 50: The Men and Moments That Made the Boston Bruins*. Chicago: Triumph, 2016.

Shuker, Ronnie. *Hockey's Powerbrokers: The Game's 100 Most Influential People of All-Time*. Montreal, QC: Juniper Publishing, 2017.

Silverman, Steve. *Who's Better, Who's Best in Hockey?* New York: Sports Publishing, 2015.

Simpson, Rob. *Black and Gold: Four Decades of the Boston Bruins in Photographs*. Mississauga, ON: John Wiley & Sons Canada, 2008.

Sinden, Harry. *Hockey Showdown: The Canada–Russia Hockey Series*. Don Mills, ON: Paper-Jacks, 1972.

———, and Dick Grace. *The Picture History of the Boston Bruins: From Shore to Orr and the Years Between*. New York: Bobbs-Merrill, 1976.

Sorensen, Ted. *Counselor: A Life at the Edge of History*. New York: Harper Perennial, 2008.

Spitz, Bob. *The Beatles: The Biography*. New York: Little, Brown and Company, 2005.

Stark, Steven D. *Meet the Beatles: A Cultural History of the Band that Shook Youth, Gender, and the World*. New York: HarperCollins, 1988.

Vautour, Kevin, and Kerry Keene. *Number 4 Bobby Orr: A Chronicle of the Boston Bruins' Greatest Decade Led by their Legendary Superstar, 1966–1976*. New York: Page, 2018.

Ward, Geoffrey C., and Ken Burns. *Baseball: An Illustrated History*. New York: Alfred A. Knopf, 1994.

———. *The Vietnam War: An Intimate History*. New York: Penguin Random House, 2017.

Wenner, Jann, ed. *20 Years of Rolling Stones: What a Long, Strange Trip It's Been*. New York: Straight Arrow, 1987.

Whalen, Thomas J. *Dynasty's End: Bill Russell and the 1968–69 World Champion Boston Celtics*. Boston: Northeastern University Press, 2004.

Willes, Ed. *The Rebel League: The Short and Unruly Life of the World Hockey Association*. Toronto: McClelland & Stewart, 2004.

Wills, Garry. *The Kennedy Imprisonment: A Meditation on Power*. Boston: Little, Brown and Company, 1981.

Woolf, Bob. *Behind Closed Doors*. New York: Atheneum, 1976.

Zweig, Eric. *Art Ross: The Hockey Legend Who Built the Bruins*. Toronto: Dundurn, 2015.

HOCKEY HALL OF FAME PLAYER AND INDUCTEE CLIPPING FILES

Weston Adams
Al Arbour
Don Awrey
Irvine Wallace "Ace" Bailey
Scotty Bowman
Johnny Bucyk
Wayne Carleton
Wayne Cashman
Gerry Cheevers
Phil Esposito
Tony Esposito
Ed Giacomin
Ted Green
Glenn Hall
Ken Hodge
Bobby Hull
Wayne Maki
John McKenzie
Stan Mikita
Willie O'Ree
Bobby Orr
Brad Park
Noel Picard
Jacques Plante
Derek Sanderson
Eddie Shore
Harry Sinden
Fred Stanfield

SPORTS MUSEUM OF NEW ENGLAND BRUINS NEWSPAPER SCRAPBOOKS

February 23, 1969–December 31, 1969
January 1, 1970–April 29, 1970
April 30, 1970–October 11, 1970

October 12, 1970–February 8, 1971

NEWSPAPERS, PERIODICALS, AND WEBSITES

Associated Press
Atlantic
Beverly Times
Boston Globe
Boston Herald
Boston Herald-American
Boston Herald-Traveler
Boston Record American
Buffalo Courier-Express
Canadian
Canadian Press
Canadian Weekly
CBS Sports
Chicago American
Chicago Tribune
CNN.com
Deadspin.com
ESPN.com
Globe and Mail
Greatesthockeylegends.com
Hockey
Hockey Illustrated
Hockey News
Hockey Pictorial
Hockey World
Hockeywriters.com
Huffington Post
Maclean's Magazine
Maple Leafs Program
Montreal Gazette
NASA.gov
National Police Gazette
National Post
New York Times
Newsweek
NHL.com
Ottawa Journal
Pro Sports
Rolling Stone
Salem Evening News
San Jose Mercury News
Saskatoon Star Phoenix
Saturday Night
Scotia Bank Hockey College News
Spokesman Review
Sport
Sport and Leisure Magazine
Sporting News
Sports Guide

Sports Illustrated
Sportsnet.ca
Springfield Republican
St. Louis Globe-Democrat
St. Louis Post-Dispatch
Standard
SuperSports
Time
Toro
Toronto Daily Star
Toronto Star
Toronto Sun
Toronto Telegram
USA Today
Vanity Fair
Weekend Magazine

INDEX

ABOUT THE AUTHOR

Thomas J. Whalen is associate professor of social science at Boston University. His social/political commentary has appeared in the *New York Times*, the *Wall Street Journal*, *USA Today*, the *Boston Globe*, the *Los Angeles Times*, and the AP, as well as on ABCNews.com. Whalen has also appeared on several national broadcast outlets, including CNN, NPR, and Reuters TV. He is author of six other books, among them *Spirit of '67: The Cardiac Kids, El Birdos, and the World Series That Captivated America* (2017); *Dynasty's End: Bill Russell and the 1968–69 World Champion Boston Celtics* (2003); and *JFK and His Enemies: A Portrait of Power* (2014). He resides on Boston's North Shore.